Reading for a

Purpose

Kate Parry

Hunter College
City University of New York

St. Martin's Press, New York

Editor: Karen Allanson
Director of Development: Richard Steins
Project Management: Gene Crofts
Production Supervisor: Alan Fischer
Text Design: Gene Crofts
Cover Design: Judy Forster
Cover Photograph: Victor Schrager

Manufactured in the United States of America.

6 5 4 3 2
f e d c b a

ISBN: 0–312–03627–2

For information, write to:
St. Martin's Press, Inc.
175 Fifth Avenue
New York, NY 10010

Acknowledgments

"How Much Money Does It Take to Enjoy the American Dream?" from AMERICAN DEMOGRAPHICS. © American Demographics, April 1987. Reprinted with permission.

"Emissions Making Car World Sick" by M. Renner. Reprinted from USA TODAY MAGAZINE, June 1989. Copyright 1989 by the Society for the Advancement of Education.

"Hope Wins When the Homeless Run" by David S. Wilson. Copyright © 1988 by The New York Times Company. Reprinted by permission.

"In a Bronx School, a '38 Free Speech Victory" by Bern Friedelson. Copyright © 1988 by The New York Times Company. Reprinted by permission.

"At the Frontline: Foundation for International Community Assistance" by Marjorie Kelly, editor, BUSINESS ETHICS, 1107 Hazeltine Blvd., Suite 530, Chaske, MN 55318. Reprinted by permission.

"How the Smallpox War Was Won" from THE OBSERVER COLOUR MAGAZINE. Copyright 1979 by The Observer. Reprinted by permission.

Acknowledgments and copyrights are continued at the back of the book on page 287, which constitutes an extension of the copyright page.

Preface

This book is intended for upper-level classes in developmental reading programs; a student who has satisfactorily worked through it should be able to proceed directly to regular undergraduate courses.

The material is varied and arranged by genre: newspaper and magazine articles in Chapter 1, selections from novels in Chapter 2, college textbook material in Chapter 3, philosophical essays in Chapter 4, and sample test passages and items in Chapter 5. Each chapter begins with an introduction, and each selection is accompanied by exercises; the introductions and exercises together reinforce the point made by the arrangement of the book as a whole: that reading is a diverse activity, and in reading different material for different purposes one must be able to adopt a variety of strategies. Nevertheless, the skills necessary for reading of all kinds, such as perceiving the overall structure of a text and inferring the meanings of unfamiliar words, are discussed fully in the introduction to Chapter 1.

The selections cover a wide range of issues, though there are a number of recurring themes, such as the status of women in relation to men, the problems of poverty in both advanced and developing economies, and the relationship between individuals and the social groups to which they belong. The issues are serious ones and are seriously discussed, for though developmental students may not read easily, they are adults and can be expected to have a mature appreciation of social problems. Particular emphasis has been placed on subjects of international concern, in order to provide for those classes that include foreign or immigrant students as well as students born and raised in the United States.

The book provides sufficient material for a two-semester course, although, assuming that instructors will want to pick and choose among the selections, it would probably be more suitable for a single semester. It lends itself to a variety of pedagogical approaches, ranging from systematically sequenced instruction in a series of skills to a more open-ended method in which students set their own pace and choose much of their reading material for themselves. But whatever the method of instruction, the emphasis is always on the students' own work, and the need for them to extend their reading beyond this book to the diverse materials they will come across as students and as professional workers.

Acknowledgments

I should like to thank my colleagues at Hunter College, especially Harriet Johnson and Martin Ostrofsky, for their valuable advice and encouragement in producing this book. I should also like to express my gratitude to those students who allowed me to print extracts from their journals. Finally, and most importantly, I acknowledge with appreciation the students in my classes, who contributed to the book by working through the material, giving me feedback, and making suggestions of their own. Any deficiencies that remain are entirely my responsibility.

Kate Parry

Contents

Contents

xi

CHAPTER FIVE

Reading for Testing 265

To the Student

Before you start using this book, you might take a moment to think about what you read and why you read it. What exactly have you read today? If you make a list, including every bit of print or writing that you have responded to, you will probably find that it includes a variety of material—not only textbooks, but also advertisements, newspaper and magazine articles, schedules, notes on the blackboard. Then think about why you have read all these things, and you will probably find that your reasons are as varied as the material. Finally, think about how you read them. Do you pay the same kind of attention to an advertisement as to a chapter in a textbook? Do you go through a shedule in the same way as you go through a novel? The answer to these questions is almost certainly "no"; your purpose is different in reading these different materials, and therefore you read in a different way.

That is the principle behind this book. Each chapter represents one of the major purposes that you, as an educated person, are likely to have in reading: *Reading for General Information, Reading for Pleasure, Reading for Study, Reading for Insight,* and *Reading for Testing.* The selections in each chapter are drawn from different sources, representing the kinds of material that most educated English-speakers read for these purposes: newspaper and magazine articles for general information, novels and memoirs for pleasure, textbooks for study, philosophical essays for insight, and sample item sets for tests. Exercises accompany all the reading selections, and these exercises also differ from chapter to chapter in order to reflect, as closely as possible, the appropriate way of treating that particular kind of material. At the beginning of each chapter there is an Introduction which explains how to use the exercises and describes some techniques that you might find useful, and it also suggests how you can go beyond the material given here.

This last point is important, because this book is only a tiny fraction of what you will read as a college student and professional worker. An ancient Hebrew thinker once wrote, "Of making many books there is no end." His remark is even more true in our time than it was in his; I hope that once you have read this book, you will have a better idea of which others you should go on to for your own purposes, and what would be the best way to approach them.

Reading for

General
Information

Reading is a major means by which people in most modern communities keep in touch with what is going on around them, especially at the national and international levels. You can, of course, hear about current affairs on the radio or television, but if you read newspapers and magazines, you have much greater choice as to where and when you will catch up on the news, and if you read efficiently, you can get more information in less time as well.

This chapter presents material typically found in newspapers and magazines. The selections are complete articles and cover topics of national and international concern. Articles of this sort are usually written rapidly and are not meant to be studied in great detail, and so they are suitable not only for working on your comprehension but also for improving your reading speed.

Reading Faster

You may feel that if you try to read faster, you will not be able to understand the material as well as you do when you read slowly. But this isn't always true: indeed, you will find that reading faster often improves your comprehension because you will more easily connect

1

the information that comes late in the text with what you read in the beginning.

The main factor in reading efficiently is *concentrating* on what you are doing. So be sure, before you begin any of the exercises in this chapter, that you are comfortable, that the light is good, and that the atmosphere is reasonably quiet. For the twenty minutes or so that it will take you to complete each exercise, put aside all thought of anything else—if you are so worried about something that you cannot put it aside, it is better not to do the exercise just then but to deal with whatever is worrying you. Try to keep your physical movements while reading to a minimum: "saying" the words silently as you read, pointing to them with your finger, or moving your head from side to side all tend to slow you down unnecessarily.

One problem that many people have when they read is the habit of looking back to points earlier in the text. If you do this, it obviously slows you down, both because you are reading some of the text twice and because it takes you extra time to find your place again when you continue reading. Sometimes looking back is necessary—if you are reading difficult and complicated material, for example—but it should be avoided as far as possible.

EXERCISE   **Reading without Looking Back**

To practice reading without looking back, take a plain sheet of paper or card and use it to cover each line of the following passage as you read it; thus it will be impossible to look back at the previous lines. Then see if you can answer the questions that follow. You may write the answers down if you like, but it is not necessary. If you cannot answer the questions, repeat the exercise: you will find that during the second reading you concentrate far more on taking in the information than you did the first time you read it, and this is exactly what you should train yourself to do. If you find this method of reading difficult, give yourself more practice; but don't try to do it with complicated material.

How Much Money Does It Take to Enjoy the American Dream?

Most of us talk about the American Dream, but few of us can define it. *The Wall Street Journal* set out to do just that recently in a survey conducted by the Roper Organization, and some of its findings are surprising. While a lot of Americans define the American Dream as getting rich, a much larger share define it as having freedom of choice, owning a home, and getting a good   5 education. Roper interviewed more than 1,500 Americans, and most of those polled—96 percent—include "freedom of choice in how to live one's life" as part of the Dream. Ninety-three percent of Americans include being "financially secure enough to have ample time for leisure pursuits" as part of the Dream. Ninety-one percent say it's the ability to start their own businesses. Only 80 percent believe that becoming wealthy defines the American Dream.

While some people scoff at the American Dream, fully 86 percent of Americans still believe in it. But is it reachable? Almost half of those polled—45 percent—say the Dream is harder to reach now than it once was. Another 23 percent say it's easier to achieve, and 32 percent say it's as easy as it has always been.

Only 5 percent of Americans say they have achieved the American Dream. Three percent say they've just begun the journey, while the rest say they are partway there. The largest group—25 percent of those polled—say they are halfway to the Dream.

You would expect that the affluent are more likely to say they're living the American Dream than those who aren't so well off. But this isn't the case. While 5 percent of people with incomes of less than $15,000 a year believe they've attained the Dream, only 6 percent of those with incomes of more than $50,000 a year say they have.

How much does the Dream cost? For most Americans, about $50,000 a year. A median income of $50,000 would enable most men and women to live the American Dream. But the cost of the American Dream increases with household income, starting at $50,000 a year for those with annual household incomes less than $15,000 and rising to $100,000 for those with incomes of $50,000 and up.

Joe Schwarz, from *American Demographics*

QUESTIONS

1. What was the survey commissioned by the *Wall Street Journal* intended to do?

_____

2. What was the single factor mentioned by most people as part of the American Dream?

_____

3. What was the attitude of most of the people surveyed toward the Dream?

_____

4. To what extent do people think they have achieved the American Dream?

_____

5. What is the difference between rich and poor people in what they say about the Dream?

_____

6. How much does the American Dream cost?

_____

Integrating the Text

One of the main problems in understanding a text is seeing how all the ideas in it are connected to one another. Reading faster will help you see the connections because you will have forgotten less of the beginning by the time you read the end, but there are also certain linguistic cues that you should be conscious of, such as *reference words, connectives, paragraph structure,* and the *overall organization.*

Understanding Reference Words

The pronouns *he, she, it, they, this, that, these,* and *those* don't have meaning in themselves. Rather, they are reference words used to tell readers or listeners to think of persons or things they already know about. In complete texts like the ones later in this chapter, these words nearly always refer to persons or things mentioned in the text, so you must be sure when you read such words that you know which persons or things they refer to. This is sometimes difficult, especially with the words *it, this,* and *that,* for they often refer to ideas rather than to concrete things—ideas that are usually expressed earlier in the text in a whole sentence or even several sentences. Examples appear in the first paragraph of the Selection 1-1 in this chapter:

> Carbon dioxide in the atmosphere has an important effect on world climate. *It* lets through most of the short-wave energy directed at the Earth by the sun, but retains a high proportion of the long-wave energy radiated back by the Earth out toward space. *This* is known as the "greenhouse effect," by analogy with the garden greenhouse whose glass windows admit solar radiation, but partially trap the infra-red radiation re-radiated from within. *This* causes the temperature in a greenhouse to rise to a higher level than that of the free air outside.

In your own words, indicate what exactly *this* refers to in each case.
Here is another example, from Selection 1-8:

> In [the past] 12 years, Americans have come a long way towards giving up smoking. In the country which tried and failed to give up drinking by means of Prohibition, in the country in which people used to walk a mile for a Camel and were never alone with a Lucky Strike, *it* is an astonishing phenomenon.

What is the astonishing phenomenon mentioned here?

You can find other examples of reference items used in this way in Selection 1-4, line 3; Selection 1-5, line 6; Selection 1-8, lines 30 and 54; and Selection 1-12, line 77.

Using Connectives

Like reference words, connectives are used to show how separate sentences are linked to one another. They are not often used in speech, but in writing—especially in journalistic and academic writing—you will find that they are common.

Connectives can be divided according to their meaning, into four groups.

The *and* Group.   Words of this group function in much the same way as *and*—that is, they tell you that the writer is adding something to whatever has already been said. On seeing one of these words, you can expect what follows to be another point of the same kind as what you have just read—a continuation of the story, an additional point in the description, or a strengthening of the argument. Following are the words in this group that you are most likely to come across:

additionally	furthermore
also	in addition
and	indeed
besides	moreover
eventually	next
first, second, etc.	then

For examples of *and* connectives, see Selection 1-1, line 26; Selection 1-2, lines 8, 15, and 24; Section 1-4, line 45; Selection 1-5, line 33; Selection 1-6, line 22; Selection 1-10, line 27; and Selection 1-12, lines 56, and 58.

The *but* Group.   But introduces an idea that contrasts—even contradicts—the idea just mentioned, and there are several more formal connectives that do the same thing. Here is a list of the most common words in this group:

actually	in fact
despite this	nevertheless
even so	on the other hand
however	still
in contrast	though (when it is not at the beginning of a clause)

Examples of *but* connectives are in Selection 1-2, line 30; Selection 1-6, lines 35, 40, 46, 58; Selection 1-7, line 24; Selection 1-8, lines 38 and 57; Selection 1-9, line 3; Selection 1-10, lines 34 and 39; and Selection 1-12, line 58.

The *so* Group. Words of this group show that the two ideas they link are causally related: the first idea is the cause of the second—or to put it another way, the second is a result of the first. The following list includes the most common of such words:

as a result	on account of this
because of this	then (notice that this connective can be used in
consequently	various ways)
for this reason	therefore
hence	thus
in consequence	

For examples of these connectives, see Selection 1-6, line 29; Selection 1-10, line 14; and Selection 1-11, lines 19 and 41.

The *e.g.* Group. The abbreviation e.g. tells a reader to expect an example or illustration of a general point that has just been made. The following phrases do the same thing:

for example
for instance

You will find these connectives used in Selection 1-4, lines 5, 35, and 45, and Selection 1-8, line 56.

EXERCISE   **Using Connectives to Make Predictions**

If you are aware of connectives and their meanings, you can use them to predict what the sentences and clauses introduced by them are likely to say. This will help you both read faster and understand better. Here are some examples from the selections that appear later in this chapter. Two or three sentences are printed in full, then only the first word or two of the next sentence, including a connective (in **bold**). Read each example, and try to predict what will come next. After you have thought about each example, and perhaps discussed it with others in your class, write what you expect to come next in the space provided. Then find out how accurate you have been by looking up the passage as it appears in the complete selection.

1. As the campaign [against smallpox] progressed the disease was gradually brought under control. By September 1976 the SEP made its first report that no new cases had been reported. **But** . . .

from Selection 1-3, Lines 21–23

_____

_____

2. Cancer is now one of the big killers of people over five years of age in the third world.
   The main reason is that the poor are living longer than they used to. **For example**, in China . . .

from Selection 1-4, Lines 3–6

_____

_____

3. There's a quiet revolution under way in Third World development, and it goes by the simple name of village banking. "It might as well be called an anti-poverty vaccine," says president John Hatch. "It works every time."
   It was a village bank loan of just $50, **for example**, that . . .

from Selection 1-2, Lines 1–4

_____

_____

4. For every kind of tragedy in the overcrowded city, Mother Teresa and her nuns managed to create a measure of consolation. They collected abandoned babies from gutters and garbage heaps and tried to nurse them back to health. They brought in the dying so they might die under care and among friends. Eventually the order built leprosariums, children's homes, havens for women, the handicapped and the old. The deepest consolation offered, **though**, was . . .

from Selection 1-5, Lines 29–34

_____

_____

5. Take education: in only 14 countries are there as many girls in primary schools as boys. In a number of developing countries, the proportion of girls attending primary school is still under 10%. **As a result**, out of an estimated 700 million illiterates, . . .

from Selection 1-7, Lines 5–8

_____

_____

6. Earlier this month the special prosecutor announced that the two nursing homes had agreed to plead guilty to lesser charges and stop soliciting contributions from the families of prospective residents.
   In addition, the Hebrew Home for the Aged agreed . . .

from Selection 1-9, Lines 76–79

_____

_____

7. "The difference between the poor who wind up homeless and those who don't seems to be a matter of having relatives to turn to when problems come up," McChesney suggests. **Yet** when families are homeless, society . . .

from Selection 1-11, Lines 66–68

_____

_____

EXERCISE   Linking Ideas without Connectives

Often the link between two sentences or two paragraphs is one of the *and, but, so,* or *e.g.* type, but it is not made explicit by the use of a connective. You can clarify such inexplicit links for yourself by deciding which of the connectives listed on pages 5–6 could be inserted. The following passages from the selections in this chapter are printed in their original form except that a blank is put in the places where you could clarify an inexplicit link by inserting a connective. Your task is to choose the connectives to insert; write your choice in the blank.

1. The pattern of cancers among the world's poorest people is still very different from that of the rich. In industrialized countries people die from lung, intestinal and prostate cancers as a consequence of smoking, alcohol abuse and high fat diets. _____ In the third world the most prevalent forms of cancer are those of the liver, mouth, esophagus and cervix, each of which claims 100,000–300,000 victims a year.

from Selection 1-4, Lines 10–15

2. A third of all cancers are preventable and a third are curable if detected early enough. _____ WHO is proposing a worldwide campaign on the link between smoking and cancer, which has only recently been acknowledged in chain-smoking China, for example; it will also press for reducing the tar content of cigarettes.

from Selection 1-4, Lines 42–45

3. For every kind of tragedy in the overcrowded city, Mother Teresa and her nuns managed to create a measure of consolation. _____ They collected abandoned babies from gutters and garbage heaps and tried to nurse them back to health.

from Selection 1-5, Lines 29–31

4. This year, with President Jimmy Carter a candidate because of his Camp David initiatives, Norwegians had visions of bomb searches, hovering helicopters and machine gun–toting guards. _____ Mother Teresa will not need them.

from Selection 1-5, Lines 50–53

5. A United Nations office, called the Center for Social Development and Humanitarian Affairs, is now assembling evidence to show just how unequal women, and particularly third-world women, are. _____ Take education: in only 14 countries are there as many girls in primary schools as boys.

from Selection 1-7, Lines 2–6

6. What was needed was an undercover team, a middle-age son and his elderly mother. _____ The New York City Department of Investigation supplied an investigator to portray the son, and at a community meeting of people concerned about nursing home issues, a representative of the Attorney General approached a 5-foot-5-inch, 108-pound woman with an engaging smile and passionate convictions about dozens of issues.

from Selection 1-9, Lines 30–35

7. As an ancient Chinese saying goes, "Bad parents produce bad children." Most single-child parents are survivors of the chaotic Cultural Revolution. _____ Many failed to finish their own schooling, and they are often ill equipped to rear children properly.

from Selection 1-10, Lines 57–60

8. We had a good reason to put this issue high on our agenda. The United States has the highest teen pregnancy rate of any similarly industrialized western nation, and we felt this was not an issue that would go away by just telling teens to say no. The rock stars and athletes speaking out against

drugs and drunk driving on TV weren't making any pitches for virginity. The situation had become even more confusing for teenagers because of the attention that abstinence was getting as the only sure way to prevent AIDS. _____ Our readers were left with a lot of unanswered questions that we felt were important to address.

from Selection 1-12, Lines 7–14

Recognizing Paragraph Structure

Often, especially in newspaper and magazine writing (and also in textbooks) paragraphs follow a typical pattern. That is, they begin with a sentence (or sometimes a question) that states the main point of the paragraph. This is called the *topic sentence*. The subsequent sentences give further detail on or explanation of the point: further detail may be introduced by an *e.g.* connective, and explanation by a phrase such as *the reason is*, but often the connection is not explicit. The following paragraph is an example from a passage quoted earlier in this introduction. The topic sentence is printed in bold type.

> **How much does the [American] Dream cost?** For most Americans, about $50,000 a year. A median income of $50,000 would enable most men and women to live the American Dream. But the cost of the American Dream increases with household income, starting at $50,000 a year for those with annual household incomes of less than $15,000, and rising to $100,000 for those with incomes of $50,000 and up.

And here is one from Selection 1-6 later in this chapter.

> **Our solution was an alternative magazine,** *Expression*. During the winter of 1937–38, a dozen or so of us wrote short stories, poetry, commentary and criticism, discarded the bulk of the material and wound up with 38 pages of typescript. Over an entire weekend in March, in the basement of a synagogue on West 85th Street, we mimeographed, collated and stapled about 300 copies. We sold them the following Monday in Clinton's corridors for a nickel each.

However, paragraphs are not always organized in this way. Another pattern starts with one or more specific illustrations and concludes with the main point expressed in a topic sentence. The following example of this pattern is taken from Selection 1-8.

> I associate New York particularly with smoking because it was there, 12 years ago almost to the day, that I at last managed to give up the habit. My last pack of king-size Kent went into the trash can at the corner

of Lexington and 76th Street. Today I thought I might go there and observe a moment's silence. In those 12 years, Americans have come a long way towards giving up smoking. In the country which tried and failed to give up drinking by means of Prohibition, in the country in which people used to walk a mile for a Camel and were never alone with a Lucky Strike, it is an astonishing phenomenon. Humphrey Bogart, who died of lung cancer, must be turning in his grave. According to Stanley Michels, the New York city councilman who sponsored the anti-smoking legislation: "This is one of the most fantastic social changes we've seen in our lifetime. **Smoking is now considered antisocial behavior**."

This pattern is much less common, however, than the one discussed earlier.

A third pattern begins a paragraph with a statement of some commonly held opinion or relatively unimportant fact. Then a *but* connective introduces the writer's own opinion or a fact that the writer considers to be important. This emphasizes the point, so you should pay attention to statements that are made in this way. You can see how the pattern works in this example from a passage quoted earlier:

You would expect that the affluent are more likely to say they're living the American Dream than those who aren't so well off. **But this isn't the case**. While 5 percent of people with incomes of less than $15,000 a year believe they've attained the Dream, only 6 percent of those with incomes of more than $50,000 a year say they have.

Again, this is a relatively uncommon pattern, and you would be unlikely to find it more than once in a single article.

Some paragraphs do not have a topic sentence. All the sentences of such a paragraph, however, are generally about the same point, and that point can be summed up in a single sentence or phrase. Consider this example from Selection 1-5:

Mother Teresa was born in 1910 to Albanian parents and baptized Agnes Gonxha Bojaxhiu in what is now Skoplje, Yugoslavia. Even at the age of twelve she wanted to "go out and give the love of Christ." By the time she was 18, Agnes had joined the Irish branch of Loreto nuns who were working in Calcutta, where she soon began teaching geography at St. Mary's High School. When the Church granted her permission to lay aside her Loreto habit and take up the blue-edged, coarse cotton white sari that became the uniform of the Missionaries of Charity, young women from St. Mary's soon joined her.

There is no topic sentence in this paragraph, but there is a clear topic:
Mother Teresa's life up to her founding of the Missionaries of Charity.

EXERCISE   **Identifying Topic Sentences**

Four of the following paragraphs have clear topic sentences; underline the
topic sentence in each case. Two paragraphs do not have topic sentences.
Write in the margin beside each of these paragraphs, "No topic sentence. The
topic is . . . ," and complete the sentence by naming the topic as you
understand it.

1. McChesney's study also revealed that homeless families have something in
   common besides poverty: they are unable to turn parents, brothers, or
   sisters for help because their families are either dead, out of state, or
   estranged. "Considering the median age of the women in the sample, they
   had a surprisingly high number of deceased parents," says McChesney.
   "Thirty percent of the women had deceased mothers, with three women not
   knowing enough about their mothers to know whether they were alive or
   dead," she writes, "making about a third of the women with no mother to turn
   to."

   from Selection 1-11, Lines 44–51

2. On my left was Seymour Krim (later, a respected writer and critic), who had
   written a short story considered by his peers to have been the best
   submitted; it was thus given the lead spot. It contained no four-letter words,
   but it did have a three-letter word referring to the buttocks. It was about a
   psychologically disturbed individual who climbed a tower on a college
   campus with a rifle (this, decades before it actually occurred in Texas) and
   shot people at random.

   from Selection 1-6, Lines 27–32

3. The world's last known case of smallpox (outside the Birmingham laboratory
   outbreak) was reported in Somalia, the Horn of Africa, in October 1977. The
   victim was a young cook called Ali Maow Maalin. His case becomes a
   landmark in medical history, for smallpox is the first communicable disease
   ever to be eradicated.

   from Selection 1-3, Lines 1–5

4. The Chinese press frequently runs cautionary tales of cozened brats. A
   cartoon in *Chinese Youth*, for example, depicts an obese child lying in a bed
   littered with toys, stuffing himself with cakes and milk served by Mother,
   while Father stands ready to dress him. In his column in the *China Daily*, Xu

Yihe writes disapprovingly of Jiajia, a friend's pampered daughter who barely budges to prepare for school in the morning. While Jiajia sits on her bed, says Xu, "her mother combs her hair, her grandmother feeds her breakfast, her grandfather is under the table putting her shoes on, and her father is getting her satchel ready." Single children are well aware of their special status. Said one: "I ride on Daddy's shoulders and ask my parents to make a circle with their arms. Then I say 'You are the sky, and I am the little red sun.'"

from Selection 1-10, Lines 17–27

5. At the first editorial meeting of *Sassy* magazine, in 1987, the staff sat around the editor-in-chief's office discussing how to make our new magazine different from other teenage publications. The unanimous first priority was to provide sex education: Since we had read the competition during our own adolescence, we knew the sex information published by teen magazines was scarce and usually couched in judgmental terms.

from Selection 1-12, Lines 1–6

6. Most people think cancer is a disease of rich western countries. No longer. More than half of the 6 million people who die from cancer each year are in developing countries. Cancer is now one of the big killers of people over five years of age in the third world.

from Selection 1-4, Lines 1–4

Patterns of Overall Organization

Articles like those reprinted in this chapter tend to follow patterns similar to those we have seen in individual paragraphs. First, the topic sentence of one of the early paragraphs (usually the first) provides a *thesis statement* for the whole article—that is, it states the main point the writer is making. The subsequent paragraphs provide illustrations or explanations of that point, and the conclusion often restates the thesis. The following article is organized in this way. To help you see the pattern, the topic sentence of each paragraph is printed in bold, and the thesis statement is underlined as well (you will notice how both the thesis statement and the topic sentences are related to the title of the piece). Try reading just the words in bold before you read the whole article, and notice that by doing this you get the main ideas without any details.

Emissions Making World "Car Sick"

Massive reliance on the automobile is exacting a heavy toll on human health and the biosphere, claims Michael Renner of the Worldwatch Institute. After slackening following the last decade's oil shocks,

car sales figures are now at record heights. Yet, as the auto industry
becomes more vigorous, the natural environment increasingly suffers.   5

    **"Cars account for a hefty portion of nearly all the major pollu-
tants found in the atmosphere.** They adversely affect human health and
the quality of urban air, forest, aquatic life, and agriculture. The automobile has already made some of the world's cities barely habitable and,
with its contribution to the greenhouse effect, could affect the habitability   10
of the planet as a whole."

    Phasing out lead has been the principal success story in the fight
against automobile air pollution. However, **other car pollutants—nitro-
gen and sulfur oxides, carbon monoxide, hydrocarbons, and particles—are more difficult to reduce because they are natural products**   15
of the combustion process. "The latest generation of catalytic converters
drastically curtail production of these substances, but only a handful of
countries require them. Even in these countries, emission levels are still
unacceptable because of the sheer number of miles being driven."

    Cars also contribute heavily to the formation of ground-level   20
ozone, a dangerous pollutant. High concentrations of ozone not only
affect urban air quality, but also are thought partially to be responsible
for the massive damage to central Europe's forests. The U.S. National
Crop Loss Assessment Program calculates that annual ozone damage to
four crops alone—corn, wheat, soybeans, and peanuts—may top   25
$4,000,000,000. In Athens, ozone-based smog is reckoned to claim as
many as 30 lives a year.

    In addition, car exhaust combines with emissions from other sources
to produce another environmental scourge*—acid rain—which is killing crops, trees, and fish in the eastern U.S. and Europe. Automotive   30
fuels account for an estimated 17% of worldwide emission of carbon
dioxide—the primary gas responsible for the greenhouse effect. A number of measures, such as new engine designs and alternative fuels, would
reduce pollution from cars. **"But if we are to make lasting reductions**
in pollution, <u>we need to go beyond technical fixes and considerways</u>   35
<u>to reduce our excessive reliance on the automobile,</u>" Renner explains.

U.S.A. Today

    News stories, however, are often organized the other way around:
they may begin with a specific example and draw the main point from
it. Stories written in this way often don't have a topic sentence in
every paragraph, as you can see in the following article; and sometimes the topic sentence refers not to the paragraph it is in but to the

---

* Technically, this is not a proper topic sentence because it mentions only one "environmental scourge," whereas the paragraph deals with two. But clearly you are expected to consider the greenhouse effect as an environmental scourge as well.

paragraph that follows. In the following selection, the topic sentences are again printed in bold face, as are those words from previous sentences that are necessary to explain the reference words. The sentence that can best be described as a thesis statement is both in boldface and underlined. Again, read just the boldface words before you read the whole article.

Hope Wins When the Homeless Run

Ernie Garcia was hot, sweaty and tired after a five-kilometer training run on Saturday. But his grin seemed wider than the running track and his happiness had little to do with the fact that he had finished the tree-lined course far ahead of his friends.

"Two months ago I couldn't have run a block," said Mr. Garcia, a 5 former high school football player who is 31 years old and lives in a skid row mission. He said he began drinking and taking cocaine heavily after separating from his wife and losing his job three years ago.

He is returning to his athletic glory days, he said, thanks to the prayer and training he began two months ago for **this weekend's fund-raising** 10 **"Run for the Homeless" at Griffith Park. About 200 skid row residents have signed up for the five-kilometer race** (about three miles), which is expected to attract at least 2,000 other runners.

This is the second year of the race. **Originally intended strictly as a fund-raising event, the race has evolved into a program for the home-** 15 **less,** organizers say. Besides raising self-esteem, the race exposes the homeless not only to the discipline of running, but also to other runners and the activities of mainstream society.

"There's a real sense of hope coming from the race," said John Dillon, executive director of **the Chrysalis Center, which tries to help the** 20 **homeless help themselves. The nonprofit center is the beneficiary and main sponsor of the race.**

"This running just gives me a chance to be free," said Andre Downs, who came in second among the homeless runners last year.

For Saturday's training run, Mr. Downs was with about 50 other 25 homeless runners and his friend Harvey Newton, 46, who also lives in a skid row hotel. Both men run whenever they can, normally on lunch hours when they do odd jobs. They train outside their downtown neighborhood, an environment that poses challenges other runners seldom face, they said. 30

"My leg has been out of the cast for less than two months," said Mr. Newton, who finished third in last year's race but does not expect to do as well this time. "I was helping to throw this rowdy guy out of the hotel," he said with a shrug. "A fight broke out and, well, somehow my leg just broke." 35

The race is one of several new actions to aid the homeless in the nation's second largest city,* where the number of people without permanent homes is estimated to range from 35,000 to 50,000.

Last week, for example, the city's Community Redevelopment Agency approved $360,000 in loans to expand shelters for the homeless. 40 And also last week, Los Angeles began its Homeless Outreach program, which employs street people to spread the word about social programs available for skid row residents.

Runners and teams pay fees to enter the race. Participants in an accompanying 10-kilometer walk pledge donations to help the homeless. 45

"But then we decided to get the homeless themselves involved," Mr. Dillon said. The homeless are provided running shoes and clothing (some of it donated), as well as box lunches and bus rides for four training runs and clinics, which stress nutrition and safety. Bus rides are also provided for the final race. 50

Mr. Dillon said he expected the race to raise $50,000, but $20,000 of that would go for race-related expenses, including prizes ranging from $150 to $200 for the top finishers.

The Chrysalis Center official is convinced that the race is well worth the expense. In addition to improving self-esteem, he said, the 55 race last year induced at least eight of the 27 homeless people who ran in it to enter job programs. A few others were hired by runners they met in the race.

"About 30 people out here are even thinking about the prize money," said George Marrett, the chairman of the race. "The rest are here for their 60 health and a sense of accomplishment." Myrtis June Hall, a stooped mother of six, all in foster homes, has lived in a skid row hotel for seven years—"things just sort of fell apart," she said.

She said she planned to walk the race. "I've enjoyed this very much, getting out of the hotel and all," she added. "Just because you live in skid 65 row, you don't have to be skid row."

David S. Wilson, the *New York Times*

As you can see, this article consists almost entirely of examples, and many of the paragraphs have no topic sentence.

Some articles give no explicit statement of their thesis—that is, the point of the story—but the thesis may be more or less clearly implied. Consider, for example, Selection 1-6. The selection ends with these two sentences:

Perhaps he [Mr. Clark] did learn something from the A.C.L.U. I like to think so.

* Los Angeles.

What did Mr. Clark learn? The writer doesn't tell you, but you are expected to figure it out for yourself. Read the article, and see what you think.

EXERCISE   **Recognizing Overall Organization**

You may find it helpful to go over a number of the selections in this chapter, trying to identify the topic sentences for those paragraphs that have them, and the overall pattern of organization in each article. You will find this easiest to do in Selections 1-1, 1-4, 1-7, 1-10, and 1-12: underline the topic sentence for each paragraph, if there is one, and put a star in the margin beside the thesis statement. You might also look at Selections 1-5 and 1-10, neither of which has an explicit thesis statement. Write down what you think the thesis is in each of these cases, and then discuss it with your classmates.

Dealing with New Vocabulary

One of the most common factors that causes difficulty in reading is unfamiliar vocabulary. If you don't know the words in a text, how can you understand what they say? And if you take the time to look up in a dictionary every new word you read, how can you remember what the passage is about? But new words need not be altogether discouraging, for if you look carefully at their relationship with other, familiar, words around them, you will find that it is often possible to work out their meanings quite accurately—without the use of a dictionary.

Ask yourself several questions when you come across a new word:

1. Judging from the word's place in the sentence, which of the following four kinds of word is it? (It is almost certainly one of them.)
   — a *noun* (a word that *names* someone or something)
   — a *verb* (a word that indicates what someone or something *experiences* or *does*)
   — an *adjective* (a word that *describes* someone or something)
   — an *adverb* (a word that gives more information about an *action*, such as how, when, where, or why it happens)
2. If it's a noun, is it the *subject* of a verb? That is, does it appear before it, as someone or something that does what the verb says? Or is it the *object* of a verb? That is, does the word appear after

it, suggesting that it receives or is affected by the action? Judging from its relationship to that verb, does it seem to name something concrete, like a person, an animal, a thing, or a place? Or does it seem to name something more abstract?

3. If it's a verb, what is its subject? What follows the verb? With such a subject and with its ending, what kind of action could the verb represent?

4. If it's an adjective, what noun does it refer to? What kind of characteristic is likely to describe whatever is named by the noun?

5. If it's an adverb, what action or event does it tell you more about? How could that action or event be described?

6. Whichever kind of word it is, can you think of another word of the same kind that you could put in its place so that the sentence makes sense?

7. When you replace the new word as suggested in (6), does the sentence then agree with whatever else is said in the paragraph?

8. If the word appears more than once, does the meaning you guess for it work for both or all the contexts in which it appears? (Often you will find that although you cannot guess the meaning of a word when you first come across it, you can when you find it a second or third time).

EXERCISE   **Word Meanings from Context**

In the following passages, some of the words have been left out. Your task is to work out word meanings from the context by asking yourself the above questions about the blank spaces. Then write down the word that you think might have been there. You are not expected to arrive at the original word (it may, in fact, be one you do not know), but you should be able to get one that has a similar, though perhaps a more general, meaning.

A "Death" Sentence

Instead of being sentenced to jail, Californians convicted of first drunk-driving offenses are being sentenced to fines, probation and (1) _____ visits to the morgue. It is not so much a shock treatment program (2) _____ say, as a lesson in the (3) _____ of human life.

Since the compulsory program was initiated by a Sacramento judge, more than four hundred young drivers have received the morgue sentence. Of those four hundred, only six had second DWI arrests. That is a pretty impressive score, considering other DWI (4) _____ rates of 30 percent to 50 percent.

Ordering drunk drivers to visit or perform volunteer work at morgues or emergency rooms has been done before. But California is the first state to encourage officially that it be routine. It is to be hoped that other states and individual judges will follow suit. A morgue visit takes horror out of the (5) _____ and gives it a face: the drunk drivers see their potential victims—or maybe themselves.

The Depression of 1990

Only two generations ago, the United States was beset by an unprecedented economic disaster that shook the very (1) _____ of Western civilization. The stock market crashed; prices, interest rates, and wages fell like dominoes; and unemployment (2) _____ engulfing 25 percent of the labor force. Suddenly there was mass poverty, and soon thousands were on the (3) _____ of starvation.

Can it happen again? Can this plague of mass poverty and unemployment (4) _____ our society again? Presumably the "great crash" of 1929 was a (5) _____ event in our history, and now we have a full (6) _____ of protective measures to guard against a recurrence. To think otherwise is to be (7) _____ a prophet of doom.

The Rise of Print Culture

The invention and widespread use of printing from moveable type—the first of the modern media—dramatically (1) _____ the entire fabric of Western culture, making literacy and education possible and (2) _____ opening the way to mass communication. The publication of books became an (3) _____ part of the excitement of the (4) _____ of learning in an age of discovery and of (5) _____ exploration. Printing helped to bring about the transition from the philosophy of the Middle Ages to the new and often (6) _____ perspectives of the modern era. Without the invention of printing, the Industrial Revolution of the nineteenth century and the contemporary electronic revolution may never have occurred.

If you compare your answers in the preceding exercise with those of your classmates, and with those that your instructor gives you, you will find that you have been able to understand the "unknown words" quite well. Try to use the context of a passage in this way to guess the meaning of most of the new words that you come across in this chapter. So when working on a selection, try not to use your dictionary—at least until you have finished reading the selection and have done your best to answer the questions; then, if you wish, check any guesses you have made.

Using the Reading Selections and Exercises

The remainder of this chapter provides twelve reading selections to help you practice increasing your reading speed and comprehension. The following points suggest how the selections and accompanying exercises should be used:

1. Take note of the time as you start to read each selection (if you are reading in class, your instructor will probably tell you when to begin).

2. Read the selection as quickly as you can, trying to concentrate fully on it.

3. As soon as you have finished reading, record how long you took; there is a space for this at the end of the selection.

4. Go through the Comprehension Check that follows the selection. For each item, choose the alternative (a,b,c, or d) that seems the most appropriate way of completing the item, and write the letter of your choice in the "1st answer" blank. Do this rapidly, and *do not look back at the text.* If you can't remember enough to make a choice, leave the space blank.

5. After you have finished writing your first answers, read the selection again, looking for the particular words or sentences that contain the answers to the items. When you find each answer, write the number(s) of the line(s) in which it appears in the space marked "Line reference(s)" after the appropriate item.

6. As you review the answers, you may find that you change your mind about some of your choices or wish to fill in an answer where you skipped it before. If so, leave what you wrote under "1st answer" untouched (including any that you left blank), but write the choice that you now prefer in the space marked "2nd answer."

7. Find out your reading speed by checking the chart that follows the Comprehension Check. First find the time you took (to the nearest fifteen seconds), and then look at the same line in the column to the right of this figure; there you will see your speed in words per minute (wpm). If the time you took is not given, find out your speed by dividing the number of words by the number of minutes. Write down the speed in the space provided after item 10 of the Comprehension Check.

8. Your instructor may ask you to discuss your answers either together as a class or in small groups; your task in that case will be to defend the choices you have made by referring to the appropriate lines of the text. If you are working in a group and there is a difference of opinion, it means that one of the group members has misinterpreted the text in some way. Go over the alternatives again carefully, trying to work out the justification for each of them: the one that is closest in meaning to the text is the right one.

9. Your instructor may wish to go over the Comprehension Check with you. Put a check (√) next to each correct alternative you wrote down in either column and a cross (X) next to each incorrect one. Do not make any alterations in your answers; instead, mark the correct alternative for each item by circling the letter by which it is identified.

10. Write down two scores for yourself in the spaces provided after Comprehension Check item 10: the number you got correct after the first reading (when you did not look back at the text), and the number you got correct after the second reading (when you did look back at the text). These scores will help your instructor give you appropriate advice for improving your comprehension.

11. Turn to the two graphs provided in the Appendix at the end of the book. Use these graphs to record your progress. On the top graph, write the selection number at the top of the first column, the date below it, and an X across the vertical bar on the horizontal line that represents your speed. Then use the bottom graph in the same way to mark your first score on the Comprehension Check. Next time you do one of these exercises record the information in the next column, and use a ruler to connect the Xs in each graph. After several weeks you may have a record that looks like the graph on the next page.

    The figures given on the sample graph are those recorded by a student who worked with an earlier version of this book. She was reading passages from both Chapter 1, Reading for General Information, and Chapter 2, Reading for Pleasure. As you can see, she was a strong student: her speed increased dramatically, and she maintained a constant first score (that is, the score for the answers she gave before she looked back at the passage) of 7 or above. This is entirely satisfactory—try to do as well yourself.

12. When you have finished the Comprehension Check, think about the Questions for Discussion, which are intended to encourage you to think about what you have read in relation to your own experience. Write your answers down briefly and hand them in to your instructor, or use them as a guide in discussion with your classmates.

22

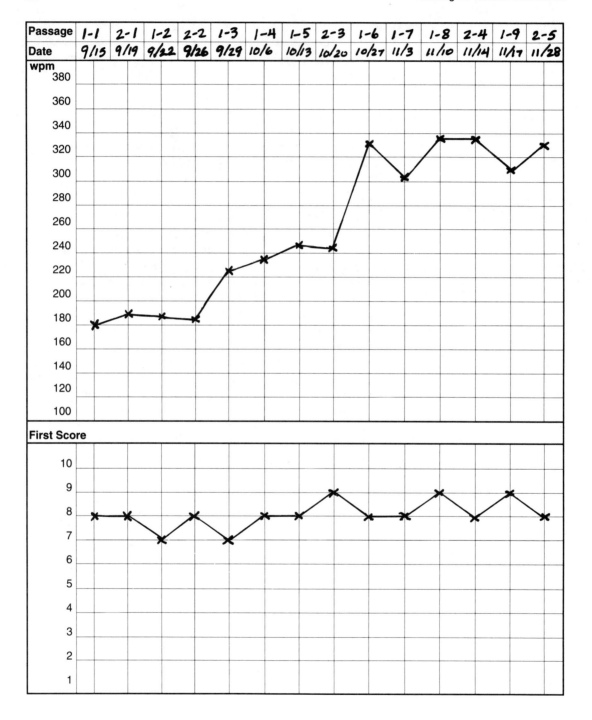

SELECTION
1-1

The Greenhouse Effect

Start time _____

Carbon dioxide in the atmosphere has an important effect on world climate. It lets through most of the short-wave energy directed at the earth by the sun, but retains a high proportion of the long-wave energy radiated back by the earth out toward space. This is known as the "greenhouse effect," by analogy with the garden greenhouse whose glass windows admit solar radiation, but partially   5
trap the infrared radiation reradiated from within. This causes the temperature in a greenhouse to rise to a higher level than that of the free air outside.

Because of the rise in carbon dioxide concentration in the atmosphere (from 265 parts per million in 1850 to 340 parts per million in 1985), due primarily to the combustion of fossil fuels (e.g., coal, oil and natural gas), scientists predict   10
that significant changes in climate patterns will occur by the end of the century. They foresee a rise in average global temperature of between 3° and 5° Centigrade before the year 2010.

Temperature increases in the polar regions could be three times the global average, which would result in rapid melting of the polar ice caps. Sea levels   15
could rise by as much as 5 to 7 meters, causing flooding of vast areas of low-lying land.

Trees normally act as a sink for carbon dioxide, which they "inhale," returning oxygen as waste to the atmosphere as they "exhale." However, when trees are cleared or burned, the carbon they contain, as well as some of the carbon in   20
the underlying soil, is oxidized and released to the atmosphere. Since 1860 some 90 to 180 thousand million tons of carbon have been released to the atmosphere as a result of forest clearing, as compared with 150 to 190 thousand million tons from the burning of coal, oil and natural gas.

Many scientists consider the warming of the atmosphere as posing one of the   25
most serious environmental threats to man. And forest clearance is doubly harmful since not only is the carbon "sink" effect of trees lost, but more carbon is released to the atmosphere.

The Courier (UNESCO)
345 words

Time Taken
(min./sec.) _____

COMPREHENSION Choose the best way of finishing each statement, according to the passage,
CHECK and write the letter on the "1st answer" blank. Then follow the directions on
pages 20–21.

1. The "greenhouse effect" refers to the process by which the earth becomes
   a. warmer.
   b. cooler.
   c. more humid.
   d. more fertile.

   _____   _____   _____
   1st answer   Line reference(s)   2nd answer

2. Carbon dioxide in the atmosphere
   a. prevents heat from passing through it.
   b. transfers heat from the sun to the earth.
   c. allows heat from the earth out but not heat from the sun in.
   d. allows heat from the sun in but not heat from the earth out.

   _____   _____   _____
   1st answer   Line reference(s)   2nd answer

3. Carbon dioxide is compared to a garden greenhouse because it
   a. conserves moisture.
   b. retains energy.
   c. admits light.
   d. provides shelter.

   _____   _____   _____
   1st answer   Line reference(s)   2nd answer

4. According to the first paragraph, carbon dioxide
   a. reflects infrared light.
   b. transmits ultraviolet light.
   c. traps long-wave energy.
   d. traps short-wave energy.

   _____   _____   _____
   1st answer   Line reference(s)   2nd answer

5. Between 1850 and 1985 the proportion of carbon dioxide in the atmosphere has

   a. remained approximately the same.
   b. multiplied several times.
   c. more than doubled.
   d. increased by nearly a third.

   _____   _____   _____
     1st answer   Line reference(s)   2nd answer

6. The main reason for the changing level of carbon dioxide is

   a. the rise in the earth's temperature.
   b. the burning of fossil fuels.
   c. the increase in the human population.
   d. the use of automobiles.

   _____   _____   _____
     1st answer   Line reference(s)   2nd answer

7. The change in the earth's climate is expected to be most intense

   a. in industrialized countries.
   b. in developing countries.
   c. in the polar regions.
   d. on the equator.

   _____   _____   _____
     1st answer   Line reference(s)   2nd answer

8. Flooding is expected because

   a. a lot of ice will melt.
   b. there will be greatly increased rainfall.
   c. less water will evaporate.
   d. trees will no longer retain water.

   _____   _____   _____
     1st answer   Line reference(s)   2nd answer

9. Trees are connected with the greenhouse effect because they

   a. make the earth warmer.
   b. absorb carbon dioxide.
   c. convert oxygen into carbon dioxide.
   d. fix oxygen in the soil.

   _____   _____   _____
     1st answer   Line reference(s)   2nd answer

10. The last paragraph suggests that

    a. deforestation should be stopped.
    b. industrialization should be slower.
    c. there will soon be no fossil fuels left.
    d. air pollution is the most serious problem.

 _____   _____   _____
    1st answer   Line reference(s)   2nd answer

CHART FOR FINDING OUT READING SPEED

Time	wpm	Time	wpm	Time	wpm	Time	wpm	Time	wpm
1:00	345	1:45	197	2:30	138	3:15	106	4:00	86
1:15	276	2:00	173	2:45	125	3:30	99	4:15	81
1:30	230	2:15	153	3:00	115	3:45	92	4:30	77

Speed in words per minute _____

Total correct on 1st reading _____

Total correct on 2nd reading _____

QUESTIONS FOR DISCUSSION

1. Does this article have any significance for your own life? Why, or why not?

2. What do you think can or should be done about the greenhouse effect?

3. If nothing is done, what do you think will happen?

**SELECTION
1-2**

Start time _____

At the Frontlines: Foundation for International Community Assistance

There's a quiet revolution under way in Third World development, and it goes by the simple name of village banking. "It might as well be called an antipoverty vaccine," says president John Hatch. "It works every time."

It was a village bank loan of just $50, for example, that enabled a group of women in Columbia to buy sewing machines for making baby clothes, which 5 they now sell commercially. It was loans of just $400 that allowed Maria Alfonsa Lopez of Honduras to expand her rope business, and afford a cement floor for her family's shack. The loans also allowed her to break the grip of the local moneylender, who had been charging her 10 percent a day.

The banks are set up by more than a dozen different groups—including 10 Hatch's Foundation for International Community Assistance (FINCA)—which get seed money from individuals, corporations, foundations, and agencies like the United Nations Development Program. They channel that money into loans to the poorest of the poor in areas as diverse as Latin America, Afrida, Central America, and Asia. And though the borrowers are often illiterate, with no prior 15 credit experience, repayment rates are typically 97 percent or better.

A number of village banks follow the model of the Grameen Bank of Bangladesh, in which borrowers must form groups of five and meet weekly with a bank officer for management advice. At first, only two members may apply for a loan, and depending on their repayments, two more may apply, then the fifth. 20 If any one member can't make payments, credit for the entire group is jeopardized.

Most loans go to women, Hatch says, because they've proven to be the most creative and productive providers for their families. And there are several groups, such as the Self Employed Women's Association in India, which focus 25 exclusively on women.

What these entrepreneurial programs demonstrate is "the magic of the marketplace," says John Sewell of the Overseas Development Council. They demonstrate the value of a trickle-up approach to development, giving aid not to governments but to small entrepreneurs. But as encouraging as the village bank 30 model is, it's not an instant panacea. "You can't throw money at it," says Robert Payton, former ambassador to Cameroon in West Africa. "You can't push it faster than it will go."

Marjorie Kelly, *Utne Reader*
387 words

**Time Taken
(min./sec.)** _____

Choose the best way of finishing each statement, according to the passage, and write the letter in the "1st answer" blank. Then follow the direction on pages 20–21.

1. The words *quiet revolution* are used in this article to describe
   a. industrial development.
   b. improved agriculture.
   c. gradual political change.
   d. investment in poor communities.

   _____   _____   _____
   1st answer   Line reference(s)   2nd answer

2. A group of women in Colombia used a $50 loan to
   a. set up business making baby clothes.
   b. buy fertilizer and seed for crops.
   c. equip their children for school.
   d. improve the buildings they live in.

   _____   _____   _____
   1st answer   Line reference(s)   2nd answer

3. Maria Alfonso Lopez had to pay the local moneylender a rate of 10 percent
   a. a year.
   b. a month.
   c. a week.
   d. a day.

   _____   _____   _____
   1st answer   Line reference(s)   2nd answer

4. FINCA is an organization that
   a. organizes international development projects.
   b. raises money to lend to poor people.
   c. sets up bank branches in villages.
   d. provides technical expertise for new industries.

   _____   _____   _____
   1st answer   Line reference(s)   2nd answer

5. The clients whom FINCA helps are often

  a. irresponsible with money.
  b. unable to read.
  c. physically disabled.
  d. unwilling to go into debt.

  _____ _____ _____
  1st answer   Line reference(s)   2nd answer

6. When FINCA lends money, it gets paid back

  a. rarely.
  b. often.
  c. usually.
  d. always.

  _____ _____ _____
  1st answer   Line reference(s)   2nd answer

7. The Grameen Bank will only lend money to

  a. heads of families.
  b. groups of five people.
  c. people with good credit.
  d. women with children.

  _____ _____ _____
  1st answer   Line reference(s)   2nd answer

8. FINCA most often helps women because

  a. they are poorer than men.
  b. they live more orderly lives.
  c. they produce more and have more ideas.
  d. they are less likely to steal.

  _____ _____ _____
  1st answer   Line reference(s)   2nd answer

9. A *trickle-up approach to development* means

  a. providing individuals with small amounts of capital.
  b. working only in remote rural areas.
  c. giving aid to the governments of small countries.
  d. educating people in business methods.

  _____ _____ _____
  1st answer   Line reference(s)   2nd answer

10. The article concludes that the kind of work that FINCA does
   a. will eventually solve the world's economic problems.
   b. represents a breakthrough in economic development.
   c. is not always as effective as it should be.
   d. is helpful but will not solve problems by itself.

_____   _____   _____
  1st answer   Line reference(s)   2nd answer

CHART FOR FINDING OUT READING SPEED

Time	wpm	Time	wpm	Time	wpm	Time	wpm	Time	wpm
1:00	387	1:45	221	2:30	155	3:15	119	4:00	97
1:15	310	2:00	194	2:45	141	3:30	111	4:15	91
1:30	258	2:15	172	3:00	129	3:45	103	4:30	86

Speed in words per minute _____

Total correct on 1st reading _____

Total correct on 2nd reading _____

QUESTIONS FOR DISCUSSION

1. Can you think of circumstances in which a small amount of capital (say $50 or $100) could contribute significantly to an individual's or a community's prosperity? How could it do so?

2. If you had money to give away, would you give it to FINCA? Why, or why not?

3. Given that FINCA lends money only to poor people, how is it that it has such a high repayment rate? What makes people pay the money back?

4. How do you account for the observation that women have "proven to be the most creative and productive providers for their families"?

**SELECTION
1-3**

How the Smallpox War Was Won

Start time _____

The world's last known case of smallpox (outside the Birmingham laboratory outbreak) was reported in Somalia, the Horn of Africa, in October 1977.
The victim was a young cook called Ali Maow Maalin. His case becomes a
landmark in medical history, for smallpox is the first communicable disease
ever to be eradicated.   5

The remarkable campaign to free the world of smallpox has been led by the
World Health Organization. The Horn of Africa, embracing the Ogaden region
of Ethiopia and Somalia, was one of the last few smallpox ridden areas of the
world when the WHO-sponsored Smallpox Eradication Program (SEP) got un-
derway there in 1971.   10

Many of the 25 million inhabitants, mostly farmers and nomads living in a
wilderness of desert, bush and mountains, already had smallpox. The problem
of tracing the disease in such formidable country was exacerbated further by the
continuous warfare in the area.

The program concentrated on an imaginative policy of "search and contain-   15
ment." Vaccination was used to reduce the widespread incidence of the disease,
but the success of the campaign depended on the work of volunteers. These
were men, paid by the day, who walked hundreds of miles in search of
"rumors"—information about possible smallpox cases.

Often these rumors turned out to be cases of measles, chicken pox or syph-   20
ilis—but nothing could be left to chance. As the campaign progressed the disease was gradually brought under control. By September 1976 the SEP made
its first report that no new cases had been reported. But that first optimism was
short-lived. A three-year-old girl called Amina Salat, from a dusty village in
the Ogaden in the south-east of Ethiopia, had given smallpox to a young nomad 25
visitor. Leaving the village the nomad had walked across the border into
Somalia. There he infected 3,000 people, and among them had been the cook,
Ali. It was a further 14 months before the elusive "target zero"—no further
cases—was reached.

Even now, the search continues in "high risk" areas and in parts of the   30
country unchecked for some time. The flow of rumors has now diminished to a
trickle—but each must still be checked by a qualified person.

Victory is in sight, but two years must pass since the "last case" before an
International Commission can declare that the world is entirely free from smallpox.   35

**Time Taken
(min./sec.)** _____

The *Observer*
390 words

Choose the best way of finishing each statement, according to the passage, and write the letter in the "1st answer" blank. Then follow the directions on pages 20–21.

1. Ali Maow Maalin is significant because he
   a. reported the last case of smallpox to the World Health Organization.
   b. was the first person in Somalia to be vaccinated.
   c. was the first smallpox victim in Somalia.
   d. was the last known case of smallpox in the world.

   _____   _____   _____
   1st answer   Line reference(s)   2nd answer

2. The eradication of smallpox was particularly difficult in Somalia because
   a. people were unwilling to report cases.
   b. people refused to be vaccinated.
   c. cases were difficult to trace.
   d. the disease was being used as a weapon of war.

   _____   _____   _____
   1st answer   Line reference(s)   2nd answer

3. The volunteers mentioned were used to
   a. find out about the reported cases of smallpox.
   b. vaccinate people in remote areas.
   c. teach people how to treat smallpox.
   d. prevent infected people from moving around.

   _____   _____   _____
   1st answer   Line reference(s)   2nd answer

4. When a case was investigated
   a. it was always found to be smallpox.
   b. it was usually found to be nothing at all.
   c. it was often found to be some other disease.
   d. it always proved to be serious.

   _____   _____   _____
   1st answer   Line reference(s)   2nd answer

5. By September 1976,

   a. smallpox had been eradicated.
   b. there were still a few known cases of smallpox.
   c. the SEP thought there were no more cases.
   d. smallpox had been successfully contained.

_____	_____	_____
1st answer	Line reference(s)	2nd answer

6. Amina Salat is mentioned because

   a. through her smallpox was spread again.
   b. she died of smallpox.
   c. the cook Ali caught it from her.
   d. she was the last recorded case of smallpox.

_____	_____	_____
1st answer	Line reference(s)	2nd answer

7. Smallpox was carried from Ethiopia into Somalia by

   a. Amina Salat.
   b. a young nomad.
   c. the cook Ali.
   d. three thousand people.

_____	_____	_____
1st answer	Line reference(s)	2nd answer

8. *Target zero* means a situation in which

   a. no one remains unvaccinated.
   b. there is no contagious disease.
   c. no one dies of smallpox.
   d. there are no further cases of smallpox.

_____	_____	_____
1st answer	Line reference(s)	2nd answer

9. At the time this article was written,

   a. there remained a few reports of smallpox to be checked.
   b. there were no further reports of smallpox.
   c. the SEP had no more work to do.
   d. there were just a few cases to be treated.

_____	_____	_____
1st answer	Line reference(s)	2nd answer

10. The International Commission cannot declare that the world is free from smallpox until

    a. there are no more known cases.
    b. everyone has been vaccinated.
    c. fourteen months have passed since the last case.
    d. two years have passed since the last case.

    _____   _____   _____
    1st answer   Line reference(s)   2nd answer

CHART FOR FINDING OUT READING SPEED

Time	wpm	Time	wpm	Time	wpm	Time	wpm	Time	wpm
1:30	396	2:30	238	3:30	170	4:30	132	5:30	108
1:45	339	2:45	216	3:45	158	4:45	125	5:45	103
2:00	299	3:00	198	4:00	149	5:00	119	6:00	99
2:15	264	3:15	183	4:15	140	5:15	113	6:15	95

Speed in words per minute _____

Total correct on 1st reading _____

Total correct on 2nd reading _____

QUESTIONS FOR DISCUSSION

1. What are the medical and organizational advances that have made the eradication of smallpox possible?

2. Why do you think the policy was described as one of "search and containment"?

3. What would you say is the significance of this story?

**SELECTION
1-4**

When Will They Ever Learn?

Start time _____

Most people think cancer is a disease of rich western countries. No longer. More than half of the 6 million people who die from cancer each year are in developing countries. Cancer is now one of the big killers of people over five years of age in the third world.

The main reason is that the poor are living longer than they used to. For   5
example, in China, life expectancy at birth is 61 today compared with 40 in the 1950s. As infectious diseases such as smallpox and typhoid are progressively contained, the poor die instead from illnesses associated with middle- and old-age.

The pattern of cancers among the world's poorest people is still very differ-   10
ent from that of the rich. In industrialized countries people die from lung, intestinal and prostate cancers as a consequence of smoking, alcohol abuse and high fat diets. In the third world the most prevalent forms of cancer are those of the liver, mouth, esophagus and cervix, each of which claims 100,000–300,000 victims a year. These cancers are associated with poor living condi-   15
tions and undernourishment.

Liver cancer in Africa, south-east Asia and the western Pacific is mostly the result of infections from hepatitis B, which causes jaundice. Yet about 80% of liver cancers could now be prevented by immunization with a new hepatitis B vaccine. In some parts of Africa and Asia there are as many as 30 new cases of   20
liver cancer annually per 100,000 people, compared with three new cases per 100,000 in North America. And China accounts for over 40% of liver cancers in the world. It plans to start building up its own supplies of the vaccine for hepatitis B.

Mouth cancer is the commonest form in southeast Asia where there are some   25
100,000 new cases yearly. Betel nut and tobacco chewing, which has been practiced for thousands of years, is thought to be the main cause. In Latin America and the Caribbean cancer of the cervix, associated with promiscuity and lack of personal hygiene, is the most common: some 32 new cases per 100,000 of the population occur every year. In Egypt the big scourge is bladder   30
cancer, stemming from bilharzia, the parasitic disease which infects the intestine.

The World Health Organization (WHO) reckons that the third world problem will get worse as the poor adopt the lifestyles of the rich and become subject to western-type cancers. For example, between 1963 and 1975 the inci-   35
dence of lung cancer doubled in Shangai. Tobacco consumption, while declining in industrialized countries, is increasing in the third world, and cigarettes marketed in some countries, such as India, contain more tar and nicotine than

those sold in industrialized countries. The incidence of breast and prostate cancers, linked with high fat and low fiber diets, has long been higher in western   40
countries; now it is on the increase in China and Japan.

A third of all cancers are preventable and a third are curable if detected early
enough. WHO is proposing a worldwide campaign on the link between smoking and cancer, which has only recently been acknowledged in chain-smoking
China, for example; it will also press for reducing the tar content of cigarettes.   45
An anti-smoking campaign, however, is bound to meet resistance both from
governments which raise big revenues from tobacco (63% of the world's tobacco is produced in developing countries) and from western cigarette manu-
facturers for whom developing countries are an increasingly important market.

WHO has managed to raise only $2 million for its cancer project. Trouble is   50
that donors are not yet convinced that cancer is no respecter of poverty.

**Time Taken
(min./sec.)** _____

The Economist
594 words

**COMPREHENSION
CHECK**

Choose the best way of finishing each statement, according to the passage,
and write the letter in the "1st answer" blank. Then follow the directions on
pages 20–21.

1. Deaths from cancer

   a. are distributed evenly across the world.
   b. occur most often in developing countries.
   c. are confined mainly to the western world.
   d. represent a serious problem only in poor countries.

   _____   _____   _____
   1st answer   Line reference(s)   2nd answer

2. Poor people are now more likely to die of cancer than they used to be
   chiefly because

   a. they have a better life expectancy.
   b. their living conditions have become worse.
   c. they have been weakened by infectious diseases.
   d. they have adopted unhealthy habits.

   _____   _____   _____
   1st answer   Line reference(s)   2nd answer

3. Different kinds of cancer are more common in certain parts of the world than in others because of differences in

   a. the hereditary characteristics of national groups.
   b. the health care available to most people.
   c. the amount and kind of exercise people get.
   d. the populations' living conditions and diet.

1st answer	Line reference(s)	2nd answer

4. Liver cancer is caused chiefly by

   a. smoking.
   b. lack of exercise.
   c. hepatitis B.
   d. poor diet.

1st answer	Line reference(s)	2nd answer

5. Mouth cancer occurs mainly in

   a. Africa.
   b. Latin America.
   c. southeast Asia.
   d. the Caribbean.

1st answer	Line reference(s)	2nd answer

6. The problem of cancer in the third world is expected to

   a. get better.
   b. get worse.
   c. remain the same.
   d. disappear.

1st answer	Line reference(s)	2nd answer

7. Most cancers are

   a. preventable but not curable.
   b. curable but not preventable.
   c. both preventable and curable.
   d. either preventable or curable.

1st answer	Line reference(s)	2nd answer

8. The World Health Organization (WHO) is proposing a campaign to

   a. publicize the association of cancer with smoking.
   b. educate people on detecting cancer.
   c. vaccinate people against cancer.
   d. get funds for cancer research.

_____   _____   _____
1st answer   Line reference(s)   2nd answer

9. The WHO campaign is likely to be resisted by

   a. the pharmaceutical industry.
   b. governments.
   c. the medical profession.
   d. uneducated people.

_____   _____   _____
1st answer   Line reference(s)   2nd answer

10. The WHO has only raised a small sum for its campaign because

   a. people don't think it will be effective.
   b. there is opposition from big business.
   c. money is needed for other medical projects.
   d. cancer is not recognized as a third-world problem.

_____   _____   _____
1st answer   Line reference(s)   2nd answer

CHART FOR FINDING OUT READING SPEED

Time	wpm	Time	wpm	Time	wpm	Time	wpm	Time	wpm
1:00	390	2:00	195	3:00	130	4:00	98	5:00	78
1:15	312	2:15	173	3:15	120	4:15	92	5:15	74
1:30	260	2:30	156	3:30	111	4:30	87	5:30	71
1:45	223	2:45	142	3:45	104	4:45	82	5:45	68

Speed in words per minute _____

Total correct on 1st reading _____

Total correct on 2nd reading _____

QUESTIONS FOR
DISCUSSION

1. Why might "most people think cancer is a disease of rich western countries"? Before reading this article, were you one of those people?

2. If eradicating infectious diseases means that people die of cancer instead, do you think it is worth the effort of fighting against smallpox, typhoid, and so on? Why, or why not?

3. Given the information in this article, what do you think individuals can do to protect themselves from cancer?

4. Do you think opposition to an anti-smoking campaign (see lines 46–49) can be justified? Why, or why not?

"I Accept in the Name of the Poor"

Start time _____

Until 1946 she was a Roman Catholic teaching nun in India, devout, dynamic, but apparently otherwise unexceptional. Then, on a train ride to Darjeeling, she felt the touch of a divine command. Its message: she must quit her cloistered existence and plunge into Calcutta's clamorous slums to care for the poorest of the poor.   5

She did just that, leaving the genteel girl's school where she had been teaching to create a new order among the poor of India's most desolate city. The Missionaries of Charity have since grown into a worldwide order numbering more than 1800 nuns, 250 brothers and thousands of lay "co-workers" who serve the sick, the lonely, the destitute and the dying in 30 countries. Last week   10
Mother Teresa of Calcutta, 69, was awarded the 1979 Nobel Prize for Peace.

Tiny, gray-eyed, her face deeply seamed with the passing years, Mother Teresa received the news with characteristic lack of fuss in the Missionaries of Charity motherhouse in Calcutta. She has won an array of international honors, and though this one carried the biggest stipend so far—$190,000—she took it   15
in her stride. "Personally, I am unworthy," she said in her first response to the award. "I accept in the name of the poor, because I believe that by giving me the prize they've recognized the presence of the poor in the world." The new Nobel prizewinner will use the money to build more hospices, "especially for the lepers."   20

Mother Teresa was born in 1910 to Albanian parents and baptized Agnes Gonxha Bojaxhiu in what is now Skoplje, Yugoslavia. Even at the age of twelve she wanted to "go out and give the love of Christ." By the time she was 18, Agnes had joined the Irish branch of Loreto nuns who were working in Calcutta, where she soon began teaching geography at St. Mary's High School.   25
When the Church granted her permission to lay aside her Loreto habit and take up the blue-edged, coarse cotton white sari that became the uniform of the Missionaries of Charity, young women from St. Mary's soon joined her.

For every kind of tragedy in the overcrowded city, Mother Teresa and her nuns managed to create a measure of consolation. They collected abandoned   30
babies from gutters and garbage heaps and tried to nurse them back to health. They brought in the dying so they might die under care and among friends. Eventually the order built leprosariums, children's homes, havens for women, the handicapped and the old. The deepest consolation offered, though, was something that went beyond physical care. "For me each one is an individual,"   35
Mother Teresa once explained. "I can give my whole heart to that person for that moment in an exchange of love. It is not social work. We must love each other. It involves emotional involvement, making people feel they are wanted."

If the peace she tries to bring passes everyday understanding, the universal and uncontroversial appeal of this year's prizewinner brought almost audible   40
sighs of joy and relief in Oslo, where the Norwegian Nobel Peace Prize Committee sits. Peace prizes all too often go to worldly statesmen who arrange temporary accommodations between bellicose neighbors. When US Secretary of State Henry Kissinger and North Vietnam negotiator Le Duc Tho won the peace prize in 1973 for their joint work on a Vietnam peace agreement, the   45
award stirred outrage throughout Norway and beyond. Last year Egyptian President Anwar Sadat and Israeli premier Menachem Begin won the prize for their Middle East peace efforts, and though Begin went alone to Oslo, security became such a problem that the award ceremonies were moved from their usual site, at Oslo University, to the Akershus, a high-walled medieval fortress. This   50
year, with President Jimmy Carter a candidate because of his Camp David initiatives, Norwegians had visions of bomb searches, hovering helicopters and machine gun–toting guards. Mother Teresa will not need them.

Time Taken   *Time*
(min./sec.) _____   **650 words**

COMPREHENSION CHECK   Choose the best way of finishing each statement, according to the passage, and write the letter in the "1st answer" blank. Then follow the directions on pages 20–21.

1. Before Mother Teresa founded the Missionaries of Charity, she was

   a. a nurse.
   b. a doctor.
   c. a teacher.
   d. a contemplative nun.

   _____   _____   _____
   1st answer   Line reference(s)   2nd answer

2. The center for the Missionaries of Charity's work is

   a. Darjeeling.
   b. Calcutta.
   c. Oslo.
   d. Loreto.

   _____   _____   _____
   1st answer   Line reference(s)   2nd answer

3. The Nobel Prize is

   a. the first public acknowledgment of Mother Teresa's work.
   b. the biggest prize, in cash terms, that she has received so far.
   c. a great honor, but insignificant in cash terms.
   d. a meaningless tribute because so many people have received it.

   _____   _____   _____
   1st answer   Line reference(s)   2nd answer

4. Mother Teresa's original nationality is

   a. Irish.
   b. Indian.
   c. Albanian.
   d. Norwegian

   _____   _____   _____
   1st answer   Line reference(s)   2nd answer

5. Mother Teresa left the Loreto nuns because

   a. she disliked their life.
   b. she was told to do so by her superiors.
   c. she thought their work was unimportant.
   d. she felt called to do something else.

   _____   _____   _____
   1st answer   Line reference(s)   2nd answer

6. The Missionaries of Charity are most concerned with

   a. people suffering from leprosy.
   b. school children in Calcutta.
   c. babies who have been abandoned.
   d. anyone with no other hope of help.

   _____   _____   _____
   1st answer   Line reference(s)   2nd answer

7. Judging from this article, Mother Teresa is certainly not

   a. self-seeking.
   b. practical.
   c. devout.
   d. strict.

   _____   _____   _____
   1st answer   Line reference(s)   2nd answer

8. The Nobel Peace Prize is awarded in

   a. the United States.
   b. India.
   c. Norway.
   d. a different place each year.

   _____ _____ _____
   1st answer   Line reference(s)   2nd answer

9. Another candidate for the prize the year Mother Teresa won was

   a. Henry Kissinger.
   b. Jimmy Carter.
   c. Anwar Sadat.
   d. Menahem Begin.

   _____ _____ _____
   1st answer   Line reference(s)   2nd answer

10. The award of the prize to Mother Teresa was received with general

    a. indifference.
    b. surprise.
    c. controversy.
    d. acclaim.

    _____ _____ _____
    1st answer   Line reference(s)   2nd answer

CHART FOR FINDING OUT READING SPEED

Time	wpm	Time	wpm	Time	wpm	Time	wpm	Time	wpm
1:30	433	2:45	236	4:00	163	5:15	124	6:30	100
1:45	371	3:00	217	4:15	153	5:30	118	6:45	96
2:00	325	3:15	200	4:30	144	5:45	113	7:00	93
2:15	289	3:30	186	4:45	137	6:00	108	7:15	90
2:30	260	3:45	173	5:00	130	6:15	104	7:30	87

Speed in words per minute _____

Total correct on 1st reading _____

Total correct on 2nd reading _____

QUESTIONS FOR DISCUSSION

1. Is Mother Teresa indeed "unexceptional" (line 2)? Explain.

2. Why does Mother Teresa claim that her work is "not social work"? (line 37)

3. Why should Mother Teresa have "universal and uncontroversial appeal" as a Nobel prizewinner? (line 39)

4. Is it appropriate that Mother Teresa should be awarded a *peace* prize for her work? Why, or why not?

*In a Bronx School,
a '38 Free Speech Victory*

Start time _____

Newfane, Vt.—The United States Supreme Court decision upholding censorship of a high school newspaper recalled an episode nearly 50 years ago. It took place at DeWitt Clinton High School in the Bronx in 1938, but it did not involve the school paper.

The school paper, The Clinton News, was perhaps one of the finest weekly   5
high school publications in the country. Under the faculty guidance of the legendary Raphael Philipson, it regularly won first prize in the Columbia Scholastic Press Association competitions and, to my knowledge, was never censored.

It was The Magpie, the school's literary magazine, that some of us thought left something to be desired. Not that it wasn't well written, designed and   10
printed; it simply did not deal with thoughts that were often uppermost in our minds.

Our solution was an alternative magazine, Expression. During the winter of 1937–38, a dozen or so of us wrote short stories, poetry, commentary and criticism, discarded the bulk of the material and wound up with 38 pages of   15
typescript. Over an entire weekend in March, in the basement of a synagogue on West 85th Street, we mimeographed, collated and stapled about 300 copies. We sold them the following Monday in Clinton's corridors for a nickel each.

While the sales force was at work, I was delegated to present the honorary first copy to A. Mortimer Clark, our principal. He shook my hand and congrat-   20
ulated all of us, through me, on our enterprise and creativity.

Then he read the magazine. More likely, he read only the first two pieces, since only their authors and I were summoned to his office later that morning. It was his opinion that our magazine was "lewd, lascivious and licentious," and he expelled us. I mean, he really marched us to the main entrance, out the   25
door, and then stepped back to close it behind us.

On my left was Seymour Krim (later, a respected writer and critic), who had written a short story considered by his peers to have been the best submitted; it was thus given the lead spot. It contained no four-letter words, but it did have a three-letter word referring to the buttocks. It was about a psychologically dis-   30
turbed individual who climbed a tower on a college campus with a rifle (this, decades before it actually occurred in Texas) and shot people at random.

On my right was Frank Gottheimer, whose older brother, Stanley, had written a poem, "Calvary," about a lynching in the South in which a character spoke the words "nigger." Fairly plausible, given the situation. But why expel   35
Frank? Well, Stanley had just graduated, and Frank was the only Gottheimer available.

Mr. Clark may never have gotten to a short story by Sid (Paddy) Chayevsky (his first "commercial" work), poems by Mel Greek or my review of Thomas Mann's novel "The Magic Mountain" further along. But he remembered me, nonetheless. His parting words were "Bring your parents!" Not an attractive prospect. 40

What we did was to take the subway from Mosholu Parkway all the way to Union Square, and then we walked to the offices of the American Civil Liberties Union on Fifth Avenue at about 16th Street. 45

Honesty forces me to say that the A.C.L.U. was not thrilled to see us. But we insisted that our First Amendment rights had been violated and, equally important, that the whole thing was of no concern to our parents.

The A.C.L.U. took our case, but it was settled out of court. It was settled by telephone, actually, when Mr. Clark came to agree that the school might be better off without the publicity and that, after all, it was our first offense. 50

In effect, we copped a plea; the charge was reduced from "selling pornography" to "selling without authorization." By the end of the week we were back in class, having promised not to "do it again."

Instead, in the spring of 1939, our senior year, we produced and appeared in our own dramatization of the short story, "The Killers," in the school auditorium. The fact that the offensive language was Hemingway's, not ours, presented a problem in ethics to Mr. Clark. But graduation came before any decision on his part. Perhaps he did learn something from the A.C.L.U. I like to think so. 60 55

Bern Friedelson, from the *New York Times*

709 words

**Time Taken
(min./sec.) _____**

**COMPREHENSION
CHECK**

Choose the best way of finishing each statement, according to the passage, and write the letter in the "1st answer" blank. Then follow the directions on pages 20–21.

1. The story is about

    a. a successful school paper.
    b. the American Civil Liberties Union.
    c. the misbehavior of some schoolboys.
    d. censorship in a high school.

    _____   _____   _____
    1st answer   Line reference(s)   2nd answer

2. The magazine edited by the writer was called

   a. the *Clinton News*.
   b. the *Magpie*.
   c. *Expression*.
   d. the *Killers*.

   _____   _____   _____
   1st answer   Line reference(s)   2nd answer

3. The writer and his friends decided to produce the magazine because

   a. they wanted to win a literary competition.
   b. the school had a newspaper but no magazine.
   c. they found the existing school magazine irrelevant.
   d. they thought they should test the school's liberalism.

   _____   _____   _____
   1st answer   Line reference(s)   2nd answer

4. The principal's first reaction on receiving the magazine was to

   a. congratulate the editor.
   b. call the writers to his office.
   c. contact the ACLU.
   d. consult the boys' parents.

   _____   _____   _____
   1st answer   Line reference(s)   2nd answer

5. After reading the magazine, the principal made the editor and his friends

   a. come to his office with their parents.
   b. go to the office of the ACLU.
   c. rewrite several of the stories.
   d. leave the school.

   _____   _____   _____
   1st answer   Line reference(s)   2nd answer

6. The principal objected to the magazine because it was

   a. badly written.
   b. indecent.
   c. too political.
   d. unauthorized.

   _____   _____   _____
   1st answer   Line reference(s)   2nd answer

7. The writer suggests that the magazine was good by

   a. describing what each of the articles was about.
   b. referring to his companions' later success as writers.
   c. reporting on the prizes the magazine won.
   d. showing how popular it was in the school.

   _____   _____   _____
   1st answer   Line reference(s)   2nd answer

8. After their interview with the principal, the writer and his friends

   a. decided to appeal to the ACLU.
   b. went home to get their parents.
   c. spent the rest of the day in the streets.
   d. returned to their regular classes.

   _____   _____   _____
   1st answer   Line reference(s)   2nd answer

9. The boys received help from

   a. Mr. Clark.
   b. Raphael Philipson.
   c. the ACLU
   d. their parents.

   _____   _____   _____
   1st answer   Line reference(s)   2nd answer

10. When the boys came back, they

    a. concentrated on their academic work.
    b. produced a new magazine of a different kind.
    c. dropped the magazine and turned to drama.
    d. lost all interest in school activities.

    _____   _____   _____
    1st answer   Line reference(s)   2nd answer

CHART FOR FINDING OUT READING SPEED

Time	wpm	Time	wpm	Time	wpm	Time	wpm	Time	wpm
1:30	473	2:45	258	4:00	177	5:15	135	6:30	109
1:45	405	3:00	236	4:15	167	5:30	129	6:45	105
2:00	354	3:15	218	4:30	158	5:45	123	7:00	101
2:15	315	3:30	203	4:45	149	6:00	118	7:15	98
2:30	284	3:45	189	5:00	142	6:15	113	7:30	95

Speed in words per minute _____

Total correct on 1st reading _____

Total correct on 2nd reading _____

QUESTIONS FOR DISCUSSION

1. Why did the principal react as he did? Do you think his actions were justified?

2. What is the First Amendment? Do you think that the rights of Bern Friedelson and his friends had indeed been violated?

3. Why do you think the ACLU was "not thrilled" to see them? Do you think it acted appropriately?

4. What can you infer about the boys in this story? Do you think they were an asset or a liability to their school? Why?

**SELECTION
1-7**

Getting to See the Invisible Woman

Start time _____

The world today is an unequal place; among unequals women are the most unequal—the poorest of the poor. A United Nations office, called the Center for Social Development and Humanitarian Affairs, is now assembling evidence to show just how unequal women, and particularly third-world women, are. Take education: in only 14 countries are there as many girls in primary schools   5
as boys. In a number of developing countries, the proportion of girls attending primary school is still under 10%. As a result, out of an estimated 700 million illiterates, nearly two thirds are female.

Just as educationists pass women by on the other side of the road, so also do development planners. The UN center points out that women are in effect invis-   10
ible to most third-world economists. In Africa, where 80% of women still live in the rural areas, it is estimated that 60%–80% of all agricultural work is done by them. But the women's work is subsistence agriculture which, like house-keeping in industrial countries, is outside the commercial sector and therefore does not figure in national statistics.   15

A report by the UN Economic Commission for Africa comments: "A male worker laying a pipe to a house in the city is considered to be economically active: a woman carrying a 40 kilo water jar for one or two hours a day is just doing a household task."

More is at stake than "woman's rights." As subsistence farmers, it is women   20
who provide the food that the poor actually eat. If development is a process meant to benefit the poor, then it would follow that planners should pay more attention to the subsistence sector, to its economic contribution and to the people who work in it. Yet, to take just one example from many, Algeria's figures on the "economically active" do not, according to a study by the International   25
Labor Organization, include 1.2 million females occupied in subsistence agriculture.

Development projects and programs inevitably concentrate on the economically active. In Africa as a whole, UN figures show an increase of 1.2% a year in total food production over the period 1970–74, but a decrease of 1.4% in   30
food production per head. There are soon going to be, literally, more people than hot dinners. The result, as in the Sahel famines of the early 1970's, can be starvation. The Economic Commission for Africa noted that "despite this ominous food supply situation, until very recently there has been little more than a whisper of attention to the high labor input and low productivity which charac-   35
terizes food production—mainly the work of women." The most fertile land and the largest share of agricultural incentives are usually allocated to cash crops—in other words to men.

All too often "modernizing influences" have failed to benefit women and have, at times, attracted their hostility or even outright opposition. An irrigated rice settlement scheme in Kenya provoked this comment: "There is no wood for fuel, or adequate space for women to grow food. They also have to work long hours on rice fields. At the end of the day the men receive all the income from their own and their wives' labor. . . . The women, reduced to begging money from their husbands to buy wood and food, are resentful about the whole rice project to the point of outright hostility, and they regard it as a place to leave as soon as possible." 40 45

In Upper Volta, pilot resettlement schemes for the Volta Valley Authority, designed as models for some multi-million-dollar projects financed by the World Bank and others, have been found to be nearly intolerable to the women because of the lack of basic facilities, such as market places, land to grow the family's food, village wells, grain mills and other facilities regarded as essentials in their home village. Many women have insisted on leaving. 50

The period 1976–85 is officially designated the UN's Decade for Women. The 10 years are supposed to be a "period for action, an opportunity and a challenge." Well, at least something is being done. Regional and national commissions on women and development have been set up in most countries to encourage governments to think more clearly about women's role and economic importance. A "voluntary fund" currently worth about $6 million is meant to give muscle to projects and programs that will benefit women. An international institute has been established to conduct research into the relationship between underdevelopment and the status of women and to provide training to help women play a more active part in their country's decision-making process. In the summer of 1980, a world conference will review progress and formulate a plan of action to 1985. By then, with a little bit of luck, the invisible women should be a bit easier to see. 55 60 65

The *Economist*
790 words

**Time Taken
(min./sec.)** _____

**COMPREHENSION
CHECK**

Choose the best way of finishing each statement, according to the passage, and write the letter in the "1st answer" blank. Then follow the directions on pages 20–21.

1. The first paragraph states that

   a. in fourteen countries, more boys than girls are in school.
   b. in the world as a whole only 10 percent of girls go to primary school.
   c. of the world's illiterates, one-third are female.
   d. of the world's illiterates, two-thirds are female.

_____   _____   _____
1st answer   Line reference(s)   2nd answer

2. In Africa, the main work of most women is

   a. housekeeping.
   b. subsistence agriculture.
   c. carrying water.
   d. trading.

   _____   _____   _____
   1st answer   Line reference(s)   2nd answer

3. Women do not appear in UN statistics on labor because

   a. they do not do any work.
   b. their work is not important.
   c. the UN is only interested in men.
   d. they are not considered to be economically active.

   _____   _____   _____
   1st answer   Line reference(s)   2nd answer

4. Development projects, at the time of writing, concentrate on people who

   a. work for cash.
   b. work for subsistence.
   c. work in the towns.
   d. do any kind of work.

   _____   _____   _____
   1st answer   Line reference(s)   2nd answer

5. Food production in Africa is

   a. remaining static.
   b. decreasing.
   c. decreasing relative to the population.
   d. increasing relative to the population.

   _____   _____   _____
   1st answer   Line reference(s)   2nd answer

6. Most of the benefits of agricultural-development schemes go to men because

   a. they do most of the agricultural work.
   b. they grow cash crops.
   c. they grow food crops.
   d. they are more efficient than women.

   _____   _____   _____
   1st answer   Line reference(s)   2nd answer

7. The irrigated rice settlement scheme in Kenya is described as

   a. unpopular with the women.
   b. unpopular with the men.
   c. unpopular with everybody.
   d. popular with everybody.

   _____   _____   _____
       1st answer   Line reference(s)   2nd answer

8. The two resettlement schemes mentioned are criticized because

   a. they waste money.
   b. they are against local traditions.
   c. they benefit only the rich.
   d. they do not benefit women.

   _____   _____   _____
       1st answer   Line reference(s)   2nd answer

9. During the years 1976 to 1985, emphasis is being placed on

   a. the role of women.
   b. subsistence agriculture.
   c. increasing the production of cash crops.
   d. collecting voluntary funds.

   _____   _____   _____
       1st answer   Line reference(s)   2nd answer

10. By 1985, "the invisible women should be a bit easier to see" because

    a. more women will have jobs.
    b. women's work will be better understood.
    c. women will have been given the vote.
    d. more women will be educated.

   _____   _____   _____
       1st answer   Line reference(s)   2nd answer

CHART FOR FINDING OUT READING SPEED

Time	wpm	Time	wpm	Time	wpm	Time	wpm	Time	wpm
1:30	527	3:00	263	4:30	176	6:00	132	7:30	105
1:45	451	3:15	243	4:45	166	6:15	126	7:45	102
2:00	395	3:30	226	5:00	158	6:30	122	8:00	99
2:15	351	3:45	211	5:15	150	6:45	117	8:15	96
2:30	316	4:00	198	5:30	144	7:00	113	8:30	93
2:45	287	4:15	186	5:45	137	7:15	109	8:45	90

Speed in words per minute _____

Total correct on 1st reading _____

Total correct on 2nd reading _____

QUESTIONS FOR DISCUSSION

1. Why, according to this article, are women's interests so often neglected? Can you think of any other reasons that are not mentioned?

2. Is the position of women in rich countries such as the United States in any way comparable to that of women in the poor countries described here?

3. This article was written more than ten years ago. Has anything changed since? How could you find out?

**SELECTION
1-8**

Only for Consenting Adults in Private

Start time _____   A couple of weeks ago New York's antismoking laws came into full force.
Smoking is forbidden in nearly all shared public places. In offices and work
premises, smokers have to huddle together in designated smoking areas which,
it is said, tend to be grotty, fuggy places littered with cigarette ends. Restau-
rants above a certain size must offer nonsmoking sections to their customers; in   5
theaters and cinemas, smoking is permitted only in segregated areas of the
lobby. Confronted with these laws, many establishments have simply banned
smoking altogether. Smoking is illegal in taxis and, theoretically, on the con-
course of Grand Central Station.

    I associate New York particularly with smoking because it was there, 12   10
years ago almost to the day, that I at last managed to give up the habit. My last
pack of king-size Kent went into the trash can at the corner of Lexington and
76th Street. Today I thought I might go there and observe a moment's silence.
In those 12 years, Americans have come a long way towards giving up smoking. In the country which tried and failed to give up drinking by means of   15
Prohibition, in the country in which people used to walk a mile for a Camel and
were never alone with a Lucky Strike, it is an astonishing phenomenon. Humphrey Bogart, who died of lung cancer, must be turning in his grave. According
to Stanley Michels, the New York City councilman who sponsored the anti-
smoking legislation: "This is one of the most fantastic social changes we've   20
seen in our lifetime. Smoking is now considered antisocial behavior."

    In 1964, the year of the first Surgeon General's report warning of the health
hazards of cigarette smoking, more than 50 percent of American males smoked;
fewer women. The latest figures show a decline from 30.4 percent (men and
women) in 1985 to 26.5 percent in 1986. On the basis of New York City tax   25
revenues, it is estimated that 40 million fewer packs were sold in the city last
year than in the previous. The only adverse trend is among young women,
curiously, not young men. The decline in the smoking habit is steepest among
the better educated; gradually, death or ill-health from smoking is becoming a
working-class epidemic. That is why work-place anti-smoking laws can save   30
lives.

    Of the 50 states of the Union, 42 now have some sort of antismoking laws.
Some 400 cities or counties have their own, of which New York City is the
latest. In 14 states and 200 localities, the laws apply to private business premises. Increasingly, companies are making their own rules. By last year 54 per-   35
cent of companies had work-place smoking policies, compared to 36 percent in
1986. Managements are discovering that nonsmoking regimes are good for productivity and can save money on employee health care. But the chief pressure

has come from the nonsmokers, especially since the Surgeon General spelled
out in 1986 the hazards of "second-hand smoke".   40

In Washington I lunched with an old friend, a defiant two-pack-a-day man.
He started smoking a cigarette with his cocktail but put it out when the people
at the next table got sniffy. "We've lost," he said. "There's no smoking in
government buildings in this town except in the designated smoking recesses
and your own private office, if you have one. Now they've put smoke detectors 45
in the johns so that alarm bells ring and they can rush in and shoot you in the
kneecaps. The other day, chairing a conference, I put an ashtray on the table
and said, 'I designate this conference room a private office.' They snarled at
me and said: 'You have that power?' I had to go an hour without a cigarette. In
Chicago you can't smoke in cabs any more—in Chicago! In California you'd   50
be lynched lighting up in a restaurant like this." What is remarkable is the
extent to which the antismoking laws enforce themselves through social pressure. In New York, according to a recent Gallup poll, 77 percent of people
agree that smokers should refrain in the presence of nonsmokers. That may
have something to do with the fact that 80 percent of smokers wish they could 55
give up. In San Francisco, for example, it requires only one objector in a work-
place to have it designated nonsmoking. Yet for the whole of San Francisco,
according to Athena Mueller of the nonsmokers' rights lobby, there is only one
enforcement officer, and it works. She put the success of the nonsmokers'
rights campaign down chiefly to the health consciousness of the American peo- 60
ple and their high standard of health education.

Prohibition in the 1920s was imposed by a pussy-footing, moral minority in
defiance of the customs of the people. "There's nothing of Prohibition about
this," said Ms. Mueller, "we're not opposed to smoking between consenting
adults in private." What is happening in America is not a paternalistic govern- 65
ment trying to save smokers from themselves, but nonsmokers insisting on their
rights to clean air and clear lungs.

Time Taken   the *Independent*
(min./sec.) _____   **840 words**

**COMPREHENSION
CHECK** Choose the best way of finishing each statement, according to the passage, and write the letter in the "1st answer" blank. Then follow the directions on pages 20–21.

1. New York's antismoking laws have caused many establishments to

    a. close down.
    b. move out of the city.
    c. become grotty, fuggy places.
    d. forbid smoking entirely.

   _____   _____   _____
     1st answer   Line reference(s)   2nd answer

2. The writer associates New York with smoking because

    a. that is where he had his first cigarette.
    b. he gave up smoking there.
    c. he thinks New Yorkers smoke more than most people.
    d. there are many cigarette advertisements there.

   _____   _____   _____
     1st answer   Line reference(s)   2nd answer

3. The change in attitudes towards smoking is described as

    a. inevitable.
    b. undesirable.
    c. surprising.
    d. disturbing.

   _____   _____   _____
     1st answer   Line reference(s)   2nd answer

4. The only section of the population in which smoking is increasing is

    a. young men.
    b. young women.
    c. older men.
    d. older women.

   _____   _____   _____
     1st answer   Line reference(s)   2nd answer

5. The writer says that work place antismoking laws can save lives because

    a. people usually smoke most heavily while they are at work.

    b. in most working environments there is little fresh air.

    c. most people who get sick and die from smoking are working class.

    d. such laws will educate people about the dangers of smoking.

_____	_____	_____
1st answer	Line reference(s)	2nd answer

6. Antismoking laws have been passed

    a. throughout the entire United States.

    b. in about half of the states.

    c. in most states.

    d. in New York, California, and Texas.

_____	_____	_____
1st answer	Line reference(s)	2nd answer

7. The writer's "old-friend" thinks the antismoking regulations are

    a. annoying.

    b. welcome.

    c. unimportant.

    d. ineffective.

_____	_____	_____
1st answer	Line reference(s)	2nd answer

8. The antismoking regulations are enforced, according to the writer, by

    a. strict punishment of offenders.

    b. regular inspections by official enforcers.

    c. announcements by the surgeon general.

    d. social pressure on smokers.

_____	_____	_____
1st answer	Line reference(s)	2nd answer

9. According to Athena Mueller, the campaign against smoking has been successful because of

    a. the government's backing.

    b. the customs of the people.

    c. its strong moral position.

    d. Americans' awareness of health issues.

_____	_____	_____
1st answer	Line reference(s)	2nd answer

10. The antismoking campaign of the 1980s is different from the antidrinking campaign of the 1920s because

a. it does not try to stop smoking altogether.
b. it imposes no restrictions on adults.
c. it is supported by government legislation.
d. it is against established customs.

_____   _____   _____
   1st answer   Line reference(s)   2nd answer

CHART FOR FINDING OUT READING SPEED

Time	wpm	Time	wpm	Time	wpm	Time	wpm	Time	wpm
2:00	420	3:30	240	5:00	168	6:30	129	8:00	105
2:15	373	3:45	224	5:15	160	6:45	124	8:15	102
2:30	336	4:00	210	5:30	153	7:00	120	8:30	99
2:45	305	4:15	198	5:45	146	7:15	116	8:45	96
3:00	280	4:30	187	6:00	140	7:30	112	9:00	93
3:15	258	4:45	177	6:15	134	7:45	108	9:15	91

Speed in words per minute _____

Total correct on 1st reading _____

Total correct on 2nd reading _____

QUESTIONS FOR DISCUSSION

1. What is so astonishing about the fact that people are giving up smoking?

2. How and why are smoking habits related to social class?

3. Do you think the attitude of the writer's "old friend" is justified?

4. Does the United States experience with tobacco on the one hand and alcohol on the other suggest anything that might be done about other addictive drugs?

**SELECTION
1-9**

Undercover Agent, 81, Helps Halt Nursing Home Payoffs

Start time _____

She was a top-notch undercover agent. Smart. Courageous. Flashed a smile
that could warm the coldest criminal heart.

Yet at the age of 81, Muriel Clark now says it wasn't all that hard to become
New York State's oldest undercover operative, taking on a secret pastime and
fictitious identity to help flush out illegal payoffs in the nursing home industry.   5

"The mystery excited me," Miss Clark recalls of the beginning of her career
in law enforcement at 78. "I went home and thought maybe I'll have a chance
to sneak around."

Miss Clark, a retired social worker, was recruited by the state's special
prosecutor for nursing homes in 1984 to pose as a little old lady about to be   10
placed in a nursing home by her son. As a result of a nine-month investigation,
officials of two nursing homes admitted that they accepted payoffs to take her
in as a resident, but until now Miss Clark's identity was kept secret by the
prosecutor's office.

For the first time yesterday, Miss Clark stepped out of the shadows, a petite   15
woman in a dark blue suit and ruffled white blouse who, as she spoke in a
Greenwich Village coffee shop, was still passionately angry about what she
viewed as the powerful in New York who take advantage of the poor, the frail
and the dispossessed.

"She did a really gutsy thing," said Deputy Attorney General Edward J.   20
Kuriansky, the Special Prosecutor for Nursing Homes, Health and Social Serv-
ices. "Elderly people are very vulnerable, and she performed an extremely
valuable service."

Miss Clark's exploits had their roots in the early 1980's, when the state
became aware that some nursing homes were accepting up to tens of thousands   25
of dollars in "contributions" from relatives desperate to secure a space quickly
for elderly people. The problem in prosecuting such cases was that children
who made payments did not want to come forward, particularly since their
parents might be vulnerable to retribution.

What was needed was an undercover team, a middle-age son and his elderly   30
mother. The New York City Department of Investigation supplied an investigator to portray the son, and at a community meeting of people concerned about
nursing home issues, a representative of the Attorney General approached a
5-foot-5-inch, 108-pound woman with an engaging smile and passionate convictions about dozens of issues.   35

Miss Clark retired from her career as a social worker in 1968 and at first
tried to lead a quiet life, she said. But her rage at what she considered the
inequities in the world—particularly the election of Richard M. Nixon, a Presi-

dent she considered "evil"—drove her into nearly two decades of involvement with social causes.

She worked with civil rights groups, taught youths on probation and, more recently, has spent nights sleeping at a shelter for the homeless, where she feeds and cares for people.

When she was approached by the special prosecutor and offered the chance to go undercover to catch illegal practices at nursing homes, Miss Clark said she jumped at the chance.

"I think I would do anything to help improve conditions there," she said. "I have strong feelings about nursing homes because the thought of being there myself fills me with horror."

At her first meeting with officials, she was told that, above all, the operation had to be kept secret. She would have to learn a whole new identity.

She became "Muriel Schwartz," whose parents were Russian Jewish immigrants, whose husband, Morris, died in 1957, and whose son, Sam, a wine merchant, traveled extensively and worried about leaving his aged, confused mother at home.

To Miss Clark, who came from an English Protestant family, who had never been married and had no children, this was all easy to memorize. But when a prosecutor suggested that they use her real health records as the medical history of the fictitious Mrs. Schwartz, Miss Clark said that was impossible. She had not been to a doctor in 40 years.

"I haven't felt sick, and it seems to me that when my friends go to a doctor they come back with a list of every disease under the sun," Miss Clark explained.

The undercover mother-and-son team, wired with a hidden recording device, visited four nursing homes in the spring of 1985. One of the most difficult moments during her tours of the homes and interviews by workers, Miss Clark recalled, was when she was asked about her interests.

"I didn't want to go into my real social interests—I'd be ostracized," she said. "I lied and said I love to sew, I'd like to read a bit, take a little walk, aahhh, a little TV and, ahhhhh, knitting. I tried to make it seem I was inert."

Her performance was a spectacular success, Mr. Kuriansky said. After her "son" was solicited for bribes totaling $55,000, Mr. Kuriansky said, the Hebrew Home for the Aged in the Riverdale section of the Bronx and the Menorah Nursing Home in the Manhattan Beach section of Brooklyn were indicted for illegally accepting cash and pledges.

Earlier this month the special prosecutor announced that the two nursing homes had agreed to plead guilty to lesser charges and stop soliciting contributions from the families of prospective residents.

In addition, the Hebrew Home for the Aged agreed to provide $6,000 worth of Passover packages to homebound elderly people.

Peter Kerr, the *New York Times*
886 words

**COMPREHENSION
CHECK**

Choose the best way of finishing each statement, according to the passage, and write the letter in the "1st answer" blank. Then follow the directions on pages 20–21.

1. Muriel Clark was offered a job as an undercover agent because

   a. she was interested in mysteries.
   b. she was of the right age and interests.
   c. she was the best of those who applied.
   d. she was experienced in social work.

   _____   _____   _____
   1st answer   Line reference(s)   2nd answer

2. Before retirement, Muriel Clark had worked as

   a. a social worker.
   b. an official in a nursing home.
   c. a police officer.
   d. a teacher.

   _____   _____   _____
   1st answer   Line reference(s)   2nd answer

3. The problem Muriel Clark was asked to investigate was

   a. unjust treatment of the elderly.
   b. inadequate facilities at the Hebrew Home for the Aged.
   c. criminal activities in four different nursing homes.
   d. the payment of bribes to homes for old people.

   _____   _____   _____
   1st answer   Line reference(s)   2nd answer

4. The investigator with whom Miss Clark worked

   a. acted as her supervisor.
   b. pretended to be her son.
   c. was a representative of the attorney general.
   d. was responsible for her safety.

   _____   _____   _____
   1st answer   Line reference(s)   2nd answer

5. For twenty years after her retirement, Miss Clark had

   a. led a quiet life.
   b. worked as an undercover agent.
   c. been involved in various social causes.
   d. helped at a shelter for the homeless.

   _____   _____   _____
   1st answer   Line reference(s)   2nd answer

6. When Miss Clark was approached by the special prosecutor, she was

   a. eager to help.
   b. reluctant to take the job.
   c. afraid of the work involved.
   d. horrified by what he told her.

   _____   _____   _____
   1st answer   Line reference(s)   2nd answer

7. To do the job, Miss Clark posed as

   a. a childless old lady.
   b. a member of an English Protestant family.
   c. a widow of a wine merchant.
   d. a daughter of Russian Jewish immigrants.

   _____   _____   _____
   1st answer   Line reference(s)   2nd answer

8. Miss Clark is best described as

   a. eccentric and difficult.
   b. gentle and loving.
   d. lively and intelligent.
   d. strong and hard-working.

   _____   _____   _____
   1st answer   Line reference(s)   2nd answer

9. When she visited the nursing homes, Miss Clark said that she was most interested in

   a. social issues.
   b. sewing.
   c. reading.
   d. watching TV.

   _____   _____   _____
   1st answer   Line reference(s)   2nd answer

10. The result of Miss Clark's investigation was

    a. two homes were indicted for taking bribes.

    b. the Hebrew Home for the Aged was closed.

    c. conditions in nursing homes in New York improved.

    d. nothing much happened.

| _____ | _____ | _____ |
| 1st answer | Line reference(s) | 2nd answer |

CHART FOR FINDING OUT READING SPEED

Time	wpm	Time	wpm	Time	wpm	Time	wpm	Time	wpm
2:00	443	3:30	253	5:00	177	6:30	136	8:00	111
2:15	394	3:45	236	5:15	169	6:45	131	8:15	107
2:30	354	4:00	222	5:30	161	7:00	127	8:30	104
2:45	322	4:15	208	5:45	154	7:15	122	8:45	101
3:00	295	4:30	197	6:00	148	7:30	118	9:00	98
3:15	273	4:45	187	6:15	142	7:45	114	9:15	96

Speed in words per minute _____

Total correct on 1st reading _____

Total correct on 2nd reading _____

QUESTIONS FOR DISCUSSION

1. What, to you, is the most surprising element in this story? Why is it surprising?

2. Does Miss Clark sound like an interesting person? Why, or why not?

3. What are the differences between Miss Clark and "Mrs. Schwartz"?

4. What does this story suggest about attitudes toward the elderly in New York City?

**SELECTION
1-10**

Bringing Up Baby, One by One

Start time _____

Pretty and smart, the Beijing first-grader has nonetheless become a night-mare to her doting parents. "Weiwei turns on the television to watch cartoons after doing only 15 minutes of homework," complains her father. "She eats lots of chocolate but hardly touches her meals." Last May, in full sight of her guests, Weiwei, 7, imperiously scraped off for herself all the icing on her birthday cake. When her father scolded her, she snapped, "You're a monster and a fat pig!"   5

There may be hundreds of thousands, perhaps millions, of Weiweis throw-ing tantrums throughout China. The reason: Beijing's stringent one-child-per-couple policy. As its population approached 1 billion, the People's Republic began enforcing the one-child limit in 1979. Today, of the 337 million Chinese children under 14, 30 million are without siblings. These children, called "little emperors" by the local press, have been swaddled in the love of their parents and grandparents; as a result, many Chinese fear, they are growing up spoiled, selfish and lazy. "The child cares about getting love from others but not for giving it to others," observes *Chinese Youth* magazine.   10   15

The Chinese press frequently runs cautionary tales of cozened brats. A car-toon in *Chinese Youth*, for example, depicts an obese child lying in a bed littered with toys, stuffing himself with cakes and milk served by Mother, while Father stands ready to dress him. In his column in the *China Daily*, Xu Yihe writes disapprovingly of Jiajia, a friend's pampered daughter who barely budges to prepare for school in the morning. While Jiajia sits on her bed, says Xu, "her mother combs her hair, her grandmother feeds her breakfast, her grandfather is under the table putting her shoes on, and her father is getting her satchel ready." Single children are well aware of their special status. Said one: "I ride on Daddy's shoulders and ask my parents to make a circle with their arms. Then I say, 'You are the sky, and I am the little red sun.'"   20   25

To the horror of the proletarian dictatorship, many single children seem to detest physical labor. When some 21,000 Beijing pupils were asked to write a short composition on the topic "What Do You Want to Be When You Grow Up?," only 5% indicated that they wanted to become workers. Few wanted to be farmers. Most wanted to become taxi drivers, hotel attendants or Premier, because those occupations are perceived to be easy and comfortable.   30

But the gravest sins of the imperial brats are committed against China's tradition of filial piety. When little Minmin's parents asked their only son to empty the family chamber pot, he poured out only a third of the contents. "I've done my part," Minmin said. "You're responsible for the rest." Some single children have even threatened to commit suicide if parents do not meet their   35 demands. However, most do not have to resort to such extremes. Pampering is built into what is called the "four-two-one syndrome"—four grandparents and two parents, all doting on an only child. Many Chinese fear that when such children reach adulthood, they will be unwilling to care for aging parents and geriatric grandparents, forcing the elderly into the care of the state. 40

While Chinese psychologists, sociologists and child counselors are quick to concede the shortcomings of single children, they emphatically reject the claims in the press that the little tyrants pose an alarming problem. They are certainly not cause for having more children, a development that China can do without, despite the surplus of parental love. According to Mao Yuyan, a psychology professor at the Chinese Academy of Sciences in Beijing, if parents want the atmosphere of a large family, they can organize their neighborhoods into quasi-clans. Children can also be trained in the collective spirit in nurseries and kindergartens. 45 50

In her studies, Mao found single children "faring better than those with siblings" in terms of intellectual development. She contends that some children with siblings are even worse brats. "They beat their elder brothers," Mao says. "The decisive factor is not whether one is a single child. It is a question of parental attitude and education." As an ancient Chinese saying goes, "Bad parents produce bad children." Most single-child parents are survivors of the chaotic Cultural Revolution. Many failed to finish their own schooling, and they are often ill equipped to rear children properly. Some of these parents apply immense pressure on the children to succeed where they themselves have not. Many hire experts to teach the toddlers music, calligraphy or a foreign language. A few even force their sons and daughters to parrot elegant Tang dynasty poetry. Says Fang Xiang, a retired child psychologist: "There is no need for tutoring in composition or arithmetic. What's important is moral education at home." 55 60 65

To help remedy the situation, crash courses for newlyweds and parents-to-be are being conducted across the country. Bookstores are stocking up on child-care books. Schools and summer camps teach children how to dress, cook and do household chores. Says Mao: "We ask mothers to offer a childhood that is more than just chocolate plus toys, to teach the child to be courteous, collective-oriented and self-reliant. That way, they will not become little emperors." What are parents to do when a child throws a tantrum? Do not give in to blackmail, says Fang. "Let the child cry all night. By the next day everything will be forgotten." At least until Baby learns to throw things. 70 75

Time Taken
(min./sec.) _____

Howard G. Chua-Eoan, *Time*
905 words

COMPREHENSION CHECK

Choose the best way of finishing each statement, according to the passage, and write the letter in the "1st answer" blank. Then follow the directions on pages 20–21.

1. Weiwei, mentioned in paragraph 1, is probably such a difficult child because
   a. she is usually given too much food.
   b. she is not sufficiently loved by her parents.
   c. she is not used to sharing with other children.
   d. she is frequently disturbed by nightmares.

   _____   _____   _____
   1st answer   Line reference(s)   2nd answer

2. In 1979, the Chinese government began to
   a. prevent people from having large families.
   b. encourage people to emigrate.
   c. draw up plans for a one-child-per-couple policy.
   d. make birth-control available for everybody.

   _____   _____   _____
   1st answer   Line reference(s)   2nd answer

3. At present in China, the proportion of children under fourteen who have no brothers and sisters is
   a. over 90 percent.
   b. under 10 percent.
   c. about 50 percent.
   d. about 30 percent.

   _____   _____   _____
   1st answer   Line reference(s)   2nd answer

4. The children described in this article are called "little emperors" because
   a. they come from the Chinese Royal Family.
   b. they live in imperial splendor.
   c. they have a higher standard of living than their parents.
   d. they are the center of attention in their families.

   _____   _____   _____
   1st answer   Line reference(s)   2nd answer

68

Reading for General Information

5. The quotations from the Chinese press suggest that there is public concern about

  a. the way many families continue to ignore the single-child policy.
  b. the fact that grandparents are no longer involved in child care.
  c. the effects on children's attitudes of being brought up alone.
  d. the increasing practice of leaving children in day-care centers.

_____ _____ _____
1st answer   Line reference(s)   2nd answer

6. According to their compositions, Beijing school children want to

  a. have jobs that will secure them an easy life.
  b. become revolutionaries like their parents.
  c. acquire an advanced academic education.
  d. return to the traditions of their forefathers.

_____ _____ _____
1st answer   Line reference(s)   2nd answer

7. According to the passage, a fear that many Chinese have is that

  a. population growth will become impossible to control.
  b. the economy will not be able to provide jobs for their children.
  c. the traditional means of caring for the aged will break down.
  d. the new generation will grow up ignorant of their culture.

_____ _____ _____
1st answer   Line reference(s)   2nd answer

8. The psychology professor Mao Yuyan recommends that parents should

  a. keep very strict control over their children.
  b. devote more resources to their children's education.
  c. make their families larger by having more children.
  d. arrange for children from different families to spend time together.

_____ _____ _____
1st answer   Line reference(s)   2nd answer

9. It seems that Chinese psychologists attribute the difficulties of today's single-child parents to

  a. the fact that single children are particularly naughty.
  b. the pressures parents are under because of their jobs.
  c. the unwillingness of parents to break away from tradition.
  d. the inadequate education this generation of parents received.

_____ _____ _____
1st answer   Line reference(s)   2nd answer

10. In order to address the problems discussed here, the Chinese authorities are

   a. reconsidering the one-child-per-couple policy.
   b. offering instruction to prospective parents.
   c. encouraging grandparents to take more responsibility.
   d. providing economic incentives to bring up children well.

    _____ _____ _____

      1st answer   Line reference(s)   2nd answer

CHART FOR FINDING OUT READING SPEED

Time	wpm	Time	wpm	Time	wpm	Time	wpm	Time	wpm
2:00	453	3:30	259	5:00	181	6:30	139	8:00	113
2:15	402	3:45	241	5:15	172	6:45	134	8:15	110
2:30	362	4:00	226	5:30	165	7:00	129	8:30	106
2:45	329	4:15	213	5:45	157	7:15	125	8:45	103
3:00	301	4:30	201	6:00	151	7:30	121	9:00	101
3:15	278	4:45	190	6:15	145	7:45	117	9:15	98

Speed in words per minute _____

Total correct on 1st reading _____

Total correct on 2nd reading _____

QUESTIONS FOR DISCUSSION

1. What general point are the examples of Weiwei and Jiajia used to demonstrate?

2. What do you think is the writer's opinion on the issues discussed? (Look particularly at the end of the article.)

3. Do you agree with him?

4. What can you infer from this article about Chinese society in general?

5. Is anything in what you find in the article about China comparable to what you know of North America?

SELECTION
1-11

Homeless Families:
How They Got That Way

Start time _____

Families are the fastest growing segment of the homeless population, and most homeless families are headed by single women, according to a University of Southern California (USC) researcher who has conducted an in-depth study of homeless families.

"These women are not crazy," says family sociologist Kay Young Mc-   5
Chesney, director of the Homeless Families Project at USC. "They aren't substance abusers, either. Even though most of them were very poor, they had managed to keep a roof over their children's heads until something happened to upset their already precarious economic balance."

McChesney and her research team interviewed eighty-seven mothers of chil-   10
dren under the age of eighteen in five Los Angeles County shelters. The women's median age was twenty-eight: their median number of children, two. A disproportionate number were black. About 30 percent had male partners; the rest were single mothers.

About 40 percent of the women became homeless when threatened with   15
eviction or legally evicted, McChesney found. "In Los Angeles, the median rent for a one-bedroom apartment is $491 a month," she says. "The average monthly AFDC [Aid to Families with Dependent Children] payment to a mother with one child is $448. So these women face a choice: they can buy food and diapers, or they can pay the rent. Some months, they decide to eat."   20

Money had been stolen from about 33 percent of the women, or they simply ran out of money after moving to Los Angeles. Many of the married couples interviewed were in this group. Often the husband had lost his job in another state. When his unemployment benefits ran out, the family moved to Califor-nia. "They're the Okies of the eighties," says McChesney. "Even if the man   25
finds a job, the family doesn't have enough money to cover the high cost of moving into an apartment."

Approximately 25 percent of the mothers found themselves with no place to live when they left, or were thrown out by, male partners—some of whom had abused them. "Many of these women were being supported in a reasonable   30
fashion when they suddenly found themselves in the street," McChesney says. "In trying to set up a household on their own, they were crippled by the fact that, in general, women don't make as much money as men—only about 48 cents to the dollar. What's more, they couldn't afford to pay someone to care for the kids while they were at work or looking for work."   35

McChesney found that a large number of women had been physically abused by their natural parents, then placed in foster homes where foster fathers or brothers sexually abused them. "They ran away in their teens and had been doing what they could to survive," she says. "Some had been homeless, except for short periods, for years. Then they got pregnant, and as one said, 'I can make it by myself. But what do I do with my baby?'" McChesney added. "So they wind up in Los Angeles County shelters, where they can stay for a month at most. Then they're back in the street—this time with their babies." 40

McChesney's study also revealed that homeless families have something in common besides poverty: they are unable to turn to parents, brothers, or sisters for help because their families are either dead, out of state, or estranged. "Considering the median age of the women in the sample, they had a surprisingly high number of deceased parents," says McChesney. "Thirty percent of the women had deceased mothers, with three women not knowing enough about their mothers to know whether they were alive or dead," she writes, "making about a third of the women with no mother to turn to. 45 50

"Thirty-five percent of the women's natural fathers were dead, and another six women knew so little about their fathers that they didn't know whether they were alive or dead, making a total of 43 percent effectively with no father. . . . Fully 16 percent of the women were orphans, with both parents dead. Five were not only orphans but also had no living siblings." 55

Of mothers who had living parents, many had families too far away to be of any help. Only 50 percent had a mother in the Los Angeles area, and only 35 percent had a father who lived there. Almost half had no brothers or sisters in the Los Angeles area. 60

Those who had living kin in the area were often unable to turn to their family for support. Forty-three percent of the mothers in the sample had been runaways or in foster or institutional care when they were children or teenagers. Many of these women had been abused, physically and/or sexually, by their biological parents, then abused again by foster parents. 65

"The difference between the poor who wind up homeless and those who don't seems to be a matter of having relatives to turn to when problems come up," McChesney suggests. Yet when families are homeless, society has a tendency to blame the victims themselves, instead of searching for the underlying causes of the problem. 70

McChesney argues that the primary cause of the current crisis in homelessness is an acute shortage of affordable low-cost housing. "Numerous studies document that, while the number of families living in poverty has increased in the eighties, the number of low-cost housing units available has decreased," she explains. "Nationally, for every unit available, we estimate there are two households in need of low-cost housing. Increasing the number of beds in emergency shelters is not going to solve the problem. More low-cost housing must be provided if we are to stem the rising tide of homelessness." 75

Time Taken
(min./sec.) ———

Society
936 words

Choose the best way of finishing each statement, according to the passage, and write the letter in the "1st answer" blank. Then follow the directions on pages 20–21.

1. The article is about homeless families in

   a. the United States.
   b. several US cities.
   c. California.
   d. Los Angeles.

   _____   _____   _____
   1st answer   Line reference(s)   2nd answer

2. In relation to the whole homeless population, families are, according to the article,

   a. about half.
   b. a growing proportion.
   d. a majority.
   d. a small minority.

   _____   _____   _____
   1st answer   Line reference(s)   2nd answer

3. Kay Young McChesney is

   a. a researcher.
   b. a homeless woman.
   c. a shelter administrator.
   d. a politician.

   _____   _____   _____
   1st answer   Line reference(s)   2nd answer

4. The article is based on evidence from

   a. questionnaires collected from homeless people.
   b. reports presented by shelter administrators.
   c. interviews with homeless women in shelters.
   d. an investigation of homeless people in the streets.

   _____   _____   _____
   1st answer   Line reference(s)   2nd answer

5. Most of the families discussed here consist of

   a. grandparents, parents, and children.
   b. parents and children.
   c. a single mother and children.
   d. children who are orphans.

   _____   _____   _____
   1st answer   Line reference(s)   2nd answer

6. Most of the women who are described here became homeless when they

   a. became addicted to drugs or alcohol.
   b. didn't have enough money to pay the rent.
   c. were discriminated against on grounds of race.
   d. left their husbands, who were abusing them.

   _____   _____   _____
   1st answer   Line reference(s)   2nd answer

7. The average monthly payment made as Aid to Families with Dependent Children

   a. may cover rent but not much else.
   b. covers the cost of raising one child.
   c. is barely enough to support a family.
   d. is not nearly enough to pay even the rent.

   _____   _____   _____
   1st answer   Line reference(s)   2nd answer

8. A common characteristic of homeless families is

   a. they have no relatives who can help them.
   b. the parents have a history of substance abuse.
   c. one or other parent has spent time in jail.
   d. their health is very poor.

   _____   _____   _____
   1st answer   Line reference(s)   2nd answer

9. The article suggests that a major cause of homelessness is

   a. poverty arising from widespread unemployment.
   b. failure of the education system to prepare people for society.
   c. irresponsibility on the part of homeless individuals.
   d. a mismatch between available housing and the social structure.

   _____   _____   _____
   1st answer   Line reference(s)   2nd answer

10. The solution recommended for homelessness is

    a. provision of more low-cost housing.

    b. increase in the number of beds in city shelters.

    c. counseling for homeless individuals and families.

    d. legislation to protect poor people from eviction.

| _____ | _____ | _____ |
| 1st answer | Line reference(s) | 2nd answer |

CHART FOR FINDING OUT READING SPEED

Time	wpm	Time	wpm	Time	wpm	Time	wpm	Time	wpm
2:15	416	3:45	250	5:15	178	6:45	139	8:15	113
2:30	374	4:00	234	5:30	170	7:00	134	8:30	110
2:45	340	4:15	220	5:45	163	7:15	129	8:45	107
3:00	312	4:30	208	6:00	156	7:30	125	9:00	104
3:15	288	4:45	197	6:15	150	7:45	121	9:15	101
3:30	267	5:00	187	6:30	144	8:00	117	9:30	99

Speed in words per minute _____

Total correct on 1st reading _____

Total correct on 2nd reading _____

QUESTIONS FOR DISCUSSION

1. Does any of the information in this article surprise you? Why, or why not?

2. What do you think is meant by the statement that some of the families discussed are "the Okies of the eighties" (line 25)?

3. What does the article suggest to you about the importance of the family as a social unit?

4. The article suggests that "society has a tendency to blame the victims" (line 68). Why should there be such a tendency?

5. In the light of this article, how do you think the problem of homelessness might be alleviated?

SELECTION
1-12

Start time _____

Censoring Sex Information:
The Story of Sassy

At the first editorial meeting of *Sassy* magazine, in 1987, the staff sat around the editor-in-chief's office discussing how to make our new magazine different from other teenage publications. The unanimous first priority was to provide sex education: Since we had read the competition during our own adolescence, we knew the sex information published by teen magazines was scarce and usually couched in judgmental terms. 5

We had a good reason to put this issue high on our agenda. The United States has the highest teen pregnancy rate of any similarly industrialized western nation, and we felt this was not an issue that would go away by just telling teens to say no. The rock stars and athletes speaking out against drugs and 10 drunk driving on TV weren't making any pitches for virginity. The situation had become even more confusing for teenagers because of the attention that abstinence was getting as the only sure way to prevent AIDS. Our readers were left with a lot of unanswered questions that we felt were important to address.

Sassy's initial advertisers did not feel as strongly as its editors about leading 15 the sex education of America's youth. Many were concerned about an article in the prototype issue entitled "Sex for Absolute Beginners," which had previously run in *Dolly, Sassy*'s Australian counterpart. The article answered questions ranging from "Can I get pregnant?" and "What is an orgasm?" to "Am I homosexual?" and "Is masturbation wrong?" A few advertisers were offended 20 by the thought of their own teenage daughters reading the information and decided not to advertise, while others reluctantly signed contracts, fearing that if the magazine were a huge success, they couldn't afford to be left out. It became clear to me later that their concerns were business rather than moral ones when I realized that many of the same companies who objected to "Sex 25 for Absolute Beginners" in *Sassy* nevertheless advertised without complaint in *Dolly*—the most widely read teenage magazine in the world in terms of circulation per capita. For what the advertisers understood long before the editors did is that sex may sell billions of dollars of U.S. products every year, but responsible, direct information about sex directed toward U.S. teenagers would not. 30

In the first issue, *Sassy* printed an article entitled "Losing your Virginity." We ran this because we felt that at least one reason so many teens were having sex was that the media had successfully convinced them that losing their virginity was going to be the biggest moment of their lives. Our strategy was to provide our readers with more realistic accounts to debunk the celluloid stereotype. After set- 35 ting up some alternative scenarios, we left the moral decisions to the reader while providing detailed information about birth control and sexually transmitted diseases and answers to frequently asked questions such as, "Will it hurt?" "Can he tell I'm a virgin?" "What if I change my mind?" and "How long will it take?"

The reader response to this article was phenomenal. *Sassy* and the article's   40
author received hundreds of letters saying that finally someone had spoken to
them in a way with which they felt comfortable. Mail started pouring in to the
"Help" column, which I wrote, making apparent that we had only scratched the
surface of a teenager's reality. What was most disconcerting to us was the tone
of fear and shame these letters portrayed. Many young women were desperate   45
for answers—we even received phone calls requesting advice. The next few
articles we ran on sex were in response to these frantic letters asking about
pregnancy, abortion, incest, suicide, and homosexuality.

"The Truth About Boys' Bodies," "Getting Turned On," "And They're
Gay," "My Girlfriend Got Pregnant," and "Real Stories About Incest" were   50
articles written to let girls know that whatever choices they made about their
sexuality weren't shameful as long as they were responsible about safe sex,
birth control, and emotional self-care.

Much of our reader response was positive. Mothers and even grandmothers
called to say that they had read our articles with their daughters and grand-   55
daughters and as a result felt closer to each other. There was also relief among
some parents that we had explained something important they were uncomfort-
able communicating. On the other hand, there was also a fair share of irate
screaming directed our way. Most of these callers felt the information we
printed was "pornographic" and reeled off the old saw that information just   60
encourages young women to have sex. Perhaps the most alarming phone call
came from a father who screamed, "Anything my daughter learns about sex,
she'll learn from me!" before he slammed down the receiver. These people
canceled their subscriptions—a routine response to a publication one disagrees
with and something we had counted on.   65

What we hadn't counted on was the mass reader/advertiser boycott led by a
woman whose kids didn't even read *Sassy*. As a member of a group called
Women Aglow was to show us, it is possible in this country for a vocal minority to bring about what amounts to censorship. Through the Jerry Falwell-sup-
ported publication *Focus on the Family*, Women Aglow organized a letter-   70
writing campaign aimed at our major advertisers in which they threatened to
boycott their products if those companies continued to advertise in *Sassy*.
Within a matter of months *Sassy* had lost nearly every ad account, and we were
publishing what we jokingly called *The Sassy Pamphlet*. We were told that to
stay in business we must remove the "controversial" content from the maga-   75
zine. That was reluctantly done, and today *Sassy* has regained its advertisers
but not its detailed information on sex education.

Sadly, what was to a few young editors just a sobering lesson about the
power of advertising was a great loss to young women, who need the information *Sassy* once provided.   80

Elizabeth Larsen, *Utne Reader*
968 words

Time Taken
(min./sec.) ———

COMPREHENSION CHECK

Choose the best way of finishing each statement, according to the passage, and write the letter in the "1st answer" blank. Then follow the directions on pages 20–21.

1. *Sassy* is the name of
   a. a book about sex education.
   b. a magazine for teenagers.
   c. a series of pamphlets.
   d. a newsletter for families.

   _____   _____   _____
   1st answer   Line reference(s)   2nd answer

2. *Sassy* was exceptional when it first came out because it
   a. perpetuated sexual stereotypes.
   b. published ads with sexual connotations.
   c. discouraged sexual activity.
   d. included frank articles about sex.

   _____   _____   _____
   1st answer   Line reference(s)   2nd answer

3. In choosing the distinctive characteristic of the publication, the editors were
   a. unanimously in favor of adopting it.
   b. generally in favor, but there were some doubts.
   c. reluctant to adopt it, but felt they had no choice.
   d. cynical because they knew it would not work.

   _____   _____   _____
   1st answer   Line reference(s)   2nd answer

4. Advertisers were hesitant about advertising in *Sassy* because they
   a. did not think it would be popular.
   b. felt it was morally objectionable.
   c. expected it to be controversial.
   d. were afraid of corrupting the nation's youth.

   _____   _____   _____
   1st answer   Line reference(s)   2nd answer

5. In the first issue, *Sassy* included an article entitled

    a. "The Truth About Boys' Bodies."
    b. "Real Stories About Incest."
    c. "Sex for Absolute Beginners."
    d. "Losing your Virginity."

    ———————— ———————— ————————
      1st answer   Line reference(s)   2nd answer

6. *Sassy's* articles were intended to

    a. inform without passing judgment.
    b. give clear moral directions.
    c. provide excitement for its readers.
    d. stimulate debate about sex education.

    ———————— ———————— ————————
      1st answer   Line reference(s)   2nd answer

7. Letters written in response to the first issue expressed

    a. anger about its content.
    b. desire for more information.
    c. concern about immorality.
    d. determination to take action.

    ———————— ———————— ————————
      1st answer   Line reference(s)   2nd answer

8. Among older readers, the response was

    a. divided.
    b. indifferent.
    c. positive.
    d. negative.

    ———————— ———————— ————————
      1st answer   Line reference(s)   2nd answer

9. Women Aglow campaigned against *Sassy* by

    a. canceling their subscriptions to it.
    b. writing letters to Congress about it.
    c. putting out an alternative publication.
    d. threatening to boycott its advertisers' products.

    ———————— ———————— ————————
      1st answer   Line reference(s)   2nd answer

10. As a result of Women Aglow's campaign, *Sassy*

    a. lost a great many readers.
    b. went out of business.
    c. changed its content.
    d. refused to publish advertisements.

    _____ _____ _____
    1st answer   Line reference(s)   2nd answer

CHART FOR FINDING OUT READING SPEED

Time	wpm	Time	wpm	Time	wpm	Time	wpm	Time	wpm
2:15	430	3:45	258	5:15	184	6:45	143	8:15	117
2:30	387	4:00	242	5:30	176	7:00	138	8:30	113
2:45	352	4:15	228	5:45	168	7:15	134	8:45	111
3:00	323	4:30	215	6:00	161	7:30	129	9:00	108
3:15	298	4:45	204	6:15	155	7:45	124	9:15	105
3:30	277	5:00	194	6:30	149	8:00	121	9:30	102

Speed in words per minute _____

Total correct on 1st reading _____

Total correct on 2nd reading _____

QUESTIONS FOR DISCUSSION

1. Would you have appreciated a magazine like *Sassy* when you were in high school? Why, or why not?

2. Do you think young girls should be given information about sex such as *Sassy* provided? Why, or why not?

3. What does this article suggest about the American public's attitudes towards sex?

4. Why was it possible for Women Aglow to "bring about what amounts to censorship" (line 70)? Should anything be done to make it impossible? If so, what?

CHAPTER TWO

Reading for

Pleasure

In these days of radio and television, records and videotapes, it is easy to forget how much fun you can have simply reading. Many books are written for the purpose of entertaining their readers, and reading can provide a deeper enjoyment than listening to music or watching television often does because reading requires you to do more, so you become more engaged in the story. This is not true, of course, of every book: whether you become involved in a particular book depends on the skill with which it is written, the difficulty of its language, and most of all, your own tastes and interests.

This chapter consists of material that the authors wrote in the hope that their readers would enjoy it. All the selections are taken from the first few pages of novels or autobiographical works. They represent considerable variety, and among them you will perhaps find some that you would like to follow up by reading the whole book.

Extending Your Reading

The selections in this chapter represent only a tiny proportion of the books that are available to you, and if you are to enjoy fully your ability to read, you need to go well beyond them. Following, therefore, is a list of books that college students who worked with the material in this textbook chose to read along with it—and reported that they enjoyed. The books are arranged alphabetically by author in categories that name different kinds of books. For each book, the name of the author is given first, then the title of the book in italics, and the name of the publisher in parentheses. This information will enable you to locate the book in a library or a bookshop.

Biography and Autobiography

Maya Angelou, *I Know Why the Caged Bird Sings*. (Random House)
Joan Baez, *And a Voice to Sing With*. (Plume)
Russell Baker, *Growing Up*. (New American Library)
Claude Brown, *Manchild in the Promised Land*. (New American Library)
Bette Davis and Michael Herskowitz, *This 'n That*. (Berkley)
Ann Edwards, *Vivian Leigh*. (Pocket Books)
Helen Keller, *The Story of My Life*. (New American Library)
Winnie Mandela, *Part of My Soul Went with Him*. (Norton)
Nicholas Pileggi, *Wise Guy: Life in a Mafia Family*. (Simon & Schuster)
Richard Rodriguez, *Hunger of Memory: The Education of Richard Rodriguez*. (Bantam Books)
Piri Thomas, *Down These Mean Streets*. (Knopf)
Richard Wright, *Black Boy*. (Harper & Row)

Classics of the Twentieth Century

Chinua Achebe, *Things Fall Apart*. (Fawcett)
Pearl Buck, *The Good Earth*. (Pocket Books)
F. Scott Fitzgerald, *The Great Gatsby*. (Scribner's)
William Golding, *Lord of the Flies*. (Putnam)
Graham Greene, *The Quiet American*. (Penguin)
Ernest Hemingway, *For Whom the Bell Tolls*. (Scribner's)
_____, *The Old Man and the Sea*. (Scribner's)
Aldous Huxley, *Brave New World*. (Harper & Row)
Harper Lee, *To Kill a Mockingbird*. (Warner Books)
George Orwell, *Animal Farm*. (Harcourt Brace Jovanovich)
_____, *Down and Out in Paris and London*. (Harcourt Brace Jovanovich)
_____, *Nineteen Eighty-Four*. (New American Library)
Alan Paton, *Cry, the Beloved Country*. (Macmillan)
John Steinbeck, *Of Mice and Men*. (Bantam Books)
_____, *The Pearl*. (Bantam Books)
_____, *The Red Pony*, (Bantam Books)
_____, *Tortilla Flat*. (Penguin)

Coming-of-Age Stories

Robert Cornier, *Beyond the Chocolate War*. (Dell)
Barthe De Clements, *Seventeen and In-Between*. (Scholastic)
Jamaica Kincaid, *Annie John*. (New American Library)
John Knowles, *A Separate Peace*. (Bantam Books)
Carson McCullers, *The Member of the Wedding*. (Bantam Books)
J. D. Salinger, *A Catcher In the Rye*. (Bantam Books)
Ann Hall Whilt, *Suitcases*. (New American Library)

Medical Stories

David B. Feinberg, *Eighty-Sixed*. (Penguin)
Leonore Fleischer, *Rain Man*. (New American Library)
John Gunther, *Death Be Not Proud*. (Harper & Row)
Ron Jones, *Acorn People*. (Bantam Books)
Marion Roach, *Another Name for Madness*. (Pocket Books)
Betty Rollin, *First You Cry*. (New American Library)
Oliver Sacks, *A Leg to Stand On*. (Harper & Row)
Cornelius Slater, *An Apple a Day*. (Ivy Books)

Mysteries and Thrillers

Eric Ambler, *Epitaph for a Spy*. (Berkley)
Agatha Christie, *And Then There Were None*. (Pocket Books)
_____, *Thirteen at Dinner*. (Berkley)
E. V. Cunningham, *The Case of the One-Penny Orange*. (Holt)
Doris Disney, *Only Couples Need Apply*. (Zebra)
Sue Grafton, *A Is for Alibi*. (Bantam Books)
Victoria Holt, *The Time of the Hunger's Moon*. (Fawcett)
Isabelle Holland, *A Lover Scorned*. (Fawcett)
Stephen King, *Misery*. (New American Library)
K. M. Peyton, *A Midsummer Night's Death*. (Dell)
Margaret Truman, *Murder on Embassy Row*. (Fawcett)

Romance

V. C. Andrews, *Flowers in the Attic*. (Pocket Books)
_____, *Garden of Shadows*. (Pocket Books)
_____, *Petals in the Wind*. (Pocket Books)
Cordia Byers, *Desire and Deceive*. (Fawcett)
Baroness Orczy, *The Scarlet Pimpernel*. (Penguin)
Francine Pascal, *Forbidden Love*. (Bantam)

Marilyn Sachs, *Hello . . . Wrong Number.* (Scholastic)
Betty Smith, *Joy in the Morning.* (Harper & Row)
Danielle Steele, *Fine Things.* (Dell)
————, *Once in a Lifetime.* (Dell)
————, *Remembrance.* (Dell)
————, *Zoya.* (Dell)

Social and Political Issues

James Baldwin, *If Beale Street Could Talk.* (Dell)
Dee Brown, *Bury My Heart at Wounded Knee.* (Washington Square Press)
Leo F. Buscaglia, *Living, Loving, and Learning.* (Fawcett)
Bill Cosby, *Fatherhood.* (Berkley)
————, *Time Flies.* (Bantam)
Frank Deford, *Alex—The Life of a Child.* (New American Library)
Javier Galan, *One Summer.* (Cambridge Book Company)
James McDonough, *Platoon Leader.* (Bantam Books)
Terry MacMillan, *Mama.* (Washington Square Press)
Gloria Naylor, *Women of Brewster Place.* (Penguin)
Robin Norwood, *Women Who Love Too Much.* (Pocket Books)
Nahid Rachlin, *Foreigner.* (Norton)
Ann Rule, *Small Sacrifices.* (New American Library)
Alexander Solzhenytsin, *One Day in the Life of Ivan Denisovich.* (Bantam Books)

Sports

Robert Lipsyte, *The Contender.* (Harper & Row)
Walter D. Myers, *Hoops.* (Dell)
Rick Pitino, *Born to Coach: A Season with the New York Knicks.* (New American Library)

You should aim at reading two or three books every month. This may seem like a lot, and you may think that you do not have enough time; but if you get into the habit of carrying a book with you at all times, you can use the odd moments when you have to wait for something or are traveling in a bus or train to read it. Don't waste time on books that you do not find interesting. If you choose one that looks attractive and then, when reading it, find that you are getting bored or confused, it is not usually worth forcing yourself to continue: simply drop it (or put it aside for later), and choose another one. You will be amazed at how fast you can get through an exciting book—and at how enjoyable those times when you have to wait around will become.

Keeping a Reading Journal

Your instructor may ask you to keep a record of what you read, and to make comments on it. Even if you are not asked to, you may want to do so for your own interest, for it can help you keep track of your thoughts and deepen your appreciation of your reading. Here are some suggestions for keeping a reading journal:

1. Buy a small notebook, which will keep all the entries together and be easy to carry around.
2. Write the date at the beginning of every entry you make in the journal.
3. Before you write anything about a new book, be sure that you write the name of the author and the title. You may also want to record the name of the publisher.
4. You may find it helpful to identify the book in terms of one of the categories identified above, and you should certainly make a brief statement of what the book is about and give a summary of the story. Depending on what your instructor asks you to do, you may write a single entry when you finish a book, or you may write a series of entries as you go through it. For a longer book, which may take a week or more to read, it is probably better to write several entries.
5. In addition to summarizing the story, it is particularly interesting to record your own reactions to the book. You may want to do this by making comments as you tell the story, or by writing a paragraph of comments after your summary. Alternatively, you can write the account of the story on the right-hand pages of your notebook, and then express your reactions to the various episodes on the opposite left-hand page.
6. If your instructor is going to read your journal, be sure to leave plenty of space for his or her comments: doublespace your hand-writing, leave the left-hand pages free, and/or leave very wide margins.

Obviously, different individuals vary a good deal as to what they want to record in a reading journal, just as they vary in what they choose to read. So there is no model of journal-writing that you must follow, but you may find the following students' reactions to books they have read interesting. (The entries are given exactly as they were written, except that a few spelling and punctuation mistakes have been corrected; you should understand that in this kind of work the emphasis is not on writing correctly or elegantly.)

Mehmet

The Story of a Shipwrecked Sailor, by Gabriel García Márquez

February 28 brought news that eight crew members of the destroyer Caldes, of the Colombian Navy, had fallen overboard and disappeared during a storm in the Caribbean Sea. The ship was traveling from Mobile, Alabama, in the United States, where it had docked for repairs, to the Colombian port of Cartagena, where it arrived two hours after the tragedy. A search for the seamen began immediately, with the cooperation of the US Panama Canal Authority. After four days, the search stopped and the lost sailors were declared dead. A week later, one of them turned up. His name was Luis Alejandro Velasco. Velasco struggled to survive and made it, becoming a hero.

This story was wonderful to read. When my cousin interrupted me reading it I almost hit him. I was upset that I had to stop reading the book. It is like watching a movie and the best part is about to happen then the screen goes blank. I would recommend anyone to read this book because man's struggle against the sea is breathtaking to read.

Sandra

The book I read this week is entitled *First You Cry* by Betty Rollin. This book tells a story which all women can relate to. The author is the principal character of the book. Betty Rollin, an NBC news reporter, has always been a winner. But something unpredictable would turn upside down her confidence in herself, in her successful career and love life. Betty, for a year now, knew she had a lump in her left breast. Her internist told her that it was nothing to worry about since a lot of women have them. But to be more cautious he ordered a mammogram. The diagnosis of the internist after the test did not show anything alarming. Although she did not worry about the lump, she could not forget it. In 1974, a year later, she went to see Dr. Ellby about the lump. He himself did the mammogram and recommended a surgeon. In the meantime she had to wait for the mammogram results. She describes her trust in life since she was a little girl. Everything always seemed to work out just fine for her. She had a golden life with her husband. She had a fine job at NBC. So she thought everything will always work out. The day came when she went back to see Dr. Sengeiman, the surgeon recommended by Dr. Ellby. She was devastated by the news that she had cancer. Then she realized how lucky she has been to be married to David, a wonderful man who helped her survive these hard times with his love and patience. At first, she had felt resentment toward her internist who led her to believe that the cyst in her breast was not cancerous. But after, she said she could not blame him for not recommending the removal of the lump, since in his best judgment it was not cancer. After the removal of her left breast, she stayed for a week in the hospital. She dreaded the day when she would have to leave to face the world out there. But remarkably after stages of depression, anger, and hate, she regained her sense of orientation in life. In the last sentence of the book she said it so well: "If I don't have a recurrence of cancer and die soon, all I've lost is a breast, and that's not so bad."

Henriette

2/12

I have read about ninety pages of the book *To Kill a Mockingbird*. So far I like the book very much, although I mistook the narrator for the first thirty pages for a boy. The name Scout just sounded to me much more male than female. Anyhow, I found out that Scout's real name is Jean Louise and that she is a seven-year-old girl. From this moment on I like the book even more, because it reminds me of my childhood. Like Scout I have an older brother, although he wasn't that important to me, as Jem is for Scout. Her deep affection for her brother is surely increased by the absence of a mother. But of course older brothers are very important in the life of a younger sister, and so was mine.

Harper Lee describes in a very empathetic way the thoughts and feelings of this charming little girl. It isn't only a description of a childhood; the writer gives us also a very realistic knowledge of life in a sleepy southern town. For instance the Radleys, who lock up their son for the whole life because he didn't fit in their narrow-minded view about how a young man should behave. The poor man has to atone for a stupid youthful misdeed with his life. The whole village speculates about this man and the wildest horror stories are told. Of course Boo Radley is an important figure in this novel, and I think he stands for fears and hopes that children have. Last, but not least, I think Harper Lee will tell a story about racism. It becomes apparent that the whole family will have to endure quite some trouble from the rest of the town because Atticus defends an African-American.

2/20

I have just been reading the last pages of the book *To Kill a Mockingbird*, and it was hard for me to put the book down for the last hundred pages, because I was kept so much in suspense. The novel isn't only a very good description of the tranquil life in a southern town and the causes which disturb this tranquility. It is also a very touching description of a family life.

The book is considered a masterpiece of American literature and won the Pulitzer Prize. I think—besides that the novel is very well structured and written in a very vivid way—it is because Harper Lee is really successful in putting the story of this town and Jean Louise Finch's family life together. Through the eyes of this little girl the reader follows the story. The intelligent, accurate, and innocent observation of this nice girl are very fascinating. Looking through her eyes a picture appears which is so exact that you almost feel you were there as well.

I'm struck most by the relationship between these two children and their father. There is so much love, tender care, and understanding and respect on both sides as well that one could almost suspect Harper Lee wrote the book to teach parents how to bring up their children. Of course this isn't the case; I think she simply had such a father herself.

Susana

2/25

Hunger of Memory, the second book I have chosen to read, is an autobiography of Richard Rodriquez, who was born in Mexico and moved to America when he was a child. His family is living in Sacramento, California.

In the first chapter, Richard tells us he goes to a Roman Catholic school and all of his classmates are white. He only knows fifty words in English, and that is the first problem he has to deal with at school. He then notices that only at home he hears his language, Spanish, and outside home he hears something different. He hears how people use different sounds and tones when speaking.

He also talks about his family; his father has steady work and his mother works at home. They are working-class people. His parents always speak Spanish at home, but they use their little knowledge of English outside. Richard mentions bilingual education, and it seems that he does not agree with it at all. He thinks Spanish is for him a private language whereas English is a public language. And somehow he thinks he has the need and right of learning the public language so that he can communicate with others.

At school, teachers notice Richard's silence. He is very quiet and never participates in class. Therefore, his parents are asked to speak English at home. From that moment on, Richard is sort of forced to speak English. One day, Richard volunteers for the first time to answer a question in a class. Since then he does not feel shy anymore, he feels more confident. And then, he realizes he is an American citizen.

Things at home sort of change. They still remain a united family, but they are not as close as they used to be. Richard does not talk to his parents very much because they do not understand him every time, so he has to repeat everything again.

As Richard grows older he cannot speak Spanish fluently anymore. He still understands what people say to him, but as he tries to say something he cannot do it. The words cannot come out. His parents sometimes have to explain to others why their children (Richard and his brother and sisters) are not able to speak in Spanish, why they cannot speak "their own language." Richard feels kind of guilty, and he feels that he has committed a sin of betrayal by learning English, but he is aware that his parents have encouraged him to learn the language.

Years pass and now Richard is a man. He mentions again the bilingual education. He says that proponents of bilingual education argue that children would not be so alienated if they were allowed to use their family language at school. And he also adds that bilingualists say children would maintain their own culture if they use their family language in school.

Richard completes his studies in the British Museum, and he asks himself how he has managed his success. "A primary reason for my success in the classroom was that I couldn't forget that schooling was changing me and separating me from the life I enjoyed before becoming a student."

As a young boy, Richard is under a scholarship. He gets used to reading lots of books and starts enjoying reading. His mother always asks him what he is reading.

Sometimes, Richard feels sort of embarrassed by his parents because they did not have an education. Therefore, his mother is always encouraging her children to study. Richard's father never studied either.

In the next few chapters, Richard talks about religion. His family is Catholic; they go to church every Sunday. Richard also tells us that they pray every day at school. Through the years, he learns and understands more about religion.

So far what I have read of the book is quite interesting. Somehow I compare this story with my own story. In my case, I was born in a Hispanic country and I grew up there learning the language (Spanish, too) and the culture. I also went to school and all my friends were Colombian, but I never learned the language of my parents (Chinese). I can understand a little bit, but like Richard, I cannot speak it. And somehow I feel bad about it, and I wish my parents would have encouraged us to speak Chinese at home, so that we could have kept our language, but they used to talk to us most of the time in Spanish.

3/4

As a young boy, Richard has always realized the dark color of his skin. His relatives are always reminding him about that, because it seems that he and his oldest sister are the only ones in the family whose skins are darker. Therefore, he never goes out to the sun because his skin would get darker and he wouldn't get a suntan like the Americans. He therefore grows up with the idea of being an ugly child. Throughout his adolescence the thing he is mostly concerned about is his complexion.

Richard goes to college at Stanford. One day a friend tells him about a summer construction job. He accepts it because he needs some money and he remembers his father telling him once that he doesn't know the "real world," and that his hands are too soft. At work he doesn't speak to the other Mexicans who also work there. But one day the contractor makes him his translator, assuming he knows Spanish. Shyly, Richard translates something and everybody watches him. After this first experience in the summer, Richard doesn't feel ashamed of his body anymore. I guess because he was feeling more confident of himself.

Richard goes to graduate school at Columbia and Berkeley. He is considered a minority student, which he doesn't like at first place, but later on he kind of accepts it. Few years later he is awarded a Fulbright Fellowship to study in London, and he is glad to get away from those students. He finishes his dissertation in the British Museum and then accepts to teach for one year at Berkeley, even though he becomes again part of the minority group.

The year is almost over and Richard has not looked for a job yet. One of his professors yells at him and asks him if he thinks that all the jobs are going to look for him just because he is a minority. Richard gets a lot of teaching offers, but he keeps delaying his decision. But after all, he decides not to take any teaching position.

On the last chapter of this book, Richard tells us that he has to forget about writing for a while (he likes to write) and look for other temporary jobs when the money is gone. He also tells us that his mother once asked him not to write anything about the family, since these kind of things were private for her. Nowadays, Richard sees his family two or three times every year (for Easter, Mother's Day, and Christmas).

I like the book mainly because of its topic. Richard writes about bilingualism, about his position in America as a Mexican-born. I think it was a mistake for his parents not to keep their own language, Spanish. I think one could migrate to another country and learn its language, but never forget about his/her own language and culture. It is certainly a necessity to communicate with the people and be able to move around, but that doesn't mean one has to abandon his/her own.

In my case, I definitely think it was a big mistake my parents made of not keeping the language. I wasn't able to communicate as much as I wanted to with my parents because of the language barrier.

As a young girl, I always considered myself Colombian because I thought that was the country where I was born and grew up. Outside home everything was Colombian, but at home it was Chinese. Today, I still don't know which is one is stronger, Colombian or Chinese. Therefore, the only thing I can say is that I'm Colombian-Chinese! Is it correct to say so if I was born in Colombia and have origins in China, or is it Chinese-Colombian? But one thing is for sure: I'm going to learn to speak and read Chinese.

As you see, these students wrote very different journals. All the journals, however, have these points in common: after reading them, you know something about the books the students read and how the students felt about them. Try to develop your own style of journal writing while making sure that you give a clear impression of the books you read and your own reactions to them.

Using the Reading Selections and Exercises

The selections that follow are set out in the same way as are those in Chapter 1, and the exercises take the same form, so you can use them by following the same procedure.

1. Take note of the time as you begin to read such selection.

2. Read the selection as quickly as you can.

3. Write down in the space provided at the end of the selection how much time it took you to read the selection.

4. Answer the Comprehension Check items by writing the letter of your choice in the space labeled "1st answer." Do not look back at the passage.

5. Read the selection again, looking for the answers to the multiple-choice items. For each item, indicate where you find the answer by writing the appropriate line number(s) in the space marked "Line reference(s)."

6. If you change your mind about any answer, write the letter of your new choice in the space labeled "2nd answer."

7. Find out your reading speed in words per minute by using the chart that follows the Comprehension Check, and write it in the space provided after item 10.

8. If you have an opportunity, discuss your answers with your classmates.

9. When you are told the correct answers, circle the appropriate letter in each item and indicate whether your own answers are right ($\sqrt{}$) or wrong (*X*).

10. Write the scores you achieved on 1st reading and 2nd reading in the spaces provided.

11. Record your speed and your score on 1st reading in the graphs provided in the Appendix at the end of the book. You can record your work for this chapter on the same graph used for Chapter 1, but be sure to write the selection number in the space provided at the top of the graph.

12. Write down your answers to the Questions for Discussion, and be prepared
    to give them to your instructor or to discuss them in class.

You will be using the material in this chapter for the same general purposes
as the material in Chapter 1—to develop your reading speed and comprehension skills. You will notice, however, that the exercises, especially the
Questions for Discussion, direct your attention to different issues—the
personalities of the people mentioned, the implications of the descriptions, and
the clues as to what will come next. In other words, you are asked to consider
not only what the passage says but also how you personally relate to the book
from which it is taken, and whether you want to read it. It is as if you were in a
bookshop or library and have to choose a book in a hurry by reading the first
page or so. It is for this reason that the only information you are given about the
book is its title and the name of its author. Your instructor, however, can tell you
more about both if you ask—just as you could find out more by reading the
blurb printed on the back of the book or on the dust jacket, and, of course, by
reading the whole work.

**SELECTION
2-1**

from *Go Tell It on the Mountain*

James Baldwin

Start time _____

I looked down the line, And I wondered.

Everyone had always said that John would be a preacher when he grew up, just like his father. It had been said so often that John, without ever thinking about it, had come to believe it himself. Not until the morning of his fourteenth birthday did he really begin to think about it, and by then it was already too late.   5

His earliest memories—which were in a way, his only memories—were of the hurry and brightness of Sunday mornings. They all rose together on that day; his father who did not have to go to work, and led them in prayer before breakfast; his mother, who dressed up on that day, and looked almost young, with her hair straightened, and on her head the close-fitting white cap that was   10 the uniform of holy women; his younger brother, Roy, who was silent that day because his father was home. Sarah, who wore a red ribbon in her hair that day, and was fondled by her father. And the baby, Ruth, who was dressed in pink and white, and rode in her mother's arms to church.

The church was not very far away, four blocks up Lenox Avenue, on a   15 corner not far from the hospital. It was to this hospital that his mother had gone when Roy, and Sarah, and Ruth were born. John did not remember very clearly the first time she had gone, to have Roy; folks said that he had cried and carried on the whole time his mother was away; he remembered only enough to be afraid every time her belly began to swell, knowing that each time the   20 swelling began it would not end until she was taken from him, to come back with a stranger. Each time this happened she became a little more of a stranger herself. She would soon be going away again, Roy said—he knew much more about such things than John. John had observed his mother closely, seeing no swelling yet, but his father had prayed one morning for the "little voyager soon   25 to be among them," and so John knew that Roy spoke the truth.

Every Sunday morning, then, since John could remember, they had taken to the streets, the Grimes family on their way to church. Sinners along the avenue watched them—men still wearing their Saturday-night clothes, wrinkled and dusty now, muddy-eyed and muddy-faced; and women with harsh voices and   30 tight, bright dresses, cigarettes between their fingers or held tightly in the corners of their mouths. They talked, and laughed, and fought together, and the women fought like the men. John and Roy, passing these men and women, looked at one another briefly, John embarrassed and Roy amused. Roy would be like them when he grew up, if the Lord did not change his heart. These men   35 and women they passed on Sunday mornings had spent the night in bars, or in cat houses, or on the streets, or on rooftops, or under the stairs. They had been drinking. They had gone from cursing to laughter, to anger, to lust. Once he and Roy had watched a man and woman in the basement of a condemned house. They did it standing up. The woman had wanted fifty cents, and the 40 man had flashed a razor.

John had never watched again; he had been afraid. But Roy had watched them many times, and he told John he had done it with some girls down the block.

And his mother and father, who went to church on Sundays, they did it too, 45 and sometimes John heard them in the bedroom behind him, over the sound of rat's feet, and rat screams, and the music and cursing from the harlot's house downstairs.

**Time Taken
(min./sec.)** ———

564 words

**COMPREHENSION
CHECK**

Choose the best way of finishing each statement, according to the passage, and write in the letter on the "1st answer" blank. Then follow the directions on pages 91–92.

1. John had the idea that he would be a preacher because
   a. his father was one.
   b. that was what he had always wanted to be.
   c. everyone said that he would be one.
   d. both his parents wanted him to be one.

   ——————   ——————   ——————
   1st answer   Line reference(s)   2nd answer

2. In his family, John was
   a. the only son.
   b. the youngest child.
   c. the oldest child.
   d. a middle child.

   ——————   ——————   ——————
   1st answer   Line reference(s)   2nd answer

3. The family lived in a
   a. comfortable middle-class suburb.
   b. poor inner-city neighborhood.
   c. remote rural area.
   d. small village community.

   ——————   ——————   ——————
   1st answer   Line reference(s)   2nd answer

4. John's chief feeling towards his brother and sisters seems to have been

    a. resentment.

    b. affection.

    c. fear.

    d. indifference.

_____	_____	_____
1st answer	Line reference(s)	2nd answer

5. John's father is presented as

    a. affectionate.

    b. unhappy.

    c. hard-working.

    d. strict.

_____	_____	_____
1st answer	Line reference(s)	2nd answer

6. Roy could be described as

    a. unintelligent.

    b. inquisitive.

    c. careless.

    d. naughty.

_____	_____	_____
1st answer	Line reference(s)	2nd answer

7. Roy knew more than John did about

    a. school.

    b. life.

    c. sex.

    d. everything.

_____	_____	_____
1st answer	Line reference(s)	2nd answer

8. The "sinners along the avenue" were people who

    a. had committed crimes.

    b. did not go to church.

    c. belonged to a different community.

    d. lived on the streets.

_____	_____	_____
1st answer	Line reference(s)	2nd answer

9. John was a boy who was

    a. troubled and timid.
    b. assertive and confident.
    c. disobedient and naughty.
    d. loyal and religious.

_____	_____	_____
1st answer	Line reference(s)	2nd answer

10. Two major themes in this passage are

    a. ambition and pride.
    b. jealousy and love.
    c. poverty and oppression.
    d. sexuality and religion.

_____	_____	_____
1st answer	Line reference(s)	2nd answer

CHART FOR FINDING OUT READING SPEED

Time	wpm	Time	wpm	Time	wpm	Time	wpm	Time	wpm
1:30	376	2:30	226	3:30	161	4:30	125	5:30	103
1:45	322	2:45	205	3:45	150	4:45	119	5:45	98
2:00	282	3:00	188	4:00	141	5:00	113	6:00	94
2:15	250	3:15	174	4:15	133	5:15	107	6:15	90

Speed in words per minute _____

Total correct on 1st reading _____

Total correct on 2nd reading _____

QUESTIONS FOR DISCUSSION

1. Can you identify with John? Why, or why not?

2. How do you interpret John's position within his family?

3. What do you know, or imagine, about the society in which John is growing up?

4. What do you think is likely to be the main theme of the novel?

5. Would it be worth your while to read the book?

SELECTION
2-2

from *Second-Class Citizen*

Buchi Emecheta

Start time ———————

It had all begun like a dream. You know the sort of dream which seems to have originated from nowhere, yet one was always aware of its existence. One could feel it, one could be directed by it; unconsciously at first, until it became a reality, a Presence.

Adah did not know for sure what gave birth to the dream, when it all started, 5
but the earliest anchor she could pin down in this drift of nothingness was when she was about eight years old. She was not even quite sure that she was exactly eight, because, you see, she was a girl. She was a girl who arrived when everyone was expecting and predicting a boy. So, since she was such a disappointment to her parents, to her immediate family, to her tribe, nobody thought 10
of recording her birth. She was so insignificant. One thing was certain, though: she was born during the Second World War. She felt eight when she was being directed by the dream, for a younger child would not be capable of so many mischiefs. Thinking back on it all now that she was grown-up, she was sorry for her parents. But it was their own fault; they should not have had her in the 15
first place, and that would have saved a lot of people a lot of headaches.

Well, Adah thought she was eight at the time when her mother and all the other society women were busying themselves to welcome the very first lawyer to their town, Ibuza. Whenever Adah was told that Ibuza was her own, she found it difficult to understand. Her parents, she was told, came from Ibuza, 20
and so did many of her aunts and uncles. Ibuza, she was told, was a beautiful town. She had been taught at an early age that the people of Ibuza were friendly, that the food there was fresh, the spring water was pure and the air was clean. The virtues of Ibuza were praised so much that Adah came to regard being born in a God-forsaken place like Lagos as a misfortune. Her parents said 25
that Lagos was a bad place, bad for bringing up children because here they picked up the Yoruba-Ngbati accent. It was bad because it was a town with laws, a town where the Law ruled supreme. In Ibuza, they said, you took the law into your own hands. If a woman abused your child, you went straight into her hut, dragged her out, beat her up or got beaten up, as the case might be. So 30
if you didn't want to be dragged out and beaten up you wouldn't abuse another woman's child. Lagos was bad because this type of behavior was not allowed. You had to learn to control your temper, which Adah was taught was against the law of nature.

The Ibuza women who lived in Lagos were preparing for the arrival of the 35
town's first lawyer from the United Kingdom. The title "United Kingdom" when pronounced by Adah's father sounded so heavy, like the type of noise one associated with bombs. It was so deep, so mysterious, that Adah's father

always voiced it in hushed tones, wearing such a respectful expression as if he were speaking of God's Holiest of Holies. Going to the United Kingdom must surely be like paying God a visit. The United Kingdom, then, must be like heaven.   40

567 words

**Time Taken
(min./sec.)** _____

**COMPREHENSION
CHECK**

Choose the best way of finishing each statement, according to the passage, and write in the letter on the "1st answer" blank. Then follow the directions on pages 91–92.

1. From her birth, Adah was

   a. much loved.
   b. considered unimportant.
   c. cruelly treated.
   d. loved by her mother but ignored by her father.

   _____   _____   _____
      1st answer   Line reference(s)   2nd answer

2. The reason for this was that

   a. the family was very poor.
   b. she was the only child.
   c. she had too many brothers and sisters.
   d. she was a girl.

   _____   _____   _____
      1st answer   Line reference(s)   2nd answer

3. The family lived in

   a. Lagos.
   b. Yoruba-Ngbati.
   c. Ghana.
   d. Ibuza.

   _____   _____   _____
      1st answer   Line reference(s)   2nd answer

4. Ibuza is mentioned as

   a. their own town.
   b. the place where they were living.
   c. a place where they wanted to visit.
   d. a God-forsaken place.

   _____   _____   _____
      1st answer   Line reference(s)   2nd answer

5. Adah's parents thought that Lagos was

   a. beautiful.
   b. very pleasant.
   c. a bad place to live.
   d. dangerous.

   _____   _____   _____
     1st answer   Line reference(s)   2nd answer

6. They thought this because

   a. it was lawless.
   b. it was not good for bringing up children.
   c. there were many fine buildings.
   d. there was too much traffic.

   _____   _____   _____
     1st answer   Line reference(s)   2nd answer

7. The people of Ibuza were

   a. careful to obey the laws.
   b. strongly opposed to violence.
   c. apt to take the law into their own hands.
   d. sympathetic toward people who broke the law.

   _____   _____   _____
     1st answer   Line reference(s)   2nd answer

8. The particular occasion mentioned here is

   a. the funeral of Adah's father.
   b. Adah's betrothal.
   c. a traditional ceremony in Ibuza.
   d. the arrival of Ibuza's first lawyer from Britain.

   _____   _____   _____
     1st answer   Line reference(s)   2nd answer

9. The United Kingdom is described as

   a. a heavenly place.
   b. the hated home of the imperialists.
   c. a country where a good academic education could be obtained.
   d. a cold and cheerless country.

   _____   _____   _____
     1st answer   Line reference(s)   2nd answer

10. The dream mentioned

    a. occurred one night when Adah was a child.

    b. developed gradually from Adah's earliest childhood.

    c. was inspired by the celebrations on her eighth birthday.

    d. was instilled into Adah by her parents.

| _____ | _____ | _____ |
| 1st answer | Line reference(s) | 2nd answer |

CHART FOR FINDING OUT READING SPEED

Time	wpm	Time	wpm	Time	wpm	Time	wpm	Time	wpm
1:30	378	2:30	227	3:30	162	4:30	126	5:30	103
1:45	324	2:45	206	3:45	151	4:45	119	5:45	99
2:00	284	3:00	189	4:00	142	5:00	113	6:00	95
2:15	252	3:15	174	4:15	133	5:15	108	6:15	91

Speed in words per minute _____

Total correct on 1st reading _____

Total correct on 2nd reading _____

QUESTIONS FOR DISCUSSION

1. What do you think Adah's dream was?

2. What problem do you think the novel looks at?

3. Would you say the author was appreciative or critical of the society she describes? Why?

4. What seems likely to happen in the story?

5. Do you want to find out?

**SELECTION
2-3**

from *The Bridge of San Luis Rey*

Thornton Wilder

Start time ———

On Friday noon, July the twentieth, 1714, the finest bridge in all Peru broke and precipitated five travelers into the gulf below. This bridge was on the highroad between Lima and Cuzco and hundreds of persons passed over it every day. It had been woven of osier by the Incas more than a century before and visitors to the city were always led out to see it. It was a mere ladder of   5
thin slats swung out over the gorge, with handrails of dried vine. Horses and coaches and chairs had to go down hundreds of feet below and pass over the narrow torrent on rafts, but no one, not even the Viceroy, not even the Arch-bishop of Lima, had descended with the baggage rather than cross by the fa-mous bridge of San Luis Rey. St. Louis of France himself protected it, by his   10
name and by the little mud church on the further side. The bridge seemed to be among the things that last forever; it was unthinkable that it should break. The moment a Peruvian heard of the accident he signed himself and made a mental calculation as to how recently he had crossed by it and how soon he had in-tended crossing by it again. People wandered about in a trance-like state, mut-   15
tering; they had the hallucination of seeing themselves falling into a gulf.

There was a great service in the Cathedral. The bodies of the victims were approximately collected and approximately separated from one another, and there was great searching of hearts in the beautiful city of Lima. Servant girls returned bracelets which they had stolen from their mistresses, and usurers   20
harangued their wives angrily, in defense of usury. Yet it was rather strange that this event should have so impressed the Limeans, for in that country those catastrophes which lawyers shockingly call the "acts of God" were more than usually frequent. Tidal waves were continually washing away cities; earth-quakes arrived every week and towers fell upon good men and women all the   25
time. Diseases were forever flitting in and out of the provinces and old age carried away some of the most admirable citizens. That is why it was so sur-prising that the Peruvians should have been especially touched by the rent in the bridge of San Luis Rey.

Everyone was very deeply impressed, but only one person did anything   30
about it, and that was Brother Juniper. By a series of coincidences so extraordi-nary that one almost suspects the presence of some Intention, this little red-haired Franciscan from Northern Italy happened to be in Peru converting the Indians and happened to witness the accident.

It was a very hot noon, that fatal noon, and coming around the shoulder of a   35
hill Brother Juniper stopped to wipe his forehead and to gaze upon the screen of snowy peaks in the distance, then into the gorge below him filled with the dark plumage of green trees and green birds and traversed by its ladder of osier. Joy

was in him; things were not going badly. He had opened several little abandoned churches and the Indians were crawling in to early Mass and groaning at 40
the moment of miracle as though their hearts would break. Perhaps it was the
pure air from the snows before him; perhaps it was the memory that brushed
him for a moment of the poem that bade him raise his eyes to the helpful hills.
At all events he felt at peace. Then his glance fell upon the bridge, and at that
moment a twanging noise filled the air, as when the string of some musical   45
instrument snaps in a disused room, and he saw the bridge divide and fling five
gesticulating ants into the valley below.

Anyone else would have said to himself with secret joy: "Within ten minutes
myself. . . !" But it was another thought that visited Brother Juniper: "Why did
this happen to *those* five?" If there were any plan in the universe at all, if there 50
were any pattern in a human life, surely it could be discovered mysteriously
latent in those lives so suddenly cut off. Either we live by accident and die by
accident, or we live by plan and die by plan. And on that instant Brother
Juniper made the resolve to inquire into the secret lives of those five persons,
that moment falling through the air, and to surprise the reason of their taking 55
off.

Time Taken
(min./sec.) _____

740 words

COMPREHENSION
CHECK

Choose the best way of finishing each statement, according to the passage,
and write the letter on the "1st answer" blank. Then follow the directions on
pages 91–92.

1. The story takes place
   a. late in the sixteenth century.
   b. early in the eighteenth century.
   c. in the middle of the nineteenth century.
   d. at an unspecified time.

_____   _____   _____
1st answer   Line reference(s)   2nd answer

2. The bridge was made of
   a. vines.
   b. wood.
   c. stone.
   d. steel.

_____   _____   _____
1st answer   Line reference(s)   2nd answer

3. The bridge's falling down was especially shocking because

   a. the archbishop and the viceroy were crossing it at the time.
   b. it was such strong materials that it seemed impossible that it should break.
   c. it was old and people felt it would be there forever.
   d. the accident caused a particularly large number of deaths.

   _____   _____   _____
   1st answer   Line reference(s)   2nd answer

4. The accident made people think of

   a. the wrong they had done.
   b. those who had suffered from "acts of God."
   c. the need to build a safer bridge.
   d. the importance of building a new church of St. Louis.

   _____   _____   _____
   1st answer   Line reference(s)   2nd answer

5. The bridge was connected with St. Louis because

   a. it just happened to have the same name.
   b. St. Louis had built it.
   c. people believed that St. Louis guarded it.
   d. its builders decided to place it near the church of St. Louis.

   _____   _____   _____
   1st answer   Line reference(s)   2nd answer

6. At the moment the accident happened, it seems,

   a. nobody saw it.
   b. just one person saw it.
   c. there were five witnesses.
   d. a large crowd was watching.

   _____   _____   _____
   1st answer   Line reference(s)   2nd answer

7. The people on the bridge at the time are presented as

   a. close friends.
   b. important people.
   c. especially good people.
   d. anonymous travelers.

   _____   _____   _____
   1st answer   Line reference(s)   2nd answer

8. Brother Juniper was

    a. one of the travelers on the bridge.
    b. an observer of the accident.
    c. a historian who recorded the event.
    d. the priest in charge of the church of St. Louis.

| _____ | _____ | _____ |
| 1st answer | Line reference(s) | 2nd answer |

9. Brother Juniper was in Peru because

    a. it was his home country.
    b. he had come as a missionary.
    c. he was called to investigate the accident.
    d. he wanted to do research there.

| _____ | _____ | _____ |
| 1st answer | Line reference(s) | 2nd answer |

10. Brother Juniper wanted to find out

    a. why the accident happened to those particular people.
    b. why the bridge should have broken.
    c. what would have happened if the bridge hadn't broken.
    d. why God let so many innocent people die.

| _____ | _____ | _____ |
| 1st answer | Line reference(s) | 2nd answer |

CHART FOR FINDING OUT READING SPEED

Time	wpm	Time	wpm	Time	wpm	Time	wpm	Time	wpm
1:30	493	2:45	269	4:00	185	5:15	141	6:30	113
1:45	423	3:00	247	4:15	174	5:30	135	6:45	110
2:00	370	3:15	228	4:30	164	5:45	129	7:00	106
2:15	329	3:30	211	4:45	156	6:00	123	7:15	102
2:30	296	3:45	197	5:00	148	6:15	118	7:30	99

Speed in words per minute _____

Total correct on 1st reading _____

Total correct on 2nd reading _____

**QUESTIONS FOR
DISCUSSION**

1. What philosophical question is raised in this passage? Do you think the book will supply an answer?

2. How do you think this description of the accident will be followed up? How will the story develop?

3. Who do you think will be the main character or characters? Do you expect to identify closely with whoever it is?

4. What images and scenes does the book suggest to you so far? What impression do they make on you?

5. Do you expect to pick up any incidental geographical or historical information in this book? What about? Would it be interesting or useful to know more about these topics?

6. Do you want to read the book?

SELECTION
2-4

from *The Woman Warrior*
Maxine Hong Kingston

Start time _____

"You must not tell anyone," my mother said, "what I am about to tell you. In China your father had a sister who killed herself. She jumped into the family well. We say that your father has all brothers because it is as if she had never been born.

"In 1924 just a few days after our village celebrated seventeen hurry-up   5
weddings—to make sure that every young man who went 'out on the road' would responsibly come home—your father and his brothers and your grandfather and his brothers and your aunt's new husband sailed for America, the Gold Mountain. It was your grandfather's last trip. Those lucky enough to get contracts waved good-bye from the decks. They fed and guarded the stow-   10
aways and helped them off in Cuba, New York, Bali, Hawaii. 'We'll meet in California next year,' they said. All of them sent money home.

"I remember looking at your aunt one day when she and I were dressing; I had not noticed before that she had such a protruding melon of a stomach. But I did not think, 'She's pregnant,' until she began to look like other pregnant   15
women, her shirt pulling and the white tops of her black pants showing. She could not have been pregnant, you see, because her husband had been gone for years. No one said anything. We did not discuss it. In early summer she was ready to have the child, long after the time when it could have been possible.

"The village had also been counting. On the night the baby was to be born   20
the villagers raided our house. Some were crying. Like a great saw, teeth strung with lights, files of people walked zigzag across our land, tearing the rice. Their lanterns doubled in the disturbed black water, which drained away through the broken bunds. As the villagers closed in, we could see that some of them, probably men and women we knew well, wore white masks. The people   25
with long hair hung it over their faces. Women with short hair made it stand up on end. Some had tied white bands around their foreheads, arms, and legs.

"At first they threw mud and rocks at the house. Then they threw eggs and began slaughtering our stock. We could hear the animals scream their deaths— the roosters, the pigs, a last great roar from the ox. Familiar wild heads flared   30
in our night windows; the villagers encircled us. Some of the faces stopped to peer at us, their eyes rushing like searchlights. The hands flattened against the panes, framed heads, and left red prints.

"The villagers broke in the front and the back doors at the same time, even though we had not locked the doors against them. Their knives dripped with the   35
blood of our animals. They smeared blood on the doors and walls. One woman swung a chicken, whose throat she had slit, splattering blood in red arcs about

her. We stood together in the middle of our house, in the family hall with the pictures and tables of the ancestors around us, and looked straight ahead.

"At that time the house had only two wings. When the men came back, we would build two more to enclose our courtyard and a third one to begin a second courtyard. The villagers pushed through both wings, even your grandparents' rooms, to find your aunt's, which was also mine until the men returned. From this room a new wing for one of the younger families would grow. They ripped up her clothes and shoes and broke her combs, grinding them underfoot. They tore her work from the loom. They scattered the cooking fire and rolled the new weaving in it. We could hear them in the kitchen breaking our bowls and banging the pots. They overturned the great waist-high earthenware jugs; duck eggs, pickled fruits, vegetables burst out and mixed in acrid torrents. The old woman from the next field swept a broom through the air and loosed the spirits-of-the-broom over our heads. 'Pig.' 'Ghost.' 'Pig,' they sobbed and scolded while they ruined our house.

"When they left, they took sugar and oranges to bless themselves. They cut pieces from the dead animals. Some of them took bowls that were not broken and clothes that were not torn. Afterward we swept up the rice and sewed it back up into sacks. But the smells from the spilled preserves lasted. Your aunt gave birth in the pigsty that night. The next morning when I went for the water, I found her and the baby plugging up the family well.

"Don't let your father know that I told you. He denies her. Now that you have started to menstruate, what happened to her could happen to you. Don't humiliate us. You wouldn't like to be forgotten as if you had never been born. The villagers are watchful."

Whenever she had to warn us about life, my mother told stories that ran like this one, a story to grow up on. She tested our strength to establish realities. Those in the emigrant generations who could not reassert brute survival died young and far from home. Those of us in the first American generations have had to figure out how the invisible world the emigrants built around our childhoods fits in solid America.

**Time Taken
(min./sec.)** ⎯⎯⎯⎯⎯

870 words

**COMPREHENSION
CHECK**

Choose the best way of finishing each statement, according to the passage, and write the letter in the "1st answer" blank. Then follow the directions on pages 91–92.

1. The story in this passage is told by
   a. the writer.
   b. the writer's aunt.
   c. the writer's mother.
   d. the writer's grandmother.

   _____   _____   _____
   1st answer   Line reference(s)   2nd answer

2. The central character of the story was
   a. the only daughter in her family.
   b. one of several brothers and sisters.
   c. the daughter-in-law of the family.
   d. the youngest woman in the household.

   _____   _____   _____
   1st answer   Line reference(s)   2nd answer

3. The men of the family were away because
   a. they were out farming.
   b. they were sailors.
   c. they had gone abroad to look for work.
   d. they had contracts to work in America.

   _____   _____   _____
   1st answer   Line reference(s)   2nd answer

4. When the family realized that the woman in the story was pregnant they
   a. ignored it.
   b. punished her.
   c. gave her advice.
   d. sent her away.

   _____   _____   _____
   1st answer   Line reference(s)   2nd answer

5. The villagers attacked the family because

    a. one of its members had made a woman pregnant.
    b. its daughter was going to have an illegitimate child.
    c. all of its men had gone away.
    d. it had adopted American customs.

    _____   _____   _____
    1st answer   Line reference(s)   2nd answer

6. When the villagers attacked, they

    a. burnt down the house.
    b. killed the woman and her newborn child.
    c. stole all the family's property.
    d. killed all the livestock.

    _____   _____   _____
    1st answer   Line reference(s)   2nd answer

7. In response to the attack, the members of the family

    a. did nothing.
    b. tried to defend themselves.
    c. hid themselves in the pigsty.
    d. ran away.

    _____   _____   _____
    1st answer   Line reference(s)   2nd answer

8. The woman who was pregnant

    a. ran away to some unknown place.
    b. gave birth and then committed suicide.
    c. had a miscarriage because of the shock.
    d. begged her family for forgiveness.

    _____   _____   _____
    1st answer   Line reference(s)   2nd answer

9. The family's response was to

    a. give her all the support they could.
    b. punish her severely.
    c. treat her as if she had never lived.
    d. forget the incident entirely.

    _____   _____   _____
    1st answer   Line reference(s)   2nd answer

10. The story was told as

    a. an important part of family tradition.
    b. a warning to the writer.
    c. an interesting example of Chinese culture.
    d. a demonstration of how hard life used to be.

    _____   _____   _____
      1st answer   Line reference(s)   2nd answer

CHART FOR FINDING OUT READING SPEED

Time	wpm	Time	wpm	Time	wpm	Time	wpm	Time	wpm
2:15	387	3:30	249	4:45	183	6:00	145	7:15	120
2:30	348	3:45	232	5:00	174	6:15	139	7:30	116
2:45	316	4:00	218	5:15	166	6:30	134	7:45	112
3:00	290	4:15	205	5:30	158	6:45	129	8:00	109
3:15	268	4:30	193	5:45	151	7:00	124	8:15	105

Speed in words per minute _____

Total correct on 1st reading _____

Total correct on 2nd reading _____

QUESTIONS FOR DISCUSSION

1. What elements in this story are familiar to you? What elements are unfamiliar?

2. In what country and what kind of society is this story set?

3. Why do you think the villagers in the story reacted so strongly?

4. How do you interpret the family's reactions?

5. What seems to be the writer's perspective on this story? Why does she begin her book with it?

6. What kind of book do you think this will be? Do you want to read it?

**SELECTION
2-5**

from *The Story of a Shipwrecked Sailor*

Gabriel García Márquez

Start time _____

On February 22 we were told that we would be returning to Colombia. For eight months we had been in Mobile, Alabama, where the electronic equipment and gunnery of the *Caldas* were being repaired. While on liberty we did what all sailors do ashore: we went to the movies with our girlfriends and afterward met at a bar in the port, the Joe Palooka, where we drank whiskey and some-   5
times started brawls.

My girlfriend was named Mary Address, and I met her through another sailor's girlfriend after I had been in Mobile for two months. Mary had some fluency in Spanish, but I don't think she ever understood why my friends called her, in jest, "María Dirección." Each time we had shore leave I took her to the   10
movies, although she preferred going out for ice cream. With my half-English and her half-Spanish we could just about make ourselves understood, but we always did understand each other, at the movies or eating ice cream.

There was only one time I didn't go out with Mary: the night we saw *The Caine Mutiny*. Some of my friends had heard it was a good movie about life   15
aboard a minesweeper. That was the reason we went to see it. The best part of the movie, however, wasn't the minesweeper but the storm. We all agreed that the thing to do in a situation like that was to change the vessel's course, as the mutineers had done. But none of us had ever been in a storm like that one, so nothing in the movie impressed us as much as the storm did. When we returned   20
to the ship that night, one of the sailors, Diego Velázquez, who was very impressed by the movie, figured that in just a few days we would be at sea and wondered, "What if something like that happened to us?"

I confess that the movie also made an impression on me. In the past eight months, I had grown unaccustomed to the sea. I wasn't afraid, for an instructor   25
had shown us how to fend for ourselves in the event of a shipwreck. Nonethe-less, the uneasiness I felt the night we saw *The Caine Mutiny* wasn't normal.

I don't mean to say that from that moment I began to anticipate the catastro-phe, but I had never been so apprehensive before a voyage. When I was a child in Bogotá, looking at illustrations in books, it never occurred to me that one   30
might encounter death at sea. On the contrary, I had a great deal of faith in the sea. And from the time I had enlisted in the Navy, two years before, I had never felt anxious during a voyage.

But I'm not ashamed to say that I felt something like fear after seeing *The Caine Mutiny*. Lying face up in my bunk, the uppermost one, I thought about   35
my family and about the voyage we would have to make before reaching Car-tagena. I couldn't sleep. With my head resting in my hands, I listened to the soft splash of water against the pier and the calm breathing of forty sailors

sleeping in their quarters. Just below my bunk, Seaman First Class Luis Rengifo snored like a trombone. I don't know what he was dreaming about, but he certainly wouldn't have slept so soundly had he known that eight days later he would be dead at the bottom of the sea. 40

My uneasiness lasted all through that week. The day of departure was alarmingly close, and I tried to instill some confidence in myself by talking to my mates. We talked more insistently about our families, about Colombia, and about our plans for our return. Little by little, the ship was loaded with the gifts we would take home: radios, refrigerators, washing machines, and stoves. I had bought a radio. 45

Unable to shake off my worries, I made a resolution: as soon as I reached Cartagena I would quit the Navy. The night before we sailed I went to say goodbye to Mary. I thought I would speak to her about my fears and about my resolution. But I didn't because I had promised her I'd come back, and she wouldn't have believed me if I told her I had decided never to sail again. The only person I did tell was Seaman Second Class Ramón Herrera, who confided that he, too, had decided to leave the Navy as soon as we reached Cartagena. Sharing our misgivings, Ramón Herrera and I went with Diego Velázquez to have a whiskey and bid farewell to the Joe Palooka. 50 55

We thought we would have one whiskey, but we ended up having five bottles. Practically all our girlfriends knew we were leaving and they decided to say goodbye, get drunk, and cry to show their gratitude. The bandleader, a serious fellow who wore eyeglasses that made him look nothing like a musician, played a program of mambos and tangos in our honor, thinking this was Colombian music. Our girlfriends wept and drank whiskey at a dollar and a half a bottle. 60

Since we had been paid three times that week, we decided to raise the roof. Me, because I was worried and wanted to get drunk. Ramón Herrera, because he was happy, as always, and because he was from Arjona and knew how to play the drums and had a singular talent for imitating all the fashionable singers. 65

Shortly before we left, a North American sailor came up to our table and asked permission to dance with Ramón Herrera's girlfriend, an enormous blonde, the one who was drinking the least and crying the most—and she meant it! The North American asked permission in English and Ramón Herrera shook him, saying in Spanish, "I can't understand you, you son of a bitch!" 70

It turned out to be one of the best brawls Mobile ever had, with chairs broken over people's heads, radio patrol cars and cops. Ramón Herrera, who managed to throw a couple of good haymakers at the North American, went back to the ship at one in the morning, singing like Daniel Santos. He said it was the last time he would go aboard. And, indeed, it was. 75

At three in the morning on the twenty-fourth, the *Caldas* weighed anchor at Mobile, bound for Cartagena. We were all happy to be going home. And we were all taking along gifts. Chief Gunner's Mate Miguel Ortega seemed happi- 80 est of all. I don't think another sailor was ever as prudent as Miguel Ortega. During his eight months in Mobile he had hadn't squandered a dollar. All the money he got he invested in presents for his wife, who was waiting for him in Cartagena. As we boarded that morning, Ortega was on the bridge, talking about his wife and children, which was no coincidence, because he never talked of anything else. He had a refrigerator, an automatic washer, a radio, and a stove for them. Twelve hours later, Ortega would be stretched out in his bunk, dying of seasickness. And twenty-four hours later, he would be dead at the bottom of the sea.

85

90

1137 words

**Time Taken
(min./sec.) _____**

**COMPREHENSION
CHECK**

Choose the best way of finishing each statement, according to the passage, and write the letter in the "1st answer" blank. Then follow the directions on pages 91–92.

1. The sailor telling this story is from

   a. Alabama.
   b. Colombia.
   c. Arjona.
   d. Mexico.

   _____   _____   _____
   1st answer   Line reference(s)   2nd answer

2. Mary Address was a woman who the sailor

   a. went out with for most of his shore leave.
   b. intended to marry.
   c. picked up during his last week on shore.
   d. had left behind him at home.

   _____   _____   _____
   1st answer   Line reference(s)   2nd answer

3. The movie that the sailor and his friends went to see impressed them because

   a. it was a good representation of life on board a minesweeper.
   b. it told how sailors had mutinied against their officers.
   c. it showed what a violent storm could be like.
   d. it depicted experiences similar to their own.

   _____   _____   _____
   1st answer   Line reference(s)   2nd answer

4. The sailor was unhappy during his last week ashore because

    a. he did not want to leave Mary Address.
    b. he was always nervous before a voyage.
    c. he was sure they would encounter a storm.
    d. the film had made him vaguely apprehensive.

    _____   _____   _____
     1st answer   Line reference(s)   2nd answer

5. In describing how he could not sleep, the sailor mentions Luis Rengifo as a man who

    a. slept soundly although he would soon be dead.
    b. made the night more difficult by his snoring.
    c. would listen if the sailor told him his troubles.
    d. was also unhappy about their departure.

    _____   _____   _____
     1st answer   Line reference(s)   2nd answer

6. The sailor decided to quit the navy because

    a. he wanted to settle down.
    b. he had begun to mistrust the sea.
    c. he decided it was too much work.
    d. his family wanted him to stay at home.

    _____   _____   _____
     1st answer   Line reference(s)   2nd answer

7. During the last week on shore, the sailors

    a. bought presents for their families at home.
    b. went to the bar every night to get drunk.
    c. began training for the voyage.
    d. talked about what might happen on the journey.

    _____   _____   _____
     1st answer   Line reference(s)   2nd answer

8. Ramón Herrera was

    a. the musician who entertained them on their last night.
    b. the proprietor of the Joe Palooka.
    c. the only officer mentioned in the story.
    d. one of those who would die on the voyage to Cartagena.

    _____   _____   _____
     1st answer   Line reference(s)   2nd answer

9. In telling about the fight on the last night before sailing, the sailor makes it sound like

    a. a disaster.
    b. an amusing incident.
    c. a daily occurrence.
    d. an ominous event.

| _____ | _____ | _____ |
| 1st answer | Line reference(s) | 2nd answer |

10. Miguel Ortega is described as a man who

    a. was nervous about the coming voyage.
    b. was extravagant with his money.
    c. was especially devoted to his family.
    d. was seasick as soon as the voyage started.

| _____ | _____ | _____ |
| 1st answer | Line reference(s) | 2nd answer |

CHART FOR FINDING OUT READING SPEED

Time	wpm	Time	wpm	Time	wpm	Time	wpm	Time	wpm
3:00	379	4:30	253	6:00	190	7:30	152	9:00	126
3:15	350	4:45	239	6:15	182	7:45	147	9:15	123
3:30	325	5:00	227	6:30	175	8:00	142	9:30	120
3:45	303	5:15	217	6:45	168	8:15	138	9:45	117
4:00	284	5:30	207	7:00	162	8:30	134	10:00	114
4:15	268	5:45	198	7:15	157	8:45	130	10:15	111

Speed in words per minute _____

Total correct on 1st reading _____

Total correct on 2nd reading _____

QUESTIONS FOR DISCUSSION

1. What kind of person is the sailor who tells this story?

2. What indications are given that a disaster is about to happen?

3. Who are the different people mentioned? Which of them will be involved in the disaster?

4. What kind of disaster do you think it will be? What do you expect to happen?

5. Do you want to find out? Do you think it will be an interesting story?

from *The Dark Wind*

Tony Hillerman

Start time _____

The Flute Clan boy was the first to see it. He stopped and stared.

"Somebody lost a boot," he said.

Even from where he stood, at least fifteen yards farther down the trail, Albert Lomatewa could see that nobody had lost the boot. The boot had been placed, not dropped. It rested upright, squarely in the middle of the path, its 5 pointed toe aimed toward them. Obviously someone had put it there. And now, just beyond a dead growth of rabbit brush which crowded the trail, Lomatewa saw the top of a second boot. Yesterday when they had come this way no boots had been here.

Albert Lomatewa was the Messenger. He was in charge. Eddie Tuvi and the 10 Flute Clan boy would do exactly what he told them.

"Stay away from it," Lomatewa said. "Stay right here."

He lifted the heavy pack of spruce boughs from his back and placed it reverently beside the path. Then he walked to the boot. It was fairly new, made of brown leather, with a flower pattern stitched into it and a curved cowboy 15 heel. Lomatewa glanced past the rabbit brush at the second boot. It matched. Beyond the second boot, the path curved sharply around a weathered granite boulder. Lomatewa sucked in his breath. Jutting from behind the boulder he could see the bottom of a foot. The foot was bare and even from where Lomatewa stood he could see there was something terribly wrong with it. 20

Lomatewa looked back at the two his kiva had sent to guard him on this pilgrimage for spruce. They stood where he had told them to stand—Tuvi's face impassive, the boy's betraying his excited curiosity.

"Stay there," he ordered. "There is someone here and I must see about it."

The man was on his side, legs bent stiffly, left arm stretched rigidly for- 25 ward, right arm flexed upward with the palm resting beside his ear. He wore blue jeans, a jean jacket, and a blue-and-white-checked shirt, its sleeves rolled to the elbows. But it was a little while before Lomatewa noticed what the man was wearing. He was staring at his feet. The soles of both of them had been cut away. The bottom of the socks had been cut and the socks pushed up around 30 the ankles, where they formed ragged white cuffs. Then the heel pads, and the pads at the balls of the feet, and the undertips of the toes had been sliced away. Lomatewa had nine grandchildren, and one great-grandchild, and had lived long enough to see many things, but he had never seen this before. He sucked in his breath, exhaled it, and glanced up at the hands. He expected to find them 35 flayed, too. And he did. The skin had been sliced from them just as it had been from the feet. Only then did Lomatewa look at the man's face.

He had been young. Not a Hopi. A Navajo. At least part Navajo. There was a small, black-rimmed hole above his right eye.

Lomatewa stood looking down at the man, thinking how this would have to be handled. It had to be handled so that it would not interfere with the Niman Kachina. The sun was hot on him here, even though it was still early morning, and the smell of dust was in his nostrils. Dust, always dust. Reminding him of why nothing must interfere with the ceremonial. For almost a year the blessing of rain had been withdrawn. He had thinned his corn three times, and still what little was left was stunted and withering in the endless drought. The springs were drying. There was no grass left for the horses. The Niman Kachina must be properly done. He turned and walked back to where his guardians were waiting.

"A dead Tavasuh," he said. Literally the word meant "head-pounder." It was a term of contempt which Hopis sometimes used for Navajos and Lomatewa chose it deliberately to set the tone for what he must do.

"What happened to his foot?" the Flute Clan boy asked. "The bottom was cut off his foot."

"Put down the spruce," Lomatewa said, "Sit down. We must talk about this." He wasn't worried about Tuvi. Tuvi was a valuable man in the Antelope Kiva and a member of the One Horn Society—a prayerful man. But the Flute Clan boy was still a boy. He said nothing more, though, simply sitting on the path beside his spruce bundle. The questions remained in his eyes. Let him wait, Lomatewa thought. Let him learn patience.

"Three times Sotuknang has destroyed the world," Lomatewa began. "He destroyed the First World with fire. He destroyed the Second World with ice. He destroyed the Third World with flood. Each time he destroyed the world because his people failed to do what he told them to do." Lomatewa kept his eyes on the Flute Clan boy as he talked. The boy was his only worry. The boy had gone to school at Flagstaff and he had a job with the post office. There was talk that he did not plant his corn patches properly, that he did not properly know his role in the Kachina Society. Tuvi could be counted on but the boy must be taught. Lomatewa spoke directly to him, and the boy listened as if he had not heard the old story a thousand times before.

"Sotuknang destroyed the world because the Hopis forgot to do their duty. They forgot the songs that must be sung, the *pahos* that must be offered, the ceremonials that must be danced. Each time the world became infected with evil, people quarreled all the time. People became *powaqas*, and practiced witchcraft against one another. The Hopis left the proper Road of Life and only a few were left doing their duty in the kivas. And each time, Sotuknang gave the Hopis warning. He held back the rain so his people would know his displeasure. But everybody ignored the rainless seasons. They kept going after money, and quarreling, and gossiping, and forgetting the way of the Road of Life. And each time Sotuknang decided that the world had used up its string, and he saved a few of the best Hopis, and then he destroyed all the rest."

Lomatewa stared into the eyes of the Flute Clan boy. "You understand all this?"

"I understand," the boy said.

"We must do the Niman Kachina right this summer," Lomatewa said, 85
"Sotuknang has warned us. Our corn dies in the fields. There is no grass. The
wells are drying out. When we call the clouds, they no longer hear us. If we do
the Niman Kachina wrong, Sotuknang will have no more patience. He will
destroy the Fourth World."

Lomatewa glanced at Tuvi. His face was inscrutable. Then he spoke directly 90
to the boy again. "Very soon it will be time for the kachinas to leave this Earth
Surface World and go back to their home in the San Francisco Peaks. When we
deliver this spruce back to our kivas, it will be used to prepare for the Going
Home Dances to honor them. For days it will be very busy in the kivas. The
prayers to be planned. The *pahos* to be made. Everything to be done exactly in 95
the proper way." Lomatewa paused, allowing silence to make the effect he
wanted. "Everybody thinking in the proper way," he added. "But if we report
this body, this dead Navajo, to the police, nothing can be done right. The
police will come, the *bahana* police, to ask us questions. They will call us out
of the kivas. Everything will be interrupted. Everybody will be thinking 100
of death and anger when they should be thinking only holy thoughts. The
Niman Kachina will be messed up. The Going Home Dances would not be
done right. Nobody would be praying."

He stopped again, staring at the Flute Clan boy.

"If you were the Messenger, what would you do?" 105

"I would not tell the police," the boy said.

"Would you talk of this in the kiva?"

"I would not talk of it."

"You saw the feet of the Navajo," Lomatewa said. "Do you know what that
means?" 110

"The skin being cut away?"

"Yes. Do you know what it means?"

The Flute Clan boy looked down at his hands. "I know," he said.

"If you talk about that, it would be the worst thing of all. People would be
thinking of evil just when they should be thinking of good." 115

"I won't talk about it," the boy said.

"Not until after the Niman dances," Lomatewa said. "Not until after the
ceremonial is over and the kachinas are gone. After that you can tell about it."

Lomatewa picked up his bundle of spruce and settled the straps over his
shoulders, flinching at the soreness in his joints. He felt every one of his sev- 120
enty-three years, and he still had almost thirty miles to walk across Wepo Wash
and then the long climb up the cliffs of Third Mesa. He led his guardians down
the path past the body. Why not? They had already seen the mutilated feet and
knew the meaning of that. And this death had nothing to do with the Hopis.
This particular piece of evil was Navajo and the Navajos would have to pay for it. 125

1558 words

**Time Taken
(min./sec.)** —————

COMPREHENSION CHECK

Choose the best way of finishing each statement, according to the passage, and write the letter in the "1st answer" blank. Then follow the directions on pages 91–92.

1. Shortly before the events described in this passage,
   a. a village had been raided by the police.
   b. there had been a fight between Hopi and Navajo people.
   c. a young man had been murdered.
   d. a religious ceremony had been conducted.

   _____   _____   _____
   1st answer   Line reference(s)   2nd answer

2. The first thing described in the passage is
   a. a heavy bundle of spruce boughs.
   b. a mutilated dead body.
   c. a path overgrown with rabbit brush.
   d. a boot placed in the middle of a path.

   _____   _____   _____
   1st answer   Line reference(s)   2nd answer

3. The three people in the story were traveling in order to
   a. collect boughs of spruce.
   b. visit the grandchildren of one of them.
   c. get water for their people.
   d. visit an important shrine.

   _____   _____   _____
   1st answer   Line reference(s)   2nd answer

4. The journey was important to them because it
   a. led them to discover a murder.
   b. was in preparation for a religious ceremony.
   c. had to be kept secret from the police.
   d. would make them rich if they were successful.

   _____   _____   _____
   1st answer   Line reference(s)   2nd answer

5. The relationship between the three people was that

   a. Eddie Tuvi was Lomatewa's son and the Flute Clan boy his grandson.
   b. Lomatewa was the leader and the other two were his guardians.
   c. they were just three friends going on a journey together.
   d. they did not know each other but had met on their journey.

   _____   _____   _____
   1st answer   Line reference(s)   2nd answer

6. Lomatewa used a term of contempt to describe the dead Navajo because

   a. he thought Navajos were contemptible people.
   b. he did not want his companions to think sympathetically about the man.
   c. it was his way of expressing horror at the crime that had been committed.
   d. the body's flayed hands and feet meant that it was polluted.

   _____   _____   _____
   1st answer   Line reference(s)   2nd answer

7. Lomatewa was worried about the Flute Clan boy because the boy

   a. was not fully in touch with traditional ways.
   b. had a reputation for gossiping.
   c. was extremely sensitive and easily upset.
   d. had made mistakes in the past.

   _____   _____   _____
   1st answer   Line reference(s)   2nd answer

8. Lomatewa told the boy the story of how Sotuknang destroyed the world because

   a. he discovered that the boy had never heard the story.
   b. the dead Navajo made him think the world would be destroyed again.
   c. he could think of no other way of explaining what they had seen.
   d. he wanted to show the boy the importance of what they were doing.

   _____   _____   _____
   1st answer   Line reference(s)   2nd answer

9. After the boy heard the story, he said that

   a. now he understood what the body's flayed hands and feet meant.
   b. later he would report what they had seen to the police.
   c. he would not tell anybody about what they had seen.
   d. he would try hard to forget the whole incident.

   _____   _____   _____
   1st answer   Line reference(s)   2nd answer

10. The three people's greatest concern was to

a. avoid all contact with the dead man.
b. bring an end to the drought.
c. keep the murder a secret from the police.
d. stop the Navajos from bringing evil to them.

_____   _____   _____
1st answer   Line reference(s)   2nd answer

CHART FOR FINDING OUT READING SPEED

Time	wpm	Time	wpm	Time	wpm	Time	wpm	Time	wpm
4:30	346	6:15	249	8:00	195	9:45	160	11:30	135
4:45	328	6:30	240	8:15	189	10:00	156	11:45	133
5:00	312	6:45	231	8:30	183	10:15	152	12:00	130
5:15	297	7:00	223	8:45	178	10:30	148	12:15	127
5:30	283	7:15	215	9:00	173	10:45	145	12:30	125
5:45	271	7:30	208	9:15	168	11:00	142	12:45	122
6:00	260	7:45	201	9:30	164	11:15	138	13:00	120

Speed in words per minute_____

Total correct on 1st reading_____

Total correct on 2nd reading_____

QUESTIONS FOR DISCUSSION

1. What kind of book do you think this is going to be? Why?

2. What attitude does the writer seem to have towards traditional Hopi culture?

3. Do you think Lomatewa did the right thing in instructing the Flute Clan boy as he did? Why, or why not?

4. What questions are raised in this passage—and left unresolved?

5. Do you think you will find the answers if you read the whole book? Do you want to read it?

**SELECTION
2-7**

from *Down and Out in Paris and London*
George Orwell

Start time _____

The Rue du Coq d'Or, Paris, seven in the morning. A succession of furious, choking yells from the street. Madame Monce, who kept the little hotel opposite mine, had come out on to the pavement to address a lodger on the third floor. Her bare feet were stuck into sabots and her grey hair was streaming down.   5

Madame Monce: "Salope! Salope! How many times have I told you not to squash bugs on the wallpaper? Do you think you've bought the hotel, eh? Why can't you throw them out of the window like everyone else? *Putain! Salope!"*

The woman on the third floor: "Vache!"

Thereupon a whole variegated chorus of yells, as windows were flung open   10
on every side and half the street joined in the quarrel. They shut up abruptly ten minutes later, when a squadron of cavalry rode past and people stopped shouting to look at them.

I sketch this scene, just to convey something of the spirit of the Rue du Coq d'Or. Not that quarrels were the only thing that happened there—but still, we   15
seldom got through the morning without at least one outburst of this description. Quarrels, and the desolate cries of street hawkers, and the shouts of children chasing orange-peel over the cobbles, and at night loud singing and the sour reek of the refuse-carts, made up the atmosphere of the street.

It was a very narrow street—a ravine of tall, leprous houses, lurching to-   20
wards one another in queer attitudes, as though they had all been frozen in the act of collapse. All the houses were hotels and packed to the tiles with lodgers, mostly Poles, Arabs and Italians. At the foot of the hotels were tiny *bistros,* where you could be drunk for the equivalent of a shilling. On Saturday nights about a third of the male population of the quarter was drunk. There was fight-   25
ing over women, and the Arab navvies who lived in the cheapest hotels used to conduct mysterious feuds, and fight them out with chairs and occasionally revolvers. At night the policemen would only come through the street two together. It was a fairly rackety place. And yet amid the noise and dirt lived the usual respectable French shopkeepers, bakers and laundresses and the like,   30
keeping themselves to themselves and quietly piling up small fortunes. It was quite a representative Paris slum.

My hotel was called the Hôtel des Trois Moineaux. It was a dark, rickety warren of five storeys, cut up by wooden partitions into forty rooms. The rooms were small and inveterately dirty, for there was no maid, and Madame   35
F., the *patronne,* had no time to do any sweeping. The walls were as thin as matchwood, and to hide the cracks they had been covered with layer after layer of pink paper, which had come loose and housed innumerable bugs. Near the

ceiling long lines of bugs marched all day like columns of soldiers, and at night
came down ravenously hungry, so that one had to get up every few hours and   40
kill them in hecatombs. Sometimes when the bugs got too bad one used to burn
sulphur and drive them into the next room; whereupon the lodger next door
would retort by having *his* room sulphured, and drive the bugs back. It was a
dirty place, but homelike, for Madame F. and her husband were good sorts.
The rent of the rooms varied between thirty and fifty francs a week.   45

The lodgers were a floating population, largely foreigners, who used to turn
up without luggage, stay a week and then disappear again. They were of every
trade—cobblers, bricklayers, stonemasons, navvies, students, prostitutes, rag-
pickers. Some of them were fantastically poor. In one of the attics there was a
Bulgarian student who made fancy shoes for the American market. From six to   50
twelve he sat on his bed, making a dozen pairs of shoes and earning thirty-five
francs; the rest of the day he attended lectures at the Sorbonne. He was studying for the Church, and books of theology lay face-down on his leather-strewn
floor. In another room lived a Russian woman and her son, who called himself
an artist. The mother worked sixteen hours a day, darning socks at twenty-five   55
centimes a sock, while the son, decently dressed, loafed in the Montparnasse
cafés. One room was let to two different lodgers, one a day worker and the
other a night worker. In another room a widower shared the same bed with his
two grown-up daughters, both consumptive.

There were eccentric characters in the hotel. The Paris slums are a gather-   60
ing-place for eccentric people—people who have fallen into solitary, half-mad
grooves of life and given up trying to be normal or decent. Poverty frees them
from ordinary standards of behaviour, just as money frees people from work.
Some of the lodgers in our hotel lived lives that were curious beyond words.

There were the Rougiers, for instance, an old, ragged, dwarfish couple who   65
plied an extraordinary trade. They used to sell post cards on the Boulevard St.
Michel. The curious thing was that the post cards were sold in sealed packets as
pornographic ones, but were actually photographs of chateaux on the Loire; the
buyers did not discover this till too late, and of course never complained. The
Rougiers earned about a hundred francs a week, and by strict economy man-   70
aged to be always half starved and half drunk. The filth of their room was such
that one could smell it on the floor below. According to Madame F., neither of
the Rougiers had taken off their clothes for four years.

Or there was Henri, who worked in the sewers. He was a tall, melancholy
man with curly hair, rather romantic-looking in his long, sewer-man's boots.   75
Henri's peculiarity was that he did not speak, except for the purposes of work,
literally for days together. Only a year before he had been a chauffeur in good
employ and saving money. One day he fell in love, and when the girl refused
him he lost his temper and kicked her. On being kicked the girl fell desperately
in love with Henri, and for a fortnight they lived together and spent a thousand 80
francs of Henri's money. Then the girl was unfaithful; Henri planted a knife in
her upper arm and was sent to prison for six months. As soon as she had been

stabbed the girl fell more in love with Henri than ever, and the two made up their quarrel and agreed that when Henri came out of jail he should buy a taxi and they would marry and settle down. But a fortnight later the girl was un-faithful again, and when Henri came out she was with child. Henri did not stab her again. He drew out all his savings and went on a drinking-bout that ended in another month's imprisonment; after that he went to work in the sewers. Nothing would induce Henri to talk. If you asked him why he worked in the sewers he never answered, but simply crossed his wrists to signify handcuffs, and jerked his head southward, towards the prison. Bad luck seemed to have turned him half-witted in a single day.

Or there was R., an Englishman, who lived six months of the years in Putney with his parents and six months in France. During his time in France he drank four litres of wine a day, and six litres on Saturdays; he had once trav-elled as far as the Azores, because the wine there is cheaper than anywhere in Europe. He was a gentle, domesticated creature, never rowdy or quarrelsome, and never sober. He would lie in bed till midday, and from then till midnight he was in his corner of the *bistro*, quietly and methodically soaking. While he soaked he talked, in a refined, womanish voice, about antique furniture. Except myself, R. was the only Englishman in the quarter.

There were plenty of other people who lived lives just as eccentric as these: Monsieur Jules, the Roumanian, who had a glass eye and would not admit it, Furex the Limousin stonemason, Roucolle the miser—he died before my time, though—old Laurent the rag-merchant, who used to copy his signature from a slip of paper he carried in his pocket. It would be fun to write some of their biographies, if one had time. I am trying to describe the people in our quarter, not for the mere curiosity, but because they are all part of the story. Poverty is what I am writing about, and I had my first contact with poverty in this slum. The slum, with its dirt and its queer lives, was first an object-lesson in poverty, and then the background of my own experiences. It is for that reason that I try to give some idea of what life was like there.

Time Taken
(min./sec.) _____

1680 words

Choose the best way of finishing each statement, according to the passage, and write the letter in the "1st answer" blank. Then follow the directions on pages 91–92.

1. The quarrel described at the beginning of the passage is
   a. typical of what one might hear on the Rue du Coq d'Or.
   b. the first in a series of significant events in the story.
   c. a demonstration of the character of Madame Monce.
   d. an exceptional outburst on a normally peaceful street.

   _____   _____   _____
   1st answer   Line reference(s)   2nd answer

2. The buildings on the street were mainly
   a. factories.
   b. shops.
   c. hotels.
   d. private houses.

   _____   _____   _____
   1st answer   Line reference(s)   2nd answer

3. The people who lived on the street were
   a. all criminals and drunkards.
   b. a representative cross-section of the population of Paris.
   c. members of a few violently feuding families.
   d. a mixture of poor transients and respectable tradespeople.

   _____   _____   _____
   1st answer   Line reference(s)   2nd answer

4. The writer suggests that he found the Hôtel des Trois Moineaux
   a. quite luxurious for the price.
   b. simple but comfortable.
   c. quite pleasant, though dirty.
   d. disgustingly unhygienic.

   _____   _____   _____
   1st answer   Line reference(s)   2nd answer

5. The people who lived in the hotel were mostly

   a. foreigners of various professions.
   b. impoverished French people living on welfare.
   c. psychiatric cases who should have been in an institution.
   d. poor individuals trying hard to maintain decency.

   _____   _____   _____
   1st answer   Line reference(s)   2nd answer

6. The writer explains the eccentricity of some of these people as the result of

   a. madness.
   b. injustice.
   c. loneliness.
   d. poverty.

   _____   _____   _____
   1st answer   Line reference(s)   2nd answer

7. The Rougiers lived by

   a. darning socks.
   b. selling postcards.
   c. making shoes.
   d. working in the sewers.

   _____   _____   _____
   1st answer   Line reference(s)   2nd answer

8. Henri's life had been ruined because

   a. he fell in love with a woman who was unfaithful.
   b. he had killed a man in a fight.
   c. he had taken to drink.
   d. he had lost his job and become homeless.

   _____   _____   _____
   1st answer   Line reference(s)   2nd answer

9. The Englishman, R., was always

   a. quarrelsome.
   b. sober.
   c. drunk.
   d. sick.

   _____   _____   _____
   1st answer   Line reference(s)   2nd answer

10. The writer describes the people in the passage because they are

   a. the main characters of the story.
   b. representative of the poor.
   c. unusually impressive personalities.
   d. examples of immorality.

   _____ _____ _____
   1st answer   Line reference(s)   2nd answer

CHART FOR FINDING OUT READING SPEED

Time	wpm	Time	wpm	Time	wpm	Time	wpm	Time	wpm
4:30	373	6:30	258	8:30	198	10:30	160	12:30	134
4:45	354	6:45	249	8:45	192	10:45	156	12:45	132
5:00	336	7:00	240	9:00	187	11:00	153	13:00	129
5:15	320	7:15	232	9:15	182	11:15	149	13:15	127
5:30	305	7:30	224	9:30	177	11:30	146	13:30	124
5:45	292	7:45	217	9:45	172	11:45	143	13:45	122
6:00	280	8:00	210	10:00	168	12:00	140	14:00	120
6:15	269	8:15	204	10:15	164	12:15	137	14:15	118

Speed in words per minute _____

Total correct on 1st reading_____

Total correct on 2nd reading_____

QUESTIONS FOR DISCUSSION

1. In what ways does the description remind you of neighborhoods you know or have heard about?

2. Can you imagine yourself living in a neighborhood like the one described in the passage? How would you react to it?

3. What does the description tell you about the writer's personality and attitude? Does it tell you directly or indirectly?

4. What seems to be the writer's intention in writing this book? How do you think he will carry it out?

5. Does the book seem likely to be interesting?

from *Jane Eyre*

Charlotte Brontë

Start time _____

There was no possibility of taking a walk that day. We had been wandering, indeed, in the leafless shrubbery an hour in the morning; but since dinner (Mrs. Reed, when there was no company, dined early) the cold winter wind had brought with it clouds so sombre, and a rain so penetrating, that further out-door exercise was now out of the question. 5

I was glad of it: I never liked long walks, especially on chilly afternoons: dreadful to me was the coming home in the raw twilight, with nipped fingers and toes, and a heart saddened by the chidings of Bessie, the nurse, and hum-bled by the consciousness of my physical inferiority to Eliza, John, and Geor-giana Reed. 10

The said Eliza, John, and Georgiana were now clustered round their mama in the drawing-room: she lay reclined on a sofa by the fireside, and with her darlings about her (for the time neither quarrelling nor crying) looked perfectly happy. Me, she had dispensed from joining the group; saying, "She regretted to be under the necessity of keeping me at a distance; but that until she heard from 15 Bessie, and could discover by her own observation that I was endeavouring in good earnest to acquire a more sociable and childlike disposiiton, a more attrac-tive and sprightly manner,—something lighter, franker, more natural as it were—she really must exclude me from privileges intended only for contented, happy, little children." 20

"What does Bessie say I have done?" I asked.

"Jane, I don't like cavillers or questioners: besides, there is something truly forbidding in a child taking up her elders in that manner. Be seated somewhere; and until you can speak pleasantly, remain silent."

A small breakfast-room adjoined the drawing-room. I slipped in there. It 25 contained a book-case: I soon possessed myself of a volume, taking care that it should be one stored with pictures. I mounted into the window-seat: gathering up my feet, I sat cross-legged, like a Turk; and, having drawn the red moreen curtain nearly close, I was shrined in double retirement.

Folds of scarlet drapery shut in my view to the right hand; to the left were 30 the clear panes of glass, protecting, but not separating me from the drear No-vember day. At intervals, while turning over the leaves of my book, I studied the aspect of that winter afternoon. Afar, it offered a pale blank of mist and cloud; near, a scene of wet lawn and storm-beat shrub, with ceaseless rain sweeping away wildly before a long and lamentable blast. 35

I returned to my book—Bewick's History of British Birds: the letter-press thereof I cared little for, generally speaking; and yet there were certain intro-ductory pages that, child as I was, I could not pass quite as a blank. They were

those which treat of the haunts of sea-fowl; of "the solitary rocks and promon-
tories" by them only inhabited; of the coast of Norway, studded with isles from   40
its southern extremity, the Lindeness, or Naze, to the North Cape—

> "Where the Northern Ocean, in vast whirls,
> Boils round the naked, melancholy isles
> Of farthest Thule; and the Atlantic surge
> Pours in among the stormy Hebrides."   45

Nor could I pass unnoticed the suggestion of the bleak shores of Lapland,
Siberia, Spitzbergen, Nova Zembla, Iceland, Greenland, with "the vast sweep
of the Arctic Zone, and those forlorn regions of dreary space,—that reservoir
of frost and snow, where firm fields of ice, the accumulation of centuries of
winters, glazed in Alpine heights above heights, surround the pole, and concen-   50
tre the multiplied rigors of extreme cold." Of these death-white realms I formed
an idea of my own: shadowy, like all the half-comprehended notions that float
dim through children's brains, but strangely impressive. The words in these
introductory pages connected themselves with the succeeding vignettes, and
gave significance to the rock standing up alone in a sea of billow and spray; to   55
the broken boat stranded on a desolate coast; to the cold and ghastly moon
glancing through bars of cloud at a wreck just sinking.

I cannot tell what sentiment haunted the quiet solitary churchyard, with its
inscribed headstone; its gate, its two trees, its low horizon, girdled by a broken
wall, and its newly-risen crescent, attesting the hour of eventide.   60

The two ships becalmed on a torpid sea, I believed to be marine phantoms.

The fiend pinning down the thief's pack behind him, I passed over quickly:
it was an object of terror.

So was the black, horned thing seated aloof on a rock, surveying a distant
crowd surrounding a gallows.   65

Each picture told a story; mysterious often to my undeveloped understanding
and imperfect feelings, yet ever profoundly interesting: as interesting as the
tales Bessie sometimes narrated on winter evenings, when she chanced to be in
good humour; and when, having brought her ironing-table to the nursery-
hearth, she allowed us to sit about it, and while she got up Mrs. Reed's lace   70
frills, and crimped her night-cap borders, fed our eager attention with passages
of love and adventure taken from old fairy tales and older ballads; or (as at a
later period I discovered) from the pages of Pamela, and Henry, Earl of More-
land.

With Bewick on my knee, I was then happy: happy at least in my way. I   75
feared nothing but interruption, and that came too soon. The breakfast-room
door opened.

"Boh! Madame Mope!" cried the voice of John Reed; then he paused: he
found the room apparently empty.

"Where the dickens is she?" he continued "Lizzy! Georgy! (calling to his   80
sisters) Joan is not here: tell mama she is run out into the rain—bad animal!"

"It is well I drew the curtain," thought I: and I wished fervently he might not discover my hiding-place: nor would John Reed have found it out himself; he was not quick either of vision or conception; but Eliza just put her head in at the door, and said at once:— 85

"She is in the window-seat, to be sure, Jack."

And I came out immediately, for I trembled at the idea of being dragged forth by the said Jack.

"What do you want?" I asked, with awkward diffidence.

"Say, 'What do you want, Master Reed?'" was the answer. "I want you to 90 come here;" and seating himself in an arm-chair, he intimated by a gesture that I was to approach and stand before him.

John Reed was a schoolboy of fourteen years old; four years older than I, for I was but ten; large and stout for his age, with a dingy and unwholesome skin; thick lineaments in a spacious visage, heavy limbs and large extremities. He 95 gorged himself habitually at table, which made him bilious, and gave him a dim and bleared eye and flabby cheeks. He ought now to have been at school; but his mama had taken him home for a month or two, "on account of his delicate health." Mr. Miles, the master, affirmed that he would do very well if he had fewer cakes and sweetmeats sent him from home; but the mother's heart 100 turned from an opinion so harsh, and inclined rather to the more refined idea that John's sallowness was owing to over-application and, perhaps, to pining after home.

John had not much affection for his mother and sisters, and an antipathy to me. He bullied and punished me; not two or three times in the week, nor once 105 or twice in the day, but continually: every nerve I had feared him, and every morsel of flesh on my bones shrank when he came near. There were moments when I was bewildered by the terror he inspired, because I had no appeal whatever against either his menaces or his inflictions; the servants did not like to offend their young master by taking my part against him, and Mrs. Reed was 110 blind and deaf on the subject: she never saw him strike or heard him abuse me, though he did both now and then in her very presence; more frequently, however, behind her back.

Habitually obedient to John, I came up to his chair: he spent some three minutes in thrusting out his tongue at me as far as he could without damaging 115 the roots: I knew he would soon strike, and while dreading the blow, I mused on the disgusting and ugly appearance of him who would presently deal it. I wonder if he read that notion in my face; for, all at once, without speaking, he struck suddenly and strongly. I tottered, and on regaining my equilibrium retired back a step or two from his chair. 120

"That is for your impudence in answering mama awhile since," said he, "and for your sneaking way of getting behind curtains, and for the look you had in your eyes two minutes since, you rat!"

Accustomed to John Reed's abuse, I never had an idea of replying to it; my care was how to endure the blow which would certainly follow the insult. 125

"What were you doing behind the curtain?" he asked.

"I was reading."

"Show the book."

I returned to the window and fetched it thence.

"You have no business to take our books; you are a dependent, mama says; you have no money; your father left you none; you ought to beg, and not to live here with gentlemen's children like us, and eat the same meals we do, and wear clothes at our mama's expense. Now, I'll teach you to rummage my book-shelves: for they *are* mine; all the house belongs to me, or will do in a few years. Go and stand by the door, out of the way of the mirror and the windows."

I did so, not at first aware what was his intention; but when I saw him lift and poise the book and stand in act to hurl it, I instinctively started aside with a cry of alarm: not soon enough however; the volume was flung, it hit me, and I fell, striking my head against the door and cutting it. The cut bled, the pain was sharp; my terror had passed its climax; other feelings succeeded.

"Wicked and cruel boy!" I said. "You are like a murderer—you are like a slave driver—you are like the Roman emperors!"

I had read Goldsmith's History of Rome, and had formed my opinion of Nero, Caligula, etc. Also I had drawn parallels in silence, which I never thought thus to have declared aloud.

"What! what!" he cried. "Did you say that to me? Did you hear her, Eliza and Georgiana? Won't I tell mama? but first"—

He ran headlong at me: I felt him grasp my hair and my shoulder: he had closed with a desperate thing. I really saw in him a tyrant: a murderer. I felt a drop or two of blood from my head trickle down my neck, and was sensible of somewhat pungent sufferings: these sensations for the time predominated over fear, and I received him in frantic sort. I don't very well know what I did with my hands, but he called me "Rat! rat!" and bellowed out aloud. Aid was near him: Eliza and Georgiana had run for Mrs. Reed, who was gone upstairs; she now came upon the scene, followed by Bessie and her maid Abbot. We were parted: I heard the words:—

"Dear! dear! What a fury to fly at Master John!"

"Did ever anybody see such a picture of passion!"

Then Mrs. Reed subjoined:—

"Take her away to the red-room, and lock her in there." Four hands were immediately laid upon me, and I was borne upstairs.

1892 words

Time Taken
(min./sec.) _____

_____

COMPREHENSION   Choose the best way of finishing each statement, according to the passage,
CHECK   and write the letter in the "1st answer" blank. Then follow the directions on
                   pages 91–92.

1. In this story, Jane is
   a. a member of the Reed family.
   b. working as a servant for Mrs Reed.
   c. living in her aunt's household.
   d. staying with family friends.

   _____   _____   _____
   1st answer   Line reference(s)   2nd answer

2. Bessie is the children's
   a. elder sister.
   b. nurse.
   c. mother.
   d. teacher.

   _____   _____   _____
   1st answer   Line reference(s)   2nd answer

3. In dealing with the four children, Mrs. Reed is
   a. cruel.
   b. unfair.
   c. indulgent.
   d. affectionate.

   _____   _____   _____
   1st answer   Line reference(s)   2nd answer

4. Jane's favorite occupation seems to be
   a. reading.
   b. walking.
   c. painting pictures.
   d. telling stories.

   _____   _____   _____
   1st answer   Line reference(s)   2nd answer

5. John Reed can be described as

    a. clever and cruel.
    b. slow and shy.
    c. stupid and overbearing.
    d. strong and brave.

_____   _____   _____
1st answer   Line reference(s)   2nd answer

6. John was not at school at the time of the story because

    a. he had been suspended for misbehavior.
    b. the doctor said he needed rest.
    c. it was vacation time.
    d. his mother decided to keep him at home.

_____   _____   _____
1st answer   Line reference(s)   2nd answer

7. Jane hid in the windowseat because

    a. she was afraid Bessie would punish her.
    b. Mrs. Reed had told her to do so.
    c. she wanted to read undisturbed.
    d. it was a game she often played with John.

_____   _____   _____
1st answer   Line reference(s)   2nd answer

8. John came looking for Jane because

    a. it was part of a game.
    b. he had something to tell her.
    c. he was worried about her.
    d. he wanted to bully her.

_____   _____   _____
1st answer   Line reference(s)   2nd answer

9. When Jane compared John to the Roman emperors, she was saying that he was

    a. wealthy.
    b. powerful.
    c. magnificent.
    d. cruel.

_____   _____   _____
1st answer   Line reference(s)   2nd answer

10. Jane was taken to the red room to
   a. punish her.
   b. calm her down.
   c. protect her.
   d. treat her cut.

_____   _____   _____
   1st answer   Line reference(s)   2nd answer

CHART FOR FINDING OUT READING SPEED

Time	wpm	Time	wpm	Time	wpm	Time	wpm	Time	wpm
5:00	378	7:15	261	9:30	199	11:45	161	14:00	135
5:15	360	7:30	252	9:45	194	12:00	158	14:15	133
5:30	344	7:45	244	10:00	189	12:15	154	14:30	130
5:45	329	8:00	237	10:15	185	12:30	151	14:45	128
6:00	315	8:15	229	10:30	180	12:45	148	15:00	126
6:15	303	8:30	223	10:45	176	13:00	146	15:15	124
6:30	291	8:45	216	11:00	172	13:15	143	15:30	122
6:45	280	9:00	210	11:15	168	13:30	140	15:45	120
7:00	270	9:15	205	11:30	165	13:45	138	16:00	118

Speed in words per minute _____

Total correct on 1st reading _____

Total correct on 2nd reading _____

_____

QUESTIONS FOR DISCUSSION

1. Who are you expected to sympathize with in this story? How do you know?

2. What is your opinion of Mrs. Reed? Why.

3. Who, of all the characters mentioned in the passage, does Jane seem to like best? How can you tell?

4. How do you think the story is going to develop?

5. Do you think the book will be exciting? interesting? difficult? boring? Why?

Reading for

Study

When you are reading for general information, your emphasis is on speed, and you do not need to aim at complete comprehension. When you are reading for pleasure, you may also want to read fast, simply to find out what is going to happen next in the story; and even when you prefer to read more slowly, you are not consciously trying to understand every word. But when you are reading for study, you need to have a more thorough understanding of the material. If you are to get on well in a course and to participate fully in class, you need to become so familiar with the concepts introduced in a textbook that you can talk about them and write about them with ease. Furthermore, most courses end with an exam in which you are expected to show not only that you have understood but also that you have remembered what you have learned—and because exams often occur weeks or even months after you have read the material, you need some method of lodging the information firmly in your long-term memory. All this implies that you need to process study materials—"digest" them, as it were, in your own mind—much more than you do materials that you read for general information or for pleasure. This chapter will discuss different ways of doing this.

One essential point to realize is that studying a chapter in a textbook does not mean simply reading it through once, or even reading it several times, but rather going through the material in different ways, which will be described as a series of steps. The steps presented in this chapter are a modified version of a study technique called *SQ3R*, which stands for *Survey, Question, Read, Recite, Review*. This terminology is not used here, however, because the emphasis in this book is not on a single formula for study but rather on the need to adjust your approach according to the nature of the material that you are working with.

One final point: you should not think that studying is necessarily a solitary activity. While you must do the actual reading on your own, several of the supporting activities can be done in pairs or small groups. In fact, it is better to work with others if you can, because the more you talk about what you are studying, the more you process it in your own mind and make the material truly your own.

Steps in Studying

Finding Out What the Text Is About

If you are doing a reading assignment as a backup to what has been discussed in class, the material will already be a bit familiar; and so it should be quite possible to get a good idea of what the text covers by simply skimming it. To skim a text, glance through the whole unit assigned, noticing whatever illustrations and diagrams there may be and any particular case histories or examples printed in separate boxes. Then look at the main headings and subheadings—that is, words in bold, italic, or large type printed at the beginning of each section and subsection—and notice how the subheadings relate to the main heading under which they appear. For example, in Selection 3-1 in this chapter, the first main heading, Why We Communicate, is followed by four subheadings: Physical Needs, Ego Needs, Social Needs, Practical Needs. All these subheadings represent answers to the question posed in the main heading, *why we communicate*; and you can expect to find under each subheading an explanation of what exactly is meant by the *need* in question. If there is a summary at the end of the unit, read it at this initial skimming stage; you will find that the summary reflects the ideas suggested by the material you have already looked at.

Finally, skim the text again, looking at the first sentence or two of each paragraph and at the conclusion. These are the places where academic writers usually make their main points, so that by concentrating on these places you can get a general idea of what the text is about without reading the whole thing. This kind of skimming is especially important for reading texts, like articles from journals, that have few headings or diagrams.

As you skim, think constantly of what you know already about the subject, and be especially alert for points that have been mentioned in class. You will also find it helpful to think about other texts you have read, noticing whether, and in what respects, the text you are working on now is similar, and especially whether it seems to be organized in the same way.

Drawing Up Questions

After skimming, you will find it easier to concentrate on what you are reading if you make a list of the questions that the text seems to be answering. You should write these questions down on a sheet of paper or in the margin of the book you are reading (if the book is your own, and if you do not intend to sell it when the course is over). If you use a separate sheet of paper, you may find it helpful to draw a line down the middle of the page: Write the questions on the left side of this line, and then write the answers on the right. This will make it easy to review the material, for you can cover up the answers as you try to reproduce them from memory.

As far as you can, make up the questions on the basis of your skimming by putting into question form the ideas suggested by the headings and the first sentences of the paragraphs. If the material is totally unfamiliar, or the language particularly difficult, you may find that you cannot do this from skimming alone; if so, start reading the text, but as soon as you realize what question is being addressed in a particular paragraph, write the question down and skip to the next point—don't look for the answer yet. This method takes a lot of discipline, but it certainly helps you process the material and therefore understand and remember it.

For each of the selections in this chapter, a list of such questions is provided under the heading Questions on the Text. You are advised to skim each selection and write down your own questions on the blank pages provided or on separate sheets of paper. Then compare your questions to the ones listed under Questions on the Text. If you have a friend to study with, show your questions to each other, compare them, and perhaps modify them before you move on to the next step.

Finding Answers

At this stage, you are ready to read the text carefully. Go through it slowly, looking for the answer to each of the questions you have written down. You may want to underline or highlight the answers as you find them—but, again, do this only if the book is your own. If you find material that does not answer any of the questions you have, write down the question that it does answer and go on. If you cannot find the answer to a particular question, don't worry about it; it might, however, be worth remembering the question to ask your instructor about it later.

Recycling the Material

At this point, you should go over the material you've read again, but not by rereading the text. Instead, try to explain the information to yourself or somebody else, using your own words.

You will naturally need some prompting to do this, and one of the best tools for such prompting is your list of questions. Go through it, saying the answer to each one, or else writing the answer down as suggested earlier. If you can't remember the answer in a particular case, note which question it is, but don't look the information up yet; you may remember it as you go through the other questions. Then, after you have tried all the questions, check in the text for the ones that still cause problems. After this, go through the whole list again (if you have written the answers down, cover them up as you do this). You can't say that you have learned the material until you can answer all your questions without referring to the text at all.

Another way of recycling the material is to use any diagrams, illustrations, or boxed examples that are given. In the case of diagrams, such as those given in Selections 3-1, 3-3, and 3-5, try looking only at each diagram and explaining from your memory of the text what each part of it means. Again, this is best done by working with a friend, because you have to be clearer in your explanation. Similarly, with illustrations, identify them, if you can, without looking at the captions, and explain why the author has included them. What points in the text are they meant to illustrate? Written examples, whether printed in boxes or as set off paragraphs in the text, can be used in the same way. Read them first, and then say what general points they demonstrate.

For some subjects, you can also help yourself remember the material by thinking of your own examples for the general points that are made. The more familiar these examples are to you the better. Selections 3-1 and 3-2 are both on subjects about which you can do this easily.

Going beyond the Text

Any material is easier to remember if you can relate it to knowledge you already have, and the more personal and familiar that knowledge is the better. You should try, therefore, to think of ways in which the ideas you are reading about can be illustrated from your own experience. To help you do this, a second set of questions is supplied after each selection in this chapter, under the heading Questions beyond the Text. These questions direct you to your own observations and background, so the answers will be different for each individual; you will probably find this kind of recycling most helpful and interesting if you discuss the answers with others in your class.

Making Notes

Making notes is the most thorough and therefore the most effective way of recycling text material. Notes have the advantage of giving you the information in a more portable and more easily learned form than does the book. Finally, notes give you something to refer to when the book is no longer available, an important consideration when you work with borrowed books. But notes are only useful if they are accurate and comprehensible, so it is worth spending some time and effort learning how to make good ones.

There are several different kinds of notes, and which kind is most appropriate in a particular case depends on your own learning style, what your instructor expects of you, and the kind of material you are studying. The note-making suggestions for the selections in this chapter vary according to the last consideration; you have to make your own decisions with regard to the other two.

There is also considerable variation in the physical means of keeping notes. Should you use a book, loose sheets, index cards, or perhaps a computer disk? Again, the decision is largely personal, but different materials lend themselves to different kinds of notes, which, in turn, are most appropriately kept in different ways. Some suggestions for ways of keeping notes are in the following sections.

Outline Notes

The purpose of writing outline notes is to provide yourself with a summary of factual information. This summary is for your own use, so you do not have to write it in full sentences and you can use abbreviated forms of frequently used words. It is important, however, that the outline make a strong visual impact, because if you can remember easily what it looks like, you are likely to remember the information it contains. To make effective outline notes, follow these guidelines:

1. Use Headings and Subheadings. Just as the authors of many textbooks do, so you also should try to sort out your information by grouping it and naming briefly what each group of statements is about; the names you use are your headings and subheadings. If you are working with a text that is itself arranged under headings, you may find that the ones given are sufficient, or you may prefer to make up your own. These headings will generally correspond to the questions you ask yourself while you are studying the material. Suggestions for outline notes are given for most of the selections in this chapter; by examining these suggestions, you can see the relationship between the headings used, the study questions, and the text itself.

2. Underline Headings and Subheadings. Underlining will make headings and subheadings stand out and so make the information easier to remember.

3. Indent. Always leave a margin to the left of each heading, and then leave a wider margin to the left of each subheading that comes under it.

4. Use Numbers. Number your subheadings and your individual points, using a different type of numbering for each level of information. You may, for example, use roman numerals for main headings, arabic numbers for subheadings, and lowercase letters for the points that come under each subheading. Again, look at the suggestions made for the selections in this chapter to see some examples.

5. Space Your Material. Notes are much easier to remember if they are well spaced, so make sure that you start with an adequate supply of paper. Begin each point on a new line, and skip a line whenever you move to a new heading or subheading.

6. Abbreviate. Use abbreviations and symbols wherever possible. For example, many people use the symbol ∴ to mean "therefore," the symbol ∵ to mean "because," the abbreviation *c.* to mean "about" or "approximately," and the abbreviation *e.g.* to mean "for example." These abbreviations can be entirely personal, for nobody needs to understand them but yourself, but make sure that they are clear enough to be understood after a long period of time.

If you want a complete record of a particular chapter or article, your outline should present the material in the same order and probably under headings similar to those in the original (see, for example, the outline suggested for Selection 3-1). But if the material is very complex, or if you are working on several different sources, you may want to rearrange the material under your own headings (see the suggestions made for Selection 3-5).

Because of the importance of spacing and visual impact, outline notes are best kept on sheets of paper. If you are using only one text for the whole course, you may prefer to use a bound notebook, so that you are less likely to lose your notes. But if you are using several books, it is probably better to use loose-leaf paper. This allows you to rearrange your notes and easily compare those you have made from one book with those you have made from another. Another advantage of keeping notes on loose sheets is that you can take a sheet out and stick it up in a place where you will see it often; as soon as you know the material on it, you can replace it with another (a painless way of learning, if the people who live with you don't object). To avoid the danger of losing loose-leaf notes, keep them all together in a ring binder. A final piece of advice about using loose sheets: Never write on both sides of them. If you do, you are likely to throw unimportant material away without realizing that you have vital information written on the other side.

Outline notes can also be kept on index cards. You can use each heading as the title of a card and keep all the cards for a particular topic together in an appropriately labeled envelope or card-case. The advantage of using cards in this way is that you can carry them around easily and review them at odd moments; the disadvantage is that it is difficult to keep them so arranged that you can locate any particular information you want quickly (one way is to keep them in alphabetical order, but then you have to remember what your headings are).

Diagrams

We have already considered how the diagrams given in a text can be used in recycling the material. It is also helpful to include such diagrams in your notes, either as part of an outline or on separate sheets of paper (cards are generally not appropriate for this). You may want simply to copy the diagrams given in the text. Although a mechanical activity, copying diagrams is not a waste of time because it is another good way of fixing information in your memory. Alternatively, you can redraw the diagram in a simplified form, for printed diagrams often give more information than is necessary. Finally, you may want to construct your own diagrams: this is an economical way of recording information about processes or models, and for people with strong visual memories, it is particularly helpful for learning. An example of a diagram that you might construct for yourself is given in the exercises following Selection 3-3.

Vocabulary Notes

If you are studying in an academic field that is new to you, and especially if English is not your first language, you will find that you have to learn a lot of new vocabulary, much of which consists of technical terms. It is important to have a precise understanding of such terms, and because definitions are difficult to remember, you should write them down. The definitions, you will find, are usually given in the text: the word, when first introduced, is printed in **bold** or in *italics*, and an explanation is given of its meaning. You should record all such words, either on index cards (with one card for each word) or in a small notebook. If using cards, write the word at the top of the card and then the definition below or on the other side, in smaller letters; if you are using a notebook, draw a line down the middle of the page and write the word on the left of it and the definition on the right. It is best to put these words in alphabetical order to make it easier to look them up later. So use the first two pages of your notebook for words that begin with *a*, the second two pages for words that begin with *b*, and so on. If you are conscientious about consulting your vocabulary notes whenever you have forgotten the meaning of a word, you will find that you learn the technical terms quite easily.

Notice that this method of dealing with new vocabulary is quite different from that suggested earlier in Chapter 1. Whereas you can make a good guess at most general vocabulary, with specialized or technical words you must aim at greater precision. It is only by understanding its terms that you can get a real handle on an academic subject.

Because several of the selections in this chapter are taken from the opening chapters of textbooks, they present a good deal of such technical vocabulary. Lists of the words that you should probably make notes of are given for some selections, and paragraph references indicate where you can find the definitions.

Quotations

Academic writers often quote from other writers in order to emphasize the exact wording of the point in question, or simply to give authority to what they themselves are saying. It may be worth your while to record some quotations from the texts you read, especially if you will be asked to show what you know about the subject by writing an essay or a paper. Among the quotations that could be useful to you are extracts from famous documents (such as the United Nations Charter, quoted in Selection 3-3) or important definitions (such as the definition of "communication" given in Selection 3-1).

You may want to incorporate quotations in outline notes; this is probably the best way if you are not recording many of them. If you want to note a larger number, however, it may be more efficient to record them separately on index cards, using the names of the people who made the statements as headings for the cards. Whether you include quotations in outlines or keep them separate, make sure that you copy them accurately keeping the exact spelling and punctuation—do not, with quotations, use any abbreviations. Record exactly where you found each quotation so that you can find it again if necessary.

Bibliographical Notes

In some cases, you may need to use information from your notes in a research paper. If so, you will need all of the following information, so make sure that you record it all for any set of notes that you make:

1. the *title* of the book or article
2. the *name of the author*, exactly as it is given in the original material
3. the *date* of publication
4. the *place* of publication (for a book)
5. the *publisher* (for a book) or *the name of the publication* (for an article in a journal, newspaper, or magazine)
6. the *page numbers* from which you have made your notes. If you write down quotations, you will need the exact page number for each one.

If you are using cards, this bibliographical record could be written on a separate one and kept with the other notes from the same text. If you are using sheets of paper, write the information at the top of the first sheet of notes or at the bottom of the last one.

You may also want to make bibliographical notes of material that you have not yet read but which is referred to in your text. You will find the information in a list of references either at the end of the chapter or at the end of the book (see, for example, the one at the end of Selection 3-4).

Students who keep notes of a large number of books or articles usually find it best to keep them on cards. The last name of the author of the book or article is used as the heading for the card, so that the whole set can be arranged in alphabetical order by the authors' last names and new cards can easily be inserted. It is also useful to include on each card a brief description of the book or article. When you look for the book in a library catalog, write in the library call number as well.

Personal Index

When you come across particular names that are mentioned in many places in a text, you may find it useful to gather the information together in one place. That is, use the names as headings on individual index cards. Then write down under each heading all the information you come across about that particular person, place, or group, including a reference to where the information appears. An example of this technique is given after Selection 3-4.

Writing Essays and Papers

The best way to make information really your own is to write about it, and many instructors will require you to write essays or papers about the material you study. It is not possible in this book to explain everything about his kind of writing, but here are a few suggestions.

First, consider carefully the question you have been given to write about. If you have any doubt as to what a question means, discuss it with your instructor or at least with your classmates. Many questions have more than one part: Make sure that you recognize these parts and understand the differences between them.

Second, use your notes rather than the textbook when looking for what to write in answer to the question. In this way, you will avoid plagiarism (i.e., using another person's work as your own), and you can more easily incorporate information from a number of different texts, if necessary. Go through your notes carefully, looking for specific points that are relevant to the question; you may want to write these points out again on a separate sheet of paper to reorganize them and to avoid including irrelevant information.

Then write a new outline, not of the material you have read, but of what you expect to write: this outline should be closely related to the question you are addressing. Examples of such outlines are given in connection with Selections 3-4 and 3-5.

With your reorganized notes and new outline in hand, you can write the essay. Follow your new outline as you write, and refer back to your notes for any details you can't remember—but avoid going back to the original text. Concentrate, in the first instance, on getting the points down on paper in continuous sentences; you can leave editing for grammar and spelling until later. When you have got it all down, leave it for a day or two if possible, and then go over it again, correcting any mistakes and perhaps refining your language. Also, make sure that you have the factual details right (especially those involving statistics), that the quotations are accurate, and that the references to any books or articles are complete.

Finally, write a new copy of your revised and edited essay. Your instructor will be grateful if you type it; but if this is impossible, at least write it out neatly, leaving plenty of space for the instructor's comments.

Using the Reading Selections and Exercises

The previous discussion describes in detail the kinds of exercises that accompany the reading selections in this chapter and how you are expected to use them. In addition, the introductions to each selection offer specific suggestions about using the exercises that follow.

Interpersonal Communication

This first selection comes from *Interplay: The Process of Interpersonal Communication*, a textbook assigned for introductory courses in college communications departments. As you will see, it makes reference to a number of scholarly works, but the material that it is dealing with is essentially familiar to everyone. The selection is therefore particularly suitable for practicing how to use your own experience to illustrate the points made in the text.

Skim the selection first, as instructed on pages 138–139. Then on the left-hand side of the form provided on page 162 (or on separate pieces of paper), write down a list of questions that you think the selection will answer. For each one, include the page number where you expect to find the answer and leave at least two lines between questions so that you have plenty of room to insert more if necessary. Next, compare your questions with those your classmates have written down, and if you think your classmates have listed some good questions that you did not think of, insert them in your own list. Finally, compare your own and your classmates' lists with the one given on page 163. How many of the questions given there did you list?

After that, read the whole selection carefully, looking for the answers to each of the questions on your list. Write the answers, in brief form, on the right-hand side of the page. Then go through the list of Questions on the Text to see if you can answer those that were not included on your list; your instructor may ask you to write your answers to these as well. Discuss these answers with your classmates before going on to talk about the Questions Beyond the Text that follow. Your instructor may then ask you to do the note-making exercises as an assignment.

Everyone communicates. Students and professors, parents and children, employers and employees, friends, strangers, and enemies—all communicate. We have been communicating with others from the first weeks of life and will keep on doing so until we die. [1]

Why study an activity you've done your entire life? There are three reasons. First, studying interpersonal communication will give you a new look at a familiar topic. For instance, in a few pages you will find that some people can go years—even lifetimes—without communicating in a truly interpersonal manner. In this sense, exploring human communication is rather like studying anatomy or botany—everyday objects and processes take on new meaning. [2]

A second reason for studying the subject has to do with the staggering amount of time we spend communicating. In research at the University of Cincinnati, Rudolph Verderber and his associates (1976) measured the amount of time a sample of college students spent on various activities. The researchers found that their subjects spent an average of over 61 percent of their waking [3] time engaged in some form of communication. Whatever the occupation, the results would not be too different.

There is a third, more compelling reason for studying interpersonal communication. To put it bluntly, none of us communicate as effectively as we could. Our friendships, jobs, and studies suffer because we fail to express ourselves well and understand others accurately. If you pause now and make a mental list of communication problems you have encountered, you'll see that, no matter how successful your relationships, there is plenty of room for improvement in your everyday life. The information that follows will help you improve your communication skill with some of the people who matter most to you.

Why We Communicate

Research demonstrating the importance of communication has been around longer than you might think. Frederick II, emperor of Germany from 1196 to 1250, was called *stupor mundi*—"wonder of the world"—by his admiring subjects. Along with his administrative and military talents, Frederick was a leading scientist of his time. A medieval historian described one of his interesting, if inhumane, experiments:

> . . . He bade foster mothers and nurses to suckle the children, to bathe and wash them, but in no way to prattle with them, for he wanted to learn whether they would speak the Hebrew language, which was the oldest, or Greek, or Latin, or Arabic, or perhaps the language of their parents, of whom they had been born. But he labored in vain because all the children died. For they could not live without the petting and joyful faces and loving words of their foster mothers. (Ross and McLaughlin, 1949, p. 366)

Fortunately, contemporary researchers have found less dramatic ways to illustrate the importance of communication. In one study of isolation, subjects were paid to remain alone in a locked room. Of the five subjects, one lasted for eight days. Three held out for two days, one commenting, "Never again." The fifth subject lasted only two hours (Schachter, 1959, pp. 9–10).

You might question the value of experiments like these, arguing that solitude would be a welcome relief from the irritations of everyday life. It's true that all of us need solitude, often more than we get. On the other hand, each of us has a point beyond which we do not want to be alone. Beyond this point solitude changes from a pleasurable to a painful condition. In other words, we all need people. We all need to communicate.

Physical Needs

Communication is so important that it is necessary for physical health. In the introduction to his excellent anthology *Bridges, Not Walls*, John Stewart (1982, p. 6) cites research showing a wide range of medical hazards that result from a lack or breakdown of close relationships. For instance:

Socially isolated people are two to three times more likely to die prematurely than are those with strong social ties. The type of relationship doesn't seem to matter: marriage, friendship, and religious and community ties all seem to increase longevity.

Divorced men (before age seventy) die from heart disease, cancer, and strokes at double the rate of married men. Three times as many die from hypertension; five times as many commit suicide; seven times as many die from cirrhosis of the liver; and ten times as many die from tuberculosis.

The rate of all types of cancer is as much as five times higher for divorced men and women, compared to their single counterparts.

Poor communication can contribute to coronary disease. One Swedish study examined 32 pairs of identical twins. One sibling in each pair had heart disease, whereas the other was healthy. The researchers found that the obesity, smoking habits, and cholesterol levels of the healthy and sick twins did not differ significantly. Among the significant differences, however, were "poor childhood and adult interpersonal relationships," the ability to resolve conflicts, and the degree of emotional support given by others.

The likelihood of death increases when a close relative dies. In one Welsh village, citizens who had lost a close relative died within one year at a rate more than five times greater than those who had not suffered from a relative's death.

Such research demonstrates the importance of satisfying personal relation-   9
ships. Remember: Not everyone needs the same amount of contact, and the quality of communication is almost certainly as important as the quantity. The important point here is that personal communication is essential for our well-being. In other words, "people who need people" aren't "the luckiest people in the world" . . . they're the *only* people!

Ego Needs

Communication does more than enable us to survive. It is the *only* way we   10
learn who we are. As you'll read in Chapter 2, our sense of identity comes from the way we interact with other people. Are we smart or stupid, attractive or ugly, skillful or inept? The answers to these questions don't come from looking in the mirror. We decide who we are based on how others react to us.

Deprived of communication with others, we would have no sense of iden-   11
tity. Stewart (p. 8) dramatically illustrates this fact by citing the case of the famous "Wild Boy of Aveyron," who spent his early childhood without any apparent human contact. The boy was discovered in January 1800 while digging for vegetables in a French village garden. He showed no behaviors one would expect in a social human. The boy could not speak, but uttered only weird cries. More significant than this absence of social skills was his lack of any identity as a human being. As author Roger Shattuck (1980, p. 37) put it, "The boy had no human sense of being in the world. He had no sense of himself as a person related to other persons." Only after the influence of a

loving "mother" did the boy begin to behave—and, we can imagine, think of himself—as a human.

Like the boy of Aveyron, each of us enters the world with little or no sense 12
of identity. We gain an idea of who we are from the way others define us. As Chapter 2 explains, the messages we receive in early childhood are the strongest, but the influence of others continues throughout life.

Social Needs

Besides helping define who we are, communication is the way we relate 13
socially with others. Psychologist William Schutz (1966) describes three types of social needs we strive to fulfill by communicating. The first is *inclusion*, the need to feel a sense of belonging to some personal relationship. Inclusion needs are sometimes satisfied by informal alliances: the friends who study together, a group of runners, or neighbors who help one another with yard work. In other cases, we get a sense of belonging from formal relationships: everything from religious congregations to a job to marriage.

A second type of social need is *control*—the need to influence others, to 14
feel some sense of power over our world. Some types of control are obvious, such as the directions a boss or team captain gives. Much control, however, is more subtle. Experts in child development tell us that preschoolers who insist on staying up past bedtime or having a treat in the supermarket may be less concerned with the issue at hand than with knowing that they have at least some ability to make things happen. Even driving a parent crazy can satisfy the need for control. This fact answers the parent's question "Why are you being so stubborn?"

The third social need is *affection*—a need to care for others and know that 15
they care for us. Affection, of course, is critical for most of us. Being included and having power aren't satisfying if the important people in our lives don't care for us.

Practical Needs

We shouldn't overlook the everyday, important functions communication 16
serves. Communication is the tool that lets us tell the hair stylist to take just a little off the sides, the doctor where it hurts, and the plumber that the broken pipe needs attention *now*! Communication is the means of learning important information in school. It is the method you use to convince a prospective employer that you're the best candidate for a job, and it is the way to persuade the boss you deserve a raise. The list of common but critical jobs performed by communicating goes on and on, and it's worth noticing that the inability to express yourself clearly and effectively in every one of the above examples can prevent you from achieving your goal.

Psychologist Abraham Maslow (1968) suggested that human needs fall into 17
five categories, each of which must be satisfied before we concern ourselves with the next one. As you read on, think about the ways in which communica-

tion is often necessary to satisfy each need. The most basic of these needs are *physical:* sufficient air, water, food, and rest and the ability to reproduce as a species. The second of Maslow's needs involve *safety:* protection from threats to our well being. Beyond physical and safety concerns are the *social* needs we have mentioned already. Beyond them, Maslow suggests that each of us has *self-esteem* needs: the desire to believe that we are worthwhile, valuable people. The final category of needs involves *self-actualization:* the desire to develop our potential to the maximum, to become the best person we can be.

The Communication Process

So far we have used the word "communication" as if its meaning were perfectly clear. In fact, the process of communication isn't as simple as it might seem.   18

A Linear View

As recently as 40 years ago, researchers viewed communication as something one person "does" to another (Shannon and Weaver, 1949). In this view, communicating resembles giving an injection: a sender encodes ideas and feelings into some sort of message and then injects them by means of a channel (speech, writing, and so on) into a receiver (see Figure 1-1). If the message can get through any interference—termed *noise* in scientific jargon—communication has been successful.   19

This perspective does provide some useful information. For instance, it highlights how different channels can affect the way a receiver responds to a message. Should you say "I love you" in person? Over the phone? By renting space on a billboard? By sending flowers and a card? With a singing telegram? Each channel does have its differences.   20

The linear model also shows how noise can interfere with a message. Two types of noise can block communication: physical and psychological. As its name implies, some physical noise makes it hard to hear a message. Other distractions also can be physical noise: too much cigarette smoke in a crowded room might make it hard for you to pay attention to a speaker, and fatigue or   21

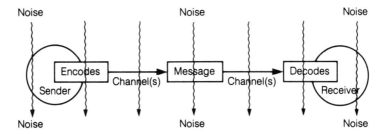

Figure 1-1 Linear Communication Model

illness might affect your concentration or make you less sympathetic than usual.

Psychological noise refers to forces within the sender and receiver that make   22
them less likely to communicate effectively. For instance, a woman who hears the word "gal" might become so irritated that she has trouble listening objectively to the rest of a speaker's message. Likewise, an insecure employee might interpret a minor suggestion the boss makes as ridicule or criticism.

An Interactive View

Despite its advantages, the linear model inaccurately suggests that communi-   23
cation flows in one direction, from sender to receiver. Although some types of messages (printed and broadcast messages, for example) do flow in a one-way, linear manner, most types of communication—especially the interpersonal variety—are two-way exchanges. To put it differently, the linear view ignores the fact that receivers *react* to messages by sending other messages of their own.

Consider, for instance, the significance of a friend's yawn as you describe   24
your romantic woes. Or imagine the blush you might see as you tell one of your raunchier jokes to a new acquaintance. Nonverbal behaviors like these show that most face-to-face communication is a two-way affair. The discernible response of a receiver to a sender's message is called *feedback*. Not all feedback is nonverbal, of course. Sometimes it is oral, as when you ask an instructor questions about an upcoming test or volunteer your opinion of a friend's new haircut. In other cases it is written, as when you answer the questions on a midterm exam or respond to a letter from a faraway friend.

When we add the element of feedback to our model, we begin to see that   25
communication is less like giving a linguistic injection than like playing a verbal and nonverbal tennis game in which messages pass back and forth between the parties (see Figure 1-2).

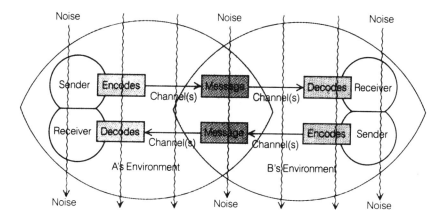

Figure 1-2 Interactive Communication Model

A quick glance at Figure 1-2 suggests that after a period of interaction, the 26
mental images of the sender and receiver ought to match. If they do, we can
say that an act of successful communication has occurred. However, your personal experience shows that misunderstandings often occur between sender and
receiver. Your constructive suggestion is taken as criticism; your friendly joke
is taken as an insult; your hints are missed entirely. These sorts of misunderstandings often occur because senders and receivers occupy different environments. In communication terminology, *environment* refers not only to a physical location, but also to the personal history that each person brings to a
conversation. Although they have some experiences in common, they each see
the situation in a unique way. Consider just some of the factors that might
contribute to different environments:

A might be well rested and B exhausted;
A might be rich and B poor;
A might be rushed and B have nowhere to go;
A might have lived a long, eventful life and B might be young and inex-
    perienced;
A might be passionately concerned with the subject and B indifferent to it.

Notice that in Figure 1-2 the environments of A and B overlap. This inter- 27
secting area represents the background and knowledge that the communicators
have in common. The size of this overlap varies between two people according
to the topic of communication: In some areas it might be rather large, whereas
on other subjects it might be extremely small. It is impossible to acquire all the
background of another person, but the kind of careful listening described in
Chapter 4 can boost the environmental overlap that leads to more accurate,
satisfying communication.

A Transactional View

Even with the addition of feedback and environment, the model in Figure 28
1-2 isn't completely satisfactory. Notice that it portrays communication as a
static activity, suggesting that there are discrete "acts" of communication that
begin and end at identifiable times, and that a sender's message causes some
effect in a receiver. Furthermore, it suggests that at any given moment a person
is either sending or receiving.

In fact, none of these characterizations is valid for most types of communi- 29
cation. The activity of communicating is usually not interactive, but *transactional*. A transactional perspective differs from the more simplistic ones we've
already discussed in several ways.

First, a transactional model reveals that communicators usually send and 30
receive messages simultaneously, so that the images of sender and receiver in
Figure 1-2 should not be separated as if a person were doing only one or the
other, but rather superimposed and redefined as "participants" (Rogers and

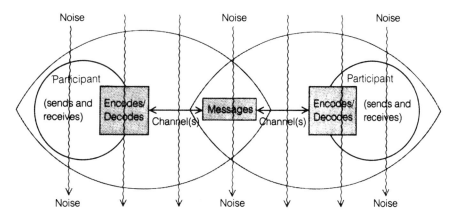

Figure 1-3 Transactional Communication Model

Kincaid, 1981) (see Figure 1-3). At a given moment we are capable of receiving, decoding, and responding to another person's behavior, while at the same time that other person is receiving and responding to ours. Consider, for example, what might occur when you and a housemate negotiate how to handle household chores. As soon as you begin to hear (receive) the words sent by your partner, "I want to talk about cleaning the bathroom . . ." you grimace and clench your jaw (sending a nonverbal message of your own while receiving the verbal one). This reaction leads your partner to interrupt himself, defensively sending a new message: "Now wait a minute. . . ."

Besides illustrating the simultaneous nature of face-to-face interaction, this example shows that it's difficult to isolate a single discrete "act" of communication from the events that precede and follow it. Your partner's comment about cleaning the bathroom (and the way it was presented) probably grew from exchanges you had in the past. Likewise, the way you'll act toward one another in the future depends on the outcome of this conversation. By now you can see that a transactional model of communication should be more like a motion picture film than a gallery of still photographs. Although Figure 1-3 does a fair job of picturing the phenomenon we call communication, an animated version in which the environments, communicators, and messages constantly changed would be an even better way of capturing the process. You can also see that communication is not something that people do *to* one another, but a process in which they create a relationship by interacting *with* each other.

Now we can summarize the definition of communication we have been developing. Communication is a *continuous, transactional process* involving *participants* who occupy different but overlapping *environments* and create a relationship by *simultaneously sending and receiving messages*, many of which are distorted by physical and psychological *noise*.

Interpersonal Communication Defined

So far we have talked about the communication process without specifically   33
discussing the interpersonal variety. What is interpersonal communication?
What distinguishes it from other types of interaction? There are two ways to
answer this question.

A Situational Definition

The most obvious distinction—although not the most useful—involves the   34
context in which the interaction occurs. We can look at how many people are
involved, whether they are close to or far from one another, and how much
access they have (for example, how much of one another they can see, hear,
and touch, and how easy it is to offer feedback). Interpersonal communication
using this approach is defined as involving a small number of communicators
who are close together and who have a great deal of access to one another.

Using a situational approach, we can easily distinguish interpersonal com-   35
munication from mass communication, which involves more people with
greater distances between them, and with very limited access to one another. In
some cases, mass communication involves feedback that takes months to process, as in the case of letters to TV stations about the most and least popular
shows.

Public communication—usually consisting of a speech given before an audi-   36
ence—is also easily distinguished from interpersonal communication. Greater
numbers of communicators at greater distances are involved in public communication, and access—especially in the form of feedback—is relatively limited,
although not so much as in the case of mass communication.

Matters become a little more confusing when we compare interpersonal and   37
small group communication. However, clear differences between these modes
do exist. For example, issues such as conformity, leadership, division of labor,
and decision making are much more prominent in groups, due to the greater
number and complexity of interrelationships.

On the other hand, there are strong similarities between one-to-one and   38
small group interaction. Both involve a small number of communicators who
are physically close and who have great access to one another. And certainly
there is a strong degree of "interpersonalness" in many group settings. Consider, for instance, a small work, study, or social group to which you've be-
longed. The relationships in such a group almost certainly involved elements
you'll be studying in this interpersonal text: resolution of conflicts, issues of
self-disclosure, the expression of feelings, changes in the emotional climate,
and so on.

A Qualitative Definition

These topics suggest another way to define interpersonal communication, one   39
that doesn't concern itself with the number of participants, but rather with the

quality of interaction between individuals, the way they deal with one another. Gerald Miller (1978) describes this second approach as "developmental." John Stewart and Gary D'Angelo (1980, p. 63) describe the qualitative difference between developmentally interpersonal and what we might call "impersonal" communication as the contrast between personifying and objectifying others. In impersonal communication we treat others as if they were objects, or things. Consider, for example, the typical way you might respond to a gas station attendant or checkout clerk at the supermarket. Most transactions of this sort are hardly personal: Except for a ritual smile and perhaps a perfunctory "How are you doing?" we might as well be interacting with a machine. Such impersonal transactions are not cruel, nor do you need to establish a warm relationship with every person you meet. The important fact to recognize is that, from a qualitative viewpoint, not all two-person interaction is interpersonal.

Several characteristics distinguish qualitatively interpersonal relationships   40
from impersonal ones.

A Minimum of Stereotyping.   In less personal relationships we tend to   41
classify the other person by using labels. We fit others into neat pigeonholes: "Anglo," "woman," "jock," and so on. Such labels may be accurate as far as they go, but they hardly describe everything that is important about the other person. On the other hand, it's almost impossible to use one or two labels to describe someone you know well. "He's not *just* a professor," you want to say. Or "Sure, she's against abortions, but there's more. . . ."

Development of Unique Rules.   When we meet someone for the first   42
time, we know how to behave because of the established social rules we have been taught. We shake hands, speak politely, and rely on socially accepted subjects: "How are you?" "What do you do?" "Lousy weather we've been having." The rules governing our interaction have little to do with us or the people with whom we interact: we are not responding to each other as individuals.

As we continue to interact, however, we sometimes gain more information   43
about each other, and use that information as the basis for our communicating. As we share experiences, the rules that govern our behavior are less determined by cultural mores, and more determined by the unique features of our own relationship. This doesn't mean that we abandon rules altogether, but rather that we often create our *own* conventions, ones that are appropriate for us. For example, one pair of friends might develop a procedure for dealing with conflicts by expressing their disagreements as soon as they arise, while another could tacitly agree to withhold a series of gripes, then clear the air periodically. In Chapter 11 we will compare such procedures: here the important point to recognize is that in both cases the individuals created their own rules.

Increased Self-Disclosure. A third qualitative characteristic of interper-   44
sonal relationships involves the amount of information the partners have about
each other. When we meet people for the first time we have little information
about them, usually no more than what others tell us and what we assume from
observing what they wear and how they handle their bodies. As we talk, we
gain more information in a variety of areas. The first topics we talk about are
usually nonthreatening, nonintimate ones. If we continue talking, however, we
may decide to discuss fewer impersonal things and to increase the number of
topics we talk about. We may also choose to be more revealing of ourselves in
doing so.

As we learn more about each other, and as our information becomes more   45
intimate, the degree to which we share an interpersonal relationship increases.
This new degree of intimacy and sharing can come almost immediately, or it
may grow slowly over a long period of time. In either case, we can say that the
relationship becomes more interpersonal as the amount of self-disclosure increases. We'll have a great deal to say about this subject in Chapter 8.

If we accept the characteristics of minimal stereotyping, creation of unique   46
rules, and sharing of personal information as criteria for a developmentally
interpersonal relationship, then several implications follow. First, many one-to-
one relationships never reach an interpersonal state. This conclusion is not surprising in itself, because establishing a close relationship takes time and effort.
In fact, such relationships are not always desirable or appropriate. Some people, however, fool themselves into thinking that they have close interpersonal
friendships when in fact their associations are interpersonal only in a situational
context.

Another implication that follows from looking at interpersonal communica-   47
tion in qualitative terms is that the ability to communicate interpersonally is a
skill that people possess in varying degrees. For example, some communicators
are adept at recognizing nonverbal messages, listening effectively, acting sup-
portively, and resolving conflicts in satisfying ways, whereas others have no
ability or no idea how to do so. The skills you will learn by studying *Interplay*
can help you become a more effective communicator.

Communication Principles and Misconceptions

Before exploring the elements of interpersonal communication in the follow-   48
ing chapters, we need to take a final look at what communication is and what it
isn't, at what it can and can't do.

Communication Principles

From this chapter you already can draw several important conclusions about   49
what communication is.

Communication Can Be Intentional or Unintentional. People usually 50
plan their words carefully before they ask the boss for a raise or offer a constructive criticism. Not all communication is so deliberate, however. Sooner or
later we all carelessly make a comment that would have better gone unsaid.
Perhaps you lose your temper and blurt out a remark that you later regret, or
maybe your private remarks are overheard by a bystander. In addition to these
slips of the tongue, we unintentionally send many nonverbal messages. You
might not be aware of your sour expression, impatient shifting, or sigh of
boredom, but others view them regardless.

It's Impossible Not to Communicate. These facial expressions, move- 51
ments, and other nonverbal behaviors mean that although we can stop talking,
we can't stop communicating. Chapter 5 introduces the multitude of ways we
send messages without saying a word, through posture, gesture, distance, body
orientation, and clothing, among others. For instance, does a friend's silence
reflect anger, contentment, or fatigue? Whether or not these sorts of messages
are understood, they do communicate constantly.

All Messages Have a Content and a Relational Dimension. Virtually 52
every verbal statement has a *content* dimension, the information it explicitly
conveys: "Please pass the salt." "Not now, I'm tired." "You forgot to buy a
quart of milk." In addition to this sort of obvious content, all messages also
have a *relational* dimension (Watzlawick, Beavin, and Jackson, 1967, pp. 51–
52). This relational component expresses how you feel about the other person;
whether you like or dislike the other person, feel in control or subordinate, feel
comfortable or anxious, and so on. For instance, consider how many different
relational messages you could communicate by simply saying "Thanks a lot" in
different ways.

Sometimes the content dimension of a message is all that matters. For exam- 53
ple, you may not care how the directory assistance operator feels about you as
long as you get the phone number you're seeking. In truly interpersonal contexts, however, the relational dimension of a message is often more important
than the content under discussion. This fact explains why disputes over apparently trivial subjects become so important. In these cases we're not really arguing over whose turn it is to take out the trash or whether to play tennis or swim.
Instead, we're disputing the nature of the relationship. Who's in control? How
important are we to each other? Chapter 10 explores several key relational
issues in detail.

Communication Is Irreversible. We sometimes wish that we could back 54
up in time, erasing words or acts and replacing them with better alternatives.
Unfortunately, such reversal is impossible. There are occasions when further
explanation can clear up another's confusion or when an apology can mollify
another's hurt feelings; but in other cases no amount of explanation can erase

the impression you have created. Despite the warnings judges issue in jury trials, it's impossible to "unreceive" a message. Words said and deeds done are irretrievable.

Communication Is Unrepeatable.   Because communication is an ongoing   55
process, it is impossible to repeat the same event. The friendly smile that worked so well meeting a stranger last week might not succeed with the person you encounter tomorrow: It might feel stale and artificial to you the second time around, or it might be wrong for the new person or occasion. Even with the same person, it's impossible to re-create an event. Why? Because neither you nor the other *is* the same person. You've both lived longer. The behavior isn't original. Your feelings about one another may have changed. You need not constantly invent new ways to act around familiar people, but you should realize that the "same" words and behavior are different each time they are spoken or performed. Chapter 7 will alert you to the stages through which a relationship progresses.

Communication Misconceptions

Now that we have spent some time describing what communication is, we   56
need to identify some things it is not (McCroskey and Wheeless, 1976, pp. 3–10). Avoiding these common misconceptions can save you a great deal of personal trouble.

Meanings Are in People, Not Words.   The biggest mistake we can make   57
is to assume that *saying* something is the same thing as *communicating* it. To use the terminology of our communication model, there's no guarantee that a receiver will decode a message in a way that matches the sender's intention. (If you doubt this proposition, list all the times you've been misunderstood in the past week.) Chapter 3 outlines the many reasons why people can interpret a statement differently from the way you intended it, and Chapter 4 describes the most common types of verbal misunderstandings and suggests ways to minimize them. Chapter 6 introduces listening skills that help insure that the way you receive a message matches the ideas a speaker is trying to convey.

More Communication Is Not Always Better.   Whereas not communicat-   58
ing enough can cause problems, there are also situations when *too much* talking is a mistake. Sometimes excessive communication is simply unproductive, as when two people "talk a problem to death," going over the same ground again and again without making progress. There are other times when talking too much actually aggravates a problem. We've all had the experience of "talking ourselves into a hole"—making a bad situation worse by pursuing it too far. As McCroskey and Wheeless put it: "More and more negative communication merely leads to more and more negative results" (p. 5).

There are even times when *no* communication is the best course. Any good   59 salesperson will testify that it's often best to stop talking and let the customer think about the product, and when two people are angry and hurt, they may say things they don't mean and will later regret. In such cases it's probably best to spend time cooling off, thinking about what to say and how to say it. Chapter 9 will help you decide when and how to share feelings.

Communication Will Not Solve All Problems. Sometimes even the best 60 planned, best timed communication won't solve a problem. Imagine for example, that you ask an instructor to explain why you received a poor grade on a project you believe deserved top marks. The professor clearly outlines the reasons why you received the low grade, and sticks to that position after listening thoughtfully to your protests. Has communication solved the problem? Hardly.

Sometimes clear communication is even the *cause* of problems. Suppose, 61 for example, that a friend asks you for an honest opinion of the $200 outfit he has just bought. Your clear and sincere answer, "I think it makes you look fat," might do more harm than good. Deciding when and how to self-disclose isn't always easy. See Chapter 8 for suggestions.

Communication Is Not a Natural Ability. Most people assume that com- 62 munication is an aptitude that people develop without the need for training— rather like breathing. Although almost everyone does manage to function passably without much formal communication training, most people operate at a level of effectiveness far below their potential. In fact, communication skills are rather like athletic ability. Even the most inept of us can learn to be more effective with training and practice.

From *Interplay: The Process of Interpersonal Communication* (1989)
by Ronald B. Adler, Lawrence B. Rosenfeld, and Neil Towne.

QUESTIONS FROM SKIMMING

In the left-hand column below, write down the questions you expect the selection will answer, along with the appropriate page number(s). Reread the selection carefully, and use the right-hand column to receord the answers to the questions after you have compared your questions to those of your classmates and to the list of Questions on the Text that follows.

QUESTIONS (put page number after question)	ANSWERS

QUESTIONS ON THE TEXT

Compare your questions to those listed here.

What are three reasons for studying communication?

What was Frederick II's experiment?

What modern experiment showed the same point?

Why is communication necessary for physical health?

What are *ego needs?*

What happens when we're deprived of communication with others?

Who was the "Wild Boy of Aveyron"? What do we learn from him?

What three *social needs* do we fulfill by communicating?

What *practical needs* do we fulfill by communicating?

What five categories of human needs did Abraham Maslow define?

What is the *linear view* of communication?

What is *noise* and how does it interfere with a message?

What is the *interactive view* of communication?

What is inaccurate about the linear view?

What is *feedback?*

What does *environment* refer to?

What is the problem with the interactive view?

What is the *transactional view* of communication?

What is the definition of communication?

What is the *situational definition* of interpersonal communication?

How does interpersonal communication differ from mass communication? from public communication?

What are the differences and similarities between interpersonal communication and small-group communication?

What is the *qualitative definition* of interpersonal communication?

What examples are given of "impersonal" communication?

What are three characteristics of qualitatively interpersonal communication?

What are the basic principles of communication?

What are some common misconceptions about communication?

**QUESTIONS
BEYOND
THE TEXT**

1. With whom have you communicated today? What needs were satisfied in each of these communicative acts?

2. Think of a particular classroom discussion (perhaps one you are engaged in at the moment) in terms of the diagram on p. 155. Who or what, in specific terms, do the various elements of the diagram represent?

3. Would you say that your classroom discussion is a form of interpersonal communication? Why, or why not?

**OUTLINE NOTES
AND DIAGRAMS**

Selection 3-1 is clearly organized, so it is easy to make an outline using roughly the same headings as are used in the text. The outline that follows is incomplete: only the main headings, some of the subheadings, and the first few points are given. You are asked to fill in the rest. Notice that abbreviations have been used and some quotations are included. There are also simplified copies of the diagrams, but only the first of these is finished; complete the other two as you fill in the outline.

  I. <u>Reasons Why We Communicate</u>
    1. <u>Physical needs</u>
       People get sick if they don't communicate.
      e.g., a. Divorced men die of stress-related diseases at much higher rates than married men.
          b. In Swedish study of identical twins (1 w/heart disease, 1 w/out), signif. variable btwn. sick and healthy twin was "poor childhood and adult interpersonal relationships."

    2. <u>Ego Needs</u>

       _____

      e.g., "Wild Boy of Aveyron"

       _____

    3. <u>Social Needs</u>
      Types
      a. Inclusion

        e.g., _____

      b. _____

         _____

      c. _____

         _____

4. _____

_____

_____

_____

II. Models of Communication

  1. Linear Model

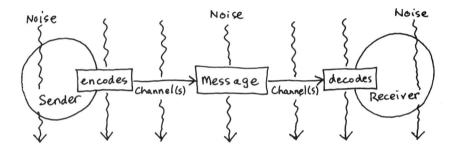

    Advantages of model
    a. Highlights importance of channel

      e.g., _____
    b. Shows how noise can interfere

      e.g., _____
    Disadvantage
      Suggests communication is only in one direction.

  2. Interactive Model

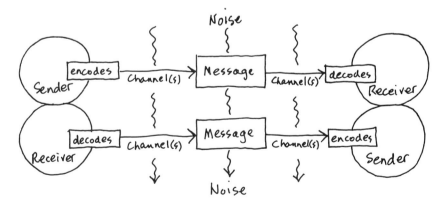

Advantages of model:

Shows

a. Interaction between communicators

b. Importance of environment

Disadvantages:

Misleading because suggests

a. Communication is static

b. Acts of communication are discrete

c. _____

d. _____

3. _____

Differs from simplified models in that it:

a. _____

b. _____

Definition of communication

" _____

_____

_____ "

III. Definitions of Interpersonal Communication

1. _____

Involves _____

2. Qualitative

Involves _____

Differences btwn. qualitatively inpersonal and impersonal relationships

a. _____

b. _____

c. _____

IV. <u>Communication Principles</u>

1. _____

_____

2. _____

_____

3. _____

_____

4. _____

_____

V. <u>Communication Misconceptions</u>

1. _____

_____

2. _____

_____

3. _____

_____

4. _____

_____

VOCABULARY NOTES

Identify and list all the technical terms introduced in the text. Then compare your list with the one below. Can you define all these terms, in the sense in which they are used in the selection? If not, write them down alphabetically in a notebook or on cards, as described on pages 143–144.

content dimension (of a message) (paragraph 54)
environment (paragraph 28)
feedback (paragraph 26)
noise (paragraph 21)
relational dimension (of a message) (paragraph 54)

QUOTATIONS   Were you able to identify the quotation suggested at the end of the section on Models of Communication in your outline? In case you could not, here it is:

"Communication is a *continuous, transactional* process involving *participants* who occupy different but overlapping *environments* and create a relationship by *simultaneously sending and receiving messages*, many of which are distorted by physical and psychological *noise*" (Adler, Rosenfeld, and Towne 1989, 9).

BIBLIOGRAPHICAL NOTES   If you record a quotation such as the one in the outline, you must be sure to keep a record of where you got it. Put a short reference in parentheses after each quotation, in which you note who wrote it, the date of the publication in which it appears, and the page number (see the example above, which gives the reference to the book in which the quotation originally appeared). Then write on a separate card or at the beginning or end of your outline notes the full bibliographic information about the book or article, like this:

Adler, Ronald B., Lawrence B. Rosenfeld, and Neil Towne. 1989.
Interplay: The Process of Interpersonal Communication. Fort Worth, TX: Holt, Rinehart and Winston.

There are variations in the exact style in which you may be required to write references to books and articles in research papers, but you will always need the pieces of information given here. It is sensible to follow the same conventions for each piece when writing bibliographical notes.

Selection 3-1 mentions another book that you might want to look up. Here is how you might write the reference on an index card:

Stewart, John. 1982. *Bridges, Not Walls*.

(Anthology on communication)

No information about the place of publication or publisher is given in the selection, so leave a space on the card as here and fill in this information when you have located the book in the library catalog. You might also write the library call number on the card (the top right-hand corner is a good place) so that you will not have to look in the catalog if you want to find the book a second time.

ESSAY TOPICS   The topics given here are intended to help you recycle the information you read in the selection and develop your own ideas about it. Read each topic carefully, and decide which one you want to work on. Then identify the categories of information asked for in the topic, name each category, and use the name as a heading. Under each heading, list the different pieces of information that you can think of in that category, decide on the order in which it would be best to present the information, and number the points in that order. In this way, you can build an outline to guide you in writing your essay. You can see what such an outline might look like from the sample given for topic 2. You might try making your own outline for this topic before looking at the sample; and, as always with this kind of exercise, it would be good to work with your classmates in doing so. After you complete the outline for topic 2, your instructor may ask you to write the whole essay: use only your outline, together with any notes you have made—do not look back at the selection. Alternatively, you might go straight on to making an outline for one of the other topics and writing an essay on it.

1. What is the importance of communication for human beings? Why is it a worthwhile subject of study?
2. What, according to the transactional model, are the elements that must be considered in an act of communication? Which of these elements are most likely to cause the communication to fail?
3. Describe an act of interpersonal communication in which you were recently engaged. On what grounds would you characterize this interaction as an interpersonal one?

Essay Outline (Topic 2)

I. Elements
   1. Participants
      a. send
      b. receive
   2. Message
   3. Channel
   4. Noise
      a. Physical
      b. Psychological

       5. <u>Environment</u>
          a. Different for each participant
          b. Overlap

II. <u>Causes of Failure</u>

       1. <u>Channel</u>
          e.g., Telephone not working

       2. <u>Noise</u>
          e.g., Distraction because worried

       3. <u>Environment</u>
          a. Affects interpretation
          b. May be little overlap

The Logical Thinker as Challenger

This selection is taken from *Thinking Logically: Basic Concepts for Reasoning*, a text designed for introductory college philosophy courses. As you will see, it focuses on how people's use of language can be examined in terms of its logic. Like Selection 3-1, this selection does not give you new information so much as suggest a new way of thinking about what you already know.

Before you read the selection, skim it and write down the questions you expect it to answer (remember to write them only on the left-hand side of the page so that you can write the answers later on the right-hand side). Then compare your questions with your classmates' and with the list of Questions on the Text. Once you have developed your questions, and so clarified what the passage is about, read it carefully and write down the answers that you find; as you will see, this passage does not answer very many questions, because it consists mostly of examples. Then move on to answer the Questions beyond the Text. For this material, these questions are particularly important, so think carefully about them, and discuss your answers with your classmates.

Finally, your instructor may ask you to complete the note-making exercises or work on the essay topics that follow.

Types of Messages: The Three Basic Functions of Language

Since different types of messages require different types of challenges, we   1
begin studying the logical thinker's role as challenger by studying the various
types of messages that may confront us. What is the difference between these
three sentences?

1. Millard Fillmore served as the thirteenth president of the United States.
2. I hate you! I hate you!! Hate!!! DEEP HATRED!!!!
3. Press in the code 109 BR.

There is a very significant difference illustrated here. Sentence 1 gives us information concerning a certain individual, Millard Fillmore. It tells us something about him, claiming to give us a fact. It makes sense to ask: Is this statement true or false? Does (2) give us any information? Is it intended to give us information? Does it express feelings and emotions? Isn't this its primary function? It is taken from an ad where a person is remonstrating with his car for breaking down more times than he could count. Finally, (3) directs behavior. It tells us to perform a specific action. Sentences 1, 2, and 3 illustrate the three basic functions of language. Language may be informative, it may express or arouse emotions or feelings, or it may direct behavior.

Let's give precise definitions of these three basic functions of language: 2

A message serves the *informative function* just in case it claims to say something about the world, just in case we can meaningfully discuss whether it is true or false.

A message serves the *expressive function* if it either purports to express some feeling or emotion or attempts to arouse feelings or emotions.

A message serves the *directive function* if it attempts to guide or direct behavior; it tells us to do something.

We must emphasize an important point about each of these definitions. Note   3
that we have said not that a message is informative just in case it says something about the world but just in case it *claims* to say something about the world. A statement need not be true to be informative. A false statement claims to say something about the world. It is giving misinformation, but its function is still to say something about the world. But notice that if a statement is informative, asking whether it is true or false must make sense. This is the crucial issue. Similarly, we can imagine someone putting on an act—screaming that he is angry, yelling, cursing—when in fact he doesn't feel any of these emotions. We can have all kinds of emotional insincerity. If we had said that a passage is expressive just in case it expresses some feeling or emotion, these cases would be problematic. How could we have expressive language without any emotion to express? But surely this behavior purports to express emotion. The person is creating a strong impression about his or her emotions and using language to foster these impressions is to use language which functions expressively. Last, a message need not actually change behavior to be directive—it's enough that it attempt to. If the person addressed doesn't pay attention or is not disposed to follow the directive, the message still serves the directive function.

How Do We Recognize Whether a Message Is Informative, Expressive, or Directive?

We may easily convert our definitions of the three basic functions of lan-   4
guage into critical questions to determine which function or functions a message serves:

Can the message be true or false?
What emotions or feelings does the message apparently express or arouse?
What specific action or actions does the message call for?

Let's apply these questions to specific examples.

4. There is a black crow in that tree.
5. All crows are black.
6. Fifty-two percent of the voters favor the Democrats.

7. Detective Most believes more strongly than Sargent Bronson that Alex committed the crime.
8. The results of the New Hampshire primary are a genuine setback for Senator Smith.

In each case, doesn't it make sense to ask whether the statement is true or false? This is enough to show that all these messages are informative. Do any of them clearly express or arouse emotions? Example 8 might dampen the enthusiasm of Senator Smith's supporters or perhaps put Senator Smith's campaign in a bad light, but otherwise these statements are emotionally neutral. Can you cite any particular emotion that the other statements express or arouse? So these messages are not expressive. Do any of them tell us to do anything? Can we cite any particular action we are told to perform? Clearly, the answer is no, and hence, none of these messages serves the directive function.

Now contrast these examples with   5

9. What a villainous deed!

Example 9 expresses outrage. There is no question of expressive function here. Does it make sense to ask whether (9) is true or false? Some particular deed or type of deed is being called villainous. Since we can specify what it means for a deed to be villainous, we can ask whether the deed satisfies the criterion. The question of truth or falsity is not completely out of place. But is the principal function of (9) to convey information? Again, since most people want to avoid what is villainous, calling an action villainous directs them to avoid similar actions. But is the primary function of (9) to guide behavior? Also, does (9) tell us to do anything about this particular deed? Is any action enjoined on us?

What about the following messages?   6

10. Please consider your plan.
11. You ought to take advanced symbolic logic.
12. It is good to clean house twice a year.
13. It is wrong to lie.

There is no question that these last examples, as did sentence 3, tell us to do something (or refrain from doing something). These messages are obviously directive. Can we meaningfully ask whether (10) is true or false? Does it arouse any emotions? Sentence 10 seems to be purely directive. Sentences 11, 12, and 13 are evaluations. Hence, the issue of their truth or falsity arises. They may also affect our attitudes concerning certain actions. So they are not completely neutral emotionally. But, again, isn't the principal function of these statements to direct behavior?

Our using the term "principal function" several times points to two very   7
important facts about language function. First, some messages may serve several functions. The three functions are not mutually exclusive. A message can be both informative and expressive, or expressive and directive. Some may

serve all three functions. Second, although on some occasions saying that a message serves several functions may be technically correct, one function may take precedence over the others. Sentence 9 is principally expressive. Sentences 11 through 13 are principally directive. Here is another example:

14. That gorgeous bouquet contains so many beautiful roses.

Sentence 14 certainly does state a fact about the bouquet: it has many roses. But a number of words in (14) have an emotional charge—"so many," "beautiful," and, most powerfully, "gorgeous." From the presence of these terms, we may judge that (14)'s principal function is not to describe the bouquet but to swoon over it. The principal function of (14) is expressive.

Although sometimes it is appropriate to identify a principal function, at other times we should recognize that we have several language functions going on. We would not be understanding the message fully if we did not recognize this. Let's look at two specific examples applying our questions to see how all the functions of language are served.   8

Many directives will try to guide behavior by saying something about the consequences of an action, consequences that should affect us emotionally. Ben Franklin's statement after the signing of the Declaration of Independence is a classic example: 9

15. We must all hang together or assuredly we shall all hang separately.

Is Franklin directing his compatriots to do anything? Surely he is telling them to put aside differences of party, geographic background, and personality and unite behind the cause of a new nation. But he does this by indicating the consequences of disunity. He is making a prediction here. Can't we ask whether Franklin's prediction is true or false? And what about the predicted consequence—hanging separately? Does that fail to arouse emotion? Isn't it necessary to recognize all three functions to appreciate this passage fully? This example is quite instructive, and we shall return to it again in the next section.

What about the following passage?   10

16. Your moral feelings really torment you for not [repaying that debt], as you well know. You say you have no duty to repay as a feeble effort to quiet your conscience, and free the expression of your crude selfishness.—Charles L. Stevenson, *Ethics and Language*.

What functions does this message serve? First, certain claims are being made about someone's psychology and motivations. Do the moral feelings really torment the person? Is his or her disclaiming any duty to repay an effort to quiet the conscience? Questions of true or false clearly enter here, making the message informative. But that is not all. To assert this message is to attempt to stir up those moral feelings and make the torment more tormenting, to disquiet the conscience, in short to make the person *feel* guilty. The message is expres-   11 sive. But again, that is not all. Doesn't the speaker want the individual addressed to repay that debt? Isn't the message intended to bring about that behavior? Clearly, then, this passage is informative, expressive, and directive.

Recognizing that a message may be true or false, or that it directs behavior,   12
is relatively straightforward, barring some pitfalls which we shall examine shortly. Recognizing that a message is expressive requires sensitivity to how language expresses and arouses emotion. We can cultivate this sensitivity by becoming aware of various factors which make language expressive.

What Are Some Specific Ways for Language to Express or Arouse Emotions?

The mere description of certain events or situations may be emotion arous-   13
ing. Consider:

17. Skies were cloudy above the Bal Harbour, Fla., meeting, which was dominated by behind-the-scenes discussion of [the president's] program, [which one labor leader called] "a high risk gamble with the future of America."—From *Time*, March 2, 1981. Copyright 1981 Time Inc. All rights reserved. Reprinted by permission from TIME.
18. The bodies of the U.S. commandos lay in the Iranian desert.—*Newsweek*, May 12, 1980. Copyright 1980, by Newsweek, Inc. All Rights Reserved. Reprinted by permission.
19. The witness was John W. Dean III, who was the White House legal counsel for three years until fired by Mr. Nixon on April 30.—*U.S. News & World Report*, July 9, 1973.

All these statements are informative, but don't they also affect us emotionally, precisely because of what they describe? *Time* conveys a distinct mood of foreboding or apprehension. Saying in particular that skies were cloudy contributes to this overall impression. Clearly, most Americans in May 1980 were not going to react very favorably to the image of U.S. soldiers lying dead *in the desert* of the very country holding American embassy personnel hostage! By presenting this image, the message arouses anger or disgust. Finally, what is the effect of knowing that John Dean was dismissed, fired from his position? Does it put him in a very good light? In all these cases, then, the information the message presents or the image it depicts is emotion arousing. Being sensitive to this helps us to determine that language is functioning expressively here.

We have noted that certain particular words are emotionally charged. Such   14
emotive words are a chief expressive tool of language. What exactly is an emotive word? We approach this by distinguishing literal meaning from emotive meaning. Many words refer to particular persons, objects, or events—President Lincoln, the commander-in-chief, John Lennon, the World Trade Center, the Capitol, the Golden Gate Bridge, the latest presidential inauguration, the first moon landing, the advent of satellite technology—all these ex-

pressions refer to something. What they refer to, their *denotations*, are their literal meaning. On the other hand, some words express attributes or relations. Green, house, animal—these are attributes which may be true of things. Parent of, to the right of, between—these relations may hold among things. Given an attribute term, we may talk of the class of objects, the class of green things, the class of houses, the class of animals, of which that term is true. Likewise, we may talk of the class of all those pairs of persons where the first is to the right of the second. These classes are the denotations of the attribute or relation terms. The denotation is part, but not all, of the literal meaning of such terms.

Associated with the terms expressing attributes and relations are "rules" or criteria, sometimes not very clearly defined or specifically spelled out, for deciding whether an attribute is true of a certain item or whether a relation holds between or among various things. For example, a skyscraper has to be a tall building, persons are old only when they have attained a certain number of years, a biological human parent is a person who has been involved in the procreation of a human being. These rules or criteria, the dictionary definitions, so to speak, are the connotations of these terms and are also part of their literal meaning. For attribute and relation terms, then, the literal meaning consists of both the denotation and connotation. 15

Over and above their literal meanings, words may have the capacity to express or arouse feelings. Consider "coolie." In the American West of the late nineteenth century, persons of oriental descent who did hard manual labor, such as building railroads, were called coolies. That definition then spells out the connotation of "coolie." The denotation is the class of all such persons. Together, these constitute the literal meaning. But to call someone a coolie was no compliment. Rather, it was a way of casting dispersion, of expressing and arousing contempt. Who are the red necks, the red skins? Are these complimentary terms? On the other hand, consider "leatherneck." The connotation is being a member of the U.S. Marines. The denotation then is the class of Marines. But to call someone a leatherneck—this shows real admiration for the macho man. The word expresses and arouses respect. What about "superstar" and "genius"? These words have literal meaning, but they also express and arouse emotions. We may say that the *emotive meaning* of a word is its dimension to express the emotions of the speaker or writer and evoke similar emotions in the hearer or reader. We can similarly speak of the emotive meaning of whole phrases or other expressions which might be parts of sentences. For convenience, we shall call any expressions possessing a distinct emotive meaning emotive words. 16

In general, there are two types of emotive words. *Laudatory* or *positive words* express or arouse positive or favorable feelings toward what they indicate. *Derogatory* or *negative words* express or arouse negative or unfavorable feelings. Words which involve little or no emotion are called *neutral words*. Hence "leatherneck," "superstar," and "genius" are all laudatory words, whereas "coolie," "red neck," and "red skin" are derogatory. We must be care- 17 ful here because some words will have different emotive meanings depending on context or on who uses them. The word "communist" in the United States has a distinct negative emotive meaning, but just the opposite in the Soviet Union. "Old" is negative at times, but in "old wine," "old castle," "very old antique," it contributes significantly to the positive emotive meaning of the expressions.

The moral of all this is that we cannot be mechanical in judging emotive   18
meaning. We must be sensitive to context—the entire passage in which the word occurs and the circumstances of its use. This touches upon a theme we shall return to again and again. In interpreting passages, we cannot be mechanical; we must be sensitive. Being aware of the issues we discuss in this book should help to develop sensitivity. Thinking specifically about emotive words and emotion-arousing images or descriptions, two specific ways for language to be expressive, should make us sensitive to the expressive power of language. But we must be prepared to exercise sensitivity.

Why Is the Informative/Expressive/Directive Distinction Important for the Logical Thinker as Challenger?

There are two significant reasons why distinguishing language function is   19
important for logical thinking. First, how we challenge a message differs, depending on the function of the message. We ask why we should believe an informative message, what evidence or data justify our accepting it as true. If a message is directive, we don't ask whether it is true. Rather, we ask whether the action it commends to us is right. Is it in accord with our moral principles? Does it violate them? What values does it promote? What values are jeopardized? If a message arouses feelings or emotions, we can ask how appropriate are those feelings or emotions. Should I feel this way? In effect, to arouse positive or negative emotions is to make a positive or negative evaluation. Should I accept this evaluation? Why is it correct?

The distinction is important for another reason. Remember our definition.   20
Logical thinking is reasonably going about deciding what to believe or do. Both informative and directive messages may come heavily laced with emotive words. These may make the beliefs or actions seem attractive. But a logical thinker wants to accept a belief because, on balance, the evidence supports it. He or she wants to perform an action if it is right or justified. Separating the expressive from the directive and informative functions of language can let us distinguish how much hard support we have for a belief or action as opposed to how forcefully someone has tried to sway our attitudes about it. The semanticist Hugh Walpole has said that appreciating the informative/expressive distinction provides "a first-rate umbrella against sales talk and propaganda." Chapters 3 and 4 will show us how apt this is. For now, we have made it plain that to challenge messages critically, we must understand their function, and for that we need the informative/expressive/directive distinction.

Summary

In this section, we have introduced a number of basic concepts concerning   21
language function. A message is *informative* when it claims to say something
about the world, when we can properly ask whether it is true or false. It is *expressive* when it either expresses or arouses some feeling or emotion. It is
directive when it attempts to influence behavior.

We may contrast the literal and emotive meanings of a word. The *literal*   22
meaning of a *referring expression* is the object to which it refers (its *denotation*). The *literal meaning* of an *attribute* or *relation* is the class of objects
(pairs of objects, triples of objects) of which the expression is true (its *denotation*) together with some rule for properly applying the expression (its *connotation*). The *emotive meaning* of a word is its capacity to express or arouse emotion. Emotive words can be *laudatory* or *derogatory*, depending on whether
they express or arouse positive or negative emotions. *Neutral words* seldom
involve much emotion.

From *Thinking Logically: Basic Concepts for Reasoning* (1988)
by James B. Freedman

**QUESTIONS
FROM SKIMMING**

In the left-hand column below, write down the questions you expect the selection will answer, along with the appropriate page number(s). Reread the selection carefully, and use the right-hand column to record the answers to the questions after you have compared your questions to those of your classmates and to the list of Questions on the Text that follows.

QUESTIONS (put page number after question)	ANSWERS

<table>
<tr><td>

**QUESTIONS
ON THE TEXT**

</td><td>

Compare your questions to those listed here.

What are the three basic functions of language?

What is an example of each?

What three questions can be used to determine which function a particular message serves?

Why is the term *principle function* important in discussing language function?

What do examples 15 and 16 illustrate about language function?

How can words arouse emotion?

What is the difference between *literal meaning* and *emotive meaning*?

What examples are given of words with these different kinds of meaning?

What examples are given of words that refer to particular things and words that express attributes and relations?

What are the *denotations* of words such as "old" and "parent," and what are their *connotations*?

What are two types of emotive meaning?

What are neutral words?

What are two reasons why it is important to distinguish language function?

</td></tr>
<tr><td>

**QUESTIONS
BEYOND
THE TEXT**

</td><td>

1. Can you give examples, from what you have heard or read today, of messages that are informative, directive, and expressive?

2. What was the very last remark that you heard before reading this selection? What would you say its principal function was?

3. Can you find in today's newspaper any examples of emotive use of language? Are the emotive words used laudatory or derogatory?

</td></tr>
<tr><td>

OUTLINE NOTES

</td><td>

This selection does not contain many points for you to put in an outline, because it mainly analyzes examples. You need to understand the examples and what is said about them, but certainly don't need to learn them; you will remember the material much better if you supply your own. As you complete the following outline, therefore, insert examples from your own experience in the places indicated by brackets. Take the examples from talk that you have recently heard—ideally, talk from this class.

</td></tr>
</table>

I. Language Functions

   1. Informative

     e.g., [————————————————————————————]
       Test question: "Can the message be true or false?"

   2. ————————————

     e.g., [————————————————————————————]
       Test question: "————————————————————"

   3. ————————————

     e.g., [————————————————————————————]
       Test question: "————————————————————"

   4. Combined Functions
     e.g., "Your moral feelings really torment you for not [repaying that debt],
     as you well know. You say you have no duty to repay as a feeble
     effort to quiet your conscience, and free the expression of your
     crude selfishness."—Charles L. Stevenson, *Ethics and Language*.
     (qtd. in Freedman 1988, p. 9).
     This message is

     a. Informative because ————————————————————

     b. Emotive because ——————————————————————

     c. Directive because ——————————————————————

II. Use of Language to Express or Arouse Emotion

   1. Description of Events That Arouse Emotion

     e.g., [————————————————————————————]

   2. Use of Emotive Words
     e.g.,"coolie"

       Literal meaning = ——————————————————————

       Emotive meaning = ————————————————————

       ["————————————"

       Literal meaning = ——————————————————————

       Emotive meaning = ————————————————————]

       ["————————————————————————————"

Literal meaning = _____

Emotive meaning = _____]

["_____"

Literal meaning = _____

Emotive meaning = _____]

Types of emotive words

a. Laudatory/positive

   e.g., ["_____"

Literal meaning = _____

Emotive meaning = _____]

["_____"

Literal meaning = _____

Emotive meaning = _____]

["_____"

Literal meaning = _____

Emotive meaning = _____]

b. Derogatory/negative

   e.g. ["_____"

Literal meaning = _____

Emotive meaning = _____]

["_____"

Literal meaning = _____

Emotive meaning = _____]

["_____"

Literal meaning = _____

Emotive meaning = _____]

VOCABULARY NOTES

In this selection, most of the words that are printed in italics are ones whose meaning you need to understand precisely. Make a list of them, and if you can't say what they mean from looking at the list, find the definitions in the text and write them down beside the words.

ESSAY TOPICS   These topics, like those given for Selection 3-1, are meant to encourage you to work more with the ideas about which you have just read. No essay outline is given here, so construct one of your own for each topic. Do this by examining the topic carefully and deciding, with the help of your classmates, what particular information the various parts of the topic ask for. Note that both topics call for examples, so draw on those you came up with when you discussed the Questions beyond the Text and on those you put in your outline notes. It is not so good to use the examples given in the text because that will show only that you have read it, not that you have understood the principles described. To remind yourself of what an essay-writing outline might look like, review the example given on pages 169–170.

After analyzing each topic, you may want to reread the selection before writing your essay. That is fine, but shut the book while you are actually writing so that you will use your own words and not those of the text.

1. Show, by giving examples, what the three basic functions of language are, and what questions can be used to test each of them. Why is it not always possible to ascribe a single function to a particular utterance?
2. What is meant by *emotive* as opposed to *literal* meaning? Give some examples of laudatory and derogatory expressions and describe how they might be used. How should statements involving such expressions be challenged?

**SELECTION
3-3**

The United Nations

This material is from *Understanding Politics: Ideas, Institutions, and Issues*, a text written for introductory courses offered to first-year undergraduates by political science departments. Unlike the other selections in this chapter, it is taken from the middle, and not the beginning, of the book: it is part of a chapter called International Law and Organization and follows a section on Nonstate Actors in Contemporary World Politics. As you can see, it is about a major international organization, one that is mentioned in several of the selections in Chapter 1, Reading for General Information, in this text. It is therefore a good example of how what you study in college can illuminate what you read in the newspaper or see on television.

As with the other selections, skim the passage first, paying particular attention to the headings, subheadings, italicized and underlined terms, and the diagram referred to in paragraph 6. In this selection, you are going to find information that is probably *not* familiar, so before you start, try to get an idea of what sort of information it is and how it is arranged. As soon as you recognize that a particular point is being addressed, write it down as a question and go on to the next point; don't try to take in the information yet. After skimming the whole selection, compare your questions with the list of Questions on the Text that follows. Finally, read the passage carefully, looking for the answers to the questions—both your own and the ones provided. You will find that using questions like this makes it much easier to understand detailed information

Impressive as the modern network of international organizations and eco- 1
nomic pacts may seem on the surface, it has not even come close to ridding the international community of quarrels and national rivalries. Many scholars and statesmen, in fact, have argued that peace and interdependence could best be promoted by one overriding organization rather than by many small international organizations. The supreme effort to found such an organization was the creation of the United Nations.

Historical Background

To understand the United Nations, we must place it in historical context. 2
Beginning in the nineteenth century, several international peacekeeping federations were founded, usually in the aftermath of increasingly destructive wars. The Holy Alliance, formed in 1815, in the wake of the Napoleonic wars, represented an attempt by Europe's major powers to control international events by means of meetings and conferences. A more elaborate organization was the League of Nations, set up in 1919, following World War I.

The League of Nations

It was with great hope and high expectations that the Covenant of the   3
League of Nations was sealed in 1919. The actual machinery of the League of
Nations included the Assembly, the Council, and the Permanent Secretariat.
The Assembly was a deliberative body made up of representatives from each
member state. Each representative in the Assembly cast one vote, and each
vote carried equal weight. Motions on the floor of the Assembly required unanimous approval for passage, meaning that virtually every member-state, no
matter how tiny, enjoyed veto power over nearly every decision. The much
smaller Council was made up of four permanent and four nonpermanent members. The role of the Council was to investigate and report on threats to the
peace and to make proposals or recommend appropriate action to the Assembly. The two bodies were coordinated and supervised by the Permanent Secretariat, the administrative arm of the League.

In addition to building world understanding and cooperation, the League of   4
Nations was charged with maintaining international peace and punishing ag-
gressor nations. In this respect, the league became the institutional embodiment
of President Woodrow Wilson's desire to replace the traditional balance of
power with "a single overwhelming, powerful group of nations who shall be
trustees of the peace of the world." It was intended that the concentrated power
of the League of Nations—the *collective security* it represented—would be so
formidable that no single challenger would stand a chance against it. The military forces of all law-abiding nations were to be ranged against any one state
that violated international peace. In the view of the League's founders, the very
existence of such an overwhelming force would make it unnecessary actually to
use it, so cowed would potential aggressors be.

In the end, however, both the concept of collective security and the League   5
itself failed. By the early 1930s, it was apparent that the League was fatally
torn by conflicting national interests and bitter rivalries.

The Founding of the UN

The vast destruction, immense casualty count, and terrifying new weapons   6
of World War II sparked renewed efforts to ensure world peace through the
establishment of a powerful international organization. (See Figure 21-1.) The
founders of the UN recognized that if the new organization were to have any
chance of succeeding, it would have to represent an organizational improvement over the League of Nations. It was widely believed that the League's
structure had had at least two fatal flaws. First, its members were all treated as
equals, irrespective of the realities of national power. In the Assembly, every
member-state had one vote, and every negative vote constituted a veto. And
even in the Council, of which the Great Powers were permanent members, the
nonpermanent members exercised veto power. Consequently, critics of the
League argued, the lesser powers had too much clout and the Great Powers too

Figure 21-1 The United Nations System (Source: United Nations Office of Public Information)

little. The other great weakness of the League was its incompleteness. The scope of the League's peace aims may have been worldwide but its membership was limited. The absence of several great powers—particularly the United States—meant that the League's mandate was universal in theory but circumscribed in practice.

The conferees who founded the United Nations in 1945 were intent on rectifying these defects in the League's collective security system. A major effort was made to ensure that no potential member-state would be excluded from the new organization. The General Assembly was designed as a deliberative body in which all UN members would have an equal voice and an equal vote. More important, the UN Charter created a Security Council entrusted with "primary responsibility for the maintenance of international peace and security." The charter specified that this body was to be made up of five permanent members (the United States, the Soviet Union, the United Kingdom, France, and China) and six nonpermanent members. Unlike their predecessors in the League, the so-called Big Five alone were given the right to veto proposed peacekeeping measures. In this manner the UN Charter sought to correct the anomaly of legal equality in the midst of political inequality. In the UN, the most powerful nations would have responsibilities commensurate with their capabilities.

Key Points in the UN Charter

Precisely how these responsibilities were conceptualized was spelled out in Chapter VII of the UN Charter, titled "Action with Respect to Threats to the Peace, Breaches of the Peace, and Acts of Aggression." Article 39 of this chapter specifies that "the Security Council shall determine the existence of any threat to the peace, breach of the peace, or act of aggression and shall make recommendations, or decide what measure shall be taken in accordance with Articles 40 and 42, to maintain or restore international peace and security." Subsequent articles spell out how the Security Council was expected to discharge its obligations. Article 41 deals with economic sanctions, including "complete or partial interruption of economic relations and of rail, sea, air, postal, telegraphic, radio, and other means of communication, and the severance of diplomatic relations." Article 42 contemplates situations in which economic sanctions may be inadequate; in such cases, the Security Council "may take action by air, sea, or land forces as may be necessary to maintain or restore international peace and security. Such action may include demonstrations, blockade, and other operations by air, sea, or land forces of Members of the United Nations." Other articles in Chapter VII deal with organizing the military components of a full-fledged collective security system, including the establishment of a Military Staff Committee (Article 47).

The machinery of international peacekeeping outlined by these articles far surpassed the comparable machinery of the League of Nations. Moreover, the UN was intended to go well beyond merely maintaining peace and security, as the establishment of its so-called specialized agencies revealed. Through these agencies, the UN plays an important role in worldwide disaster relief, resettlement of refugees, technical assistance in the areas of food and agriculture, health concerns, and many other areas. In addition, the world body actively promotes a higher world standard of living through agencies such as the Economic and Social Council (ECOSOC) and the United Nations International Children's Emergency Fund (UNICEF). Finally, financial and developmental assistance has been extended to economically troubled states through the World

Bank (more formally known as the International Bank for Reconstruction and Development, or IBRD), the International Monetary Fund (IMF) and the United Nations Conference on Trade and Development (UNCTAD). Glancing at a list of the UN's specialized agencies makes it clear that the UN was committed from the outset to promoting world welfare as well as preventing world war.

However, the UN Charter was not designed as a blueprint for a world government. Article 2, paragraph 7, of the charter makes it clear that matters "essentially within the domestic jurisdiction of any state" are beyond the purview of UN authority. In addition, Article 2 states unequivocally that the United Nations "is based on the principle of sovereign equality of all its members"— and the equality of sovereign states is a defining characteristic of *leagues*, not of *governments*.

Nevertheless, the declared equality of all members of the United Nations is undercut by other provisions of the charter that give greater weight within the organization to the most powerful or prominent member-states. The most obvious reason for these provisions was the need to guarantee the participation of the major states. But there was another, more subtle reason: Some of the UN's original supporters viewed the new international association not just as an organization of sovereign states, but also as the forerunner of a world government. And if the UN's great potential were ever to be realized fully, it was evident that the larger states would have to play a greater role than the smaller, less powerful states. The seeming inconsistencies in the charter, accordingly, represented compromises made in the present to pave the way for the future.

Stumbling Blocks and Limited Success

Unfortunately, the United Nations never fulfilled its early promise: It could not escape the same problems that had destroyed the League of Nations. Individual nations were simply not ready to commit themselves so such an organization could function properly.

On the one hand, the charter at several points obligates member-states to act in accordance with the rule of law and empowers the Security Council to punish them when they do not; on the other hand, it provides a number of loopholes and escape clauses for states that wish to evade or ignore their obligations. Article 51, for example, states that "nothing in the present Charter shall impair the inherent right of individual or collective self-defense." As long as "self-defense" is a lawful justification to resort to force, and as long as individual states are free to define self-defense broadly enough to cover virtually any action they deem to be in their national interest, such a provision invites aggression. The dilemma is obvious: Without escape clauses such as Article 51, the UN Charter would not have been acceptable; with them, it is not enforceable.

An additional problem plaguing the world body is the persistent state of

10

11

12

13

14

tension between the United States and the Soviet Union that has severely hampered the workings of the United Nations since its inception. Because each superpower maintains a coalition of allies, followers, and admirers that at one time or another have held the majority in the General Assembly, deadlock rather than decisive action has been the hallmark of most UN deliberations. The high degree of consensus so necessary to promote peace through collective security has, for the most part, simply not existed throughout the history of the United Nations. Even when consensus has been reached (as it often has among Third World states and many communist nations on a variety of issues in recent years), one or another of the permanent members of the Security Council has usually been able to block any significant action by casting a veto.

This is not to say, however, that the peace-related functions of the United   15
Nations have never been successfully exercised. At various times in the recent past, the UN has contributed to peace by sending special mediators, truce-supervision teams, and/or quasi-military forces to, among other places, Cyprus, the Middle East, and the Congo. These efforts, although limited in both scope and success, have been valuable exercises in peacekeeping. Significantly however, the more ambitious the peacekeeping operation, the more controversial the results have been. The United Nations peacekeeping efforts in the Middle East provide an excellent case in point.

The UN and the Middle East

Following the Arab-Israeli struggle for control of Palestine shortly after   16
World War II, the United Nations set up a Truce Supervision Organization (UNTSO) to observe and report on compliance with the armistice agreement between Israel and neighboring Arab states. In 1956, the *Suez Crisis* erupted into a second Arab-Israeli war and again the United Nations was called on to calm the situation—this time by establishing a peacekeeping force known as the *United Nations Emergency Force (UNEF)*, the first of its kind. At its peak, UNEF consisted of roughly six thousand troops drawn from ten countries. Its mandate was to supervise the 1956 ceasefire and the withdrawal of British, French, and Israeli forces; to patrol the border between Israel and Egypt (and the entrance to the Gulf of Aqaba at Sharm el-Sheik); and to oversee compliance with the armistice.

The UN peacekeeping force helped prevent a renewal of hostilities for a   17
decade, but in 1967 the force withdrew at the request of Egyptian President Nasser. The third Arab-Israeli war (known as the *Six-Day War*) erupted shortly after. When the smoke cleared, Israel had crushed Egypt and occupied the Sinai Peninsula (formerly Egyptian territory), the Golan Heights (formerly Syrian land), and the West Bank (formerly under Jordanian control), as well as East Jerusalem. In 1973, Egypt and Syria attacked Israel, thus sparking the *"Yom Kippur War"*—the fourth major conflict in the Middle East in twenty-five years. Israel counterattacked, driving the Syrians back and pursuing the retreating Egyptian forces across the Suez Canal. Secretary of State Henry

Kissinger, practicing what pundits called "shuttle diplomacy," flew back and forth between Egypt and Israel in an attempt to work out new ceasefire and armistice arrangements. Sending in a new UN peacekeeping force (UNEF II) was one of the first steps.

A tense "peace" lasted through the 1970s, highlighted by the _Camp David_ 18 _accords_, by which Israel gave back the Sinai to Egypt and, in return, Egypt extended diplomatic recognition to Israel. Most other Arab states, however, denounced the Egypt-Israel peace treaty, accusing Cairo of selling out to the "imperialists" and "Zionists."

In 1982, still another war broke out when Israel reacted to repeated provoca- 19 tions by the Lebanon-based _Palestine Liberation Organization (PLO)_ by bombing the PLO's strongholds across the Lebanese border and later, in a coordinated land, sea, and air attack, reinvading Lebanon. (Israel had invaded southern Lebanon for the first time in 1978 in retaliation against PLO cross-border terrorist raids.) Israel and Syrian forces engaged briefly in the Bekaa Valley but quickly agreed to a truce. The Israel army surrounded Beirut and, after a concerted bombing of PLO positions inside the city, Israel forced the PLO guerrillas, including their leader Yasir Arafat, to flee.

Unfortunately, Lebanon's troubles were far from over. In September 1982 20 Lebanon's newly elected president was assassinated and Israel troops entered West Beirut to prevent extremist factions, backed by Syria and Iran, from taking over the city.

Where was the United Nations while Lebanon was being turned into the new 21 Middle East battleground? Since 1978, a peacekeeping force has been stationed there (the _United Nations Interim Force in Lebanon_ or _UNIFL_). Like its UNEF predecessor, this force consists of about 6,000 troops drawn from numerous UN member-states, some fifteen in all. On paper, it looks impressive enough. And UNIFL's mandate is clear: to facilitate the withdrawal of Israeli troops from southern Lebanon, to restore Lebanese security; and to ensure the return of sovereignty to the Lebanese government. Unfortunately, despite the presence of UN "peacekeepers," the violence in Lebanon continues unabated, and the prospect for peace there is little more than an elusive hope.

The lesson of the Middle East is simple: Where nations in conflict exert the 22 political will to seek peace, the UN can play a useful—though limited—role. However, as the tragedy of Lebanon attests, the presence of a peacekeeping force does not guarantee peace. Today, Lebanon is no closer to self-determination or domestic tranquility than it was in 1978.

Problems Underlying Comprehensive International Organizations

Despite its successes, the United Nations obviously has not lived up to the 23 highest expectations of its founders. Although its architects sought to solve the procedural problems associated with the League of Nations—such as the unanimity rule that prevented the League's Assembly from acting unless _all_ its members could agree—the UN has not been free of procedural problems. And problems of procedure in international organizations invariably conceal more deep-seated difficulties. These must be faced by any comprehensive international organization.

The Problem of Universality

For an international body to be successful, all nations of significant size or consequence must be persuaded to join and remain part of the organization. As a minimum condition for success, all major powers must be members. The experience of the League of Nations clearly demonstrated the problems that arise when some nations are excluded or refuse to join. The history of the United Nations also illustrates the importance of including all potential member-states—especially those with the capacity to disrupt world peace. (The difficulties caused by the absence of the Peoples' Republic of China, which was excluded from the UN for two decades, was an obvious case in point.) And yet, ensuring this universality of membership in a pluralistic world has proved to be problematic. In recent years, for example, some important nations (such as South Africa) have been stripped of full membership privileges, and others (including Israel) have been threatened with expulsion.

The Problem of Inequality

Smaller nations inevitably insist on the principle of formal equality. Anything less, they contend, would be an affront to their sovereignty. By the same token, powerful nations insist that their superior strength be reflected in special procedural arrangements (such as the veto power of the permanent members of the UN Security Council). Anything less, they argue, would represent a diminution of their real importance in the world. Moreover, as the relative strengths of member-states fluctuate, the original formula governing such matters needs to be revised. Some nations that formerly were considered Great Powers have to be demoted to make room for newcomers whose stars are rising. This is more than merely a "technical" problem. No international organization can remain viable unless it resolves the problem of inequality while remaining flexible enough to change with changing circumstances.

The Problem of Competence

Organizations of this kind, by their very nature, are powerless to do any more than their least cooperative members are willing to countenance. As a result, international organizations tend to lack the competence to deal with a wide range of problems normally thought to fall within the realm of governmental action. The best they can do, as a rule, is deal with specific cases arising in general areas of common concern (for example, peacekeeping).

The Problem of Unity

In the past, the most successful international organizations have been alliances based on confronting a common enemy. The Holy Alliance, inspired by the fear of a resurgent France, was a case in point. The present-day Arab League is another: Without the unifying effect of facing a common enemy (Israel), the Arab states undoubtedly would have engaged in far more internecine squabbling over the past forty years. Similarly, without the perceived threat of communist expansion in the late 1940s and early 1950s, the North Atlantic Treaty Organization would never have been founded. When the original threat fades, however, the bonds of alliance tend to disintegrate. Disunity, or the absence of any real sense of community in the international arena is a major obstacle to *all* forms of international organization from the simplest to the most complex and comprehensive.

The Problem of Sovereignty

Underlying all four problems mentioned above is the problem of sovereignty—the supreme power a state exercises within its boundaries. In the final analysis, sovereignty is indivisible: Either a nation has the last word in its own affairs or it does not. A nation can no more be partially sovereign, the nineteenth-century U.S. political leader John C. Calhoun once noted, than a woman can be partially pregnant. It follows that the creation of an effective world government would be possible only if individual governments could be persuaded to surrender not just *part* of their sovereignty but *all* of it—a prospect that has been regarded by most nations as entirely too dangerous in a world governed by mutual fear and mistrust.

28

From *Understanding Politics: Ideas, Institutions, and Issues*, 2nd ed. (1988) by Thomas M. Magstadt and Peter M. Schotten

**QUESTIONS
FROM SKIMMING**

In the left-hand column below, write down the questions you expect the selection will answer, along with the appropriate page number(s). Reread the selection carefully, and use the right-hand column to record the answers to the questions after you have compared your questions to those of your classmates and to the list of Questions on the Text that follows.

QUESTIONS (put page number after question)	ANSWERS

Compare your questions to those noted here.

What is the historical background of the UN?

What was the League of Nations?

When was it founded?

What was the function of the Assembly? of the Council? of the Permanent
Secretariat?

What was the idea of *collective security*?

Why did the League fail?

What were the two "fatal flaws" of the League of Nations?

How was the United Nations made different?

Which were the Big Five nations?

What responsibilities did Chapter VII of the UN Charter define?

What was the UN intended to do besides keeping the peace?

What are the major agencies of the UN?

In what ways is the UN Charter inconsistent?

What problems have emerged in the working of the UN?

Where has the UN been successful?

What has been the UN role in the Middle East conflict?

What has been the UN role in Lebanon?

What does the example of the Middle East show about the UN's effectiveness?

What is the problem of *universality*?

What is the problem of *inequality*?

What is the problem of *competence*?

What is the problem of *unity*?

What is the problem of *sovereignty*?

1. How has the UN come into the news recently?

2. What UN agencies do you know of? What does each of them do?

3. What is happening at present in the Middle East? How is the UN involved?

4. Do you think the UN is becoming more or less effective? Why?

OUTLINE NOTES

This selection gives a good amount of historical information, and it is important to get the sequence of events straight in your mind. Helpful outline notes would therefore take the form of a simple chronological list. Following are the dates listed and some of the events mentioned in the selection. You are asked to fill in the rest. You will need to refer to the selection as you do so. (Note that the → symbol is used to mean "followed by" or "leading to.")

<u>The United Nations</u>

Historical Background

	Napoleonic wars
1815	Foundation of the Holy Alliance
	World War I
1919	_____
1930s	_____
	World War II
1945	_____

The UN and the Middle East

	World War II
	Arab-Israeli War _____
	UNTSO set up to _____
1956	_____
	→ 2nd Arab-Israeli War
1956	Ceasefire
	→ Establishment of UNEF (the_____
	_____)
	UNEF's mandate
	1. _____
	2. _____

3. _____

1967 _____

Six-Day War

→ _____

1973 _____

→ _____

1970s _____

1978 Israeli invasion of southern Lebanon to retaliate against PLO

→ UNIFL (i.e., _____

_____)

UNIFL's mandate

1. _____

2. _____

3. _____

1982 _____

_____

_____

_____

_____

DIAGRAMS

On page 186 there is an official United Nations diagram showing the organization's structure. You do not need to know all the details given there, but you do need to know the main features. You can learn them easily by making a simplified version of the diagram, and you can learn the most important descriptive material from the text by incorporating it in your own diagram. In the example on the next page, you will notice that the positions of the circles on the diagram have been changed to help you process the information more fully. Also, although some of the descriptive material is included, blanks are provided for you to add more from the text. For the examples, include only the names that are most familiar to you. If you know anything more about the various organs represented, you might want to add that information. You could ask your classmates for ideas and information about the UN agencies they have heard of.

The Structure of the UN

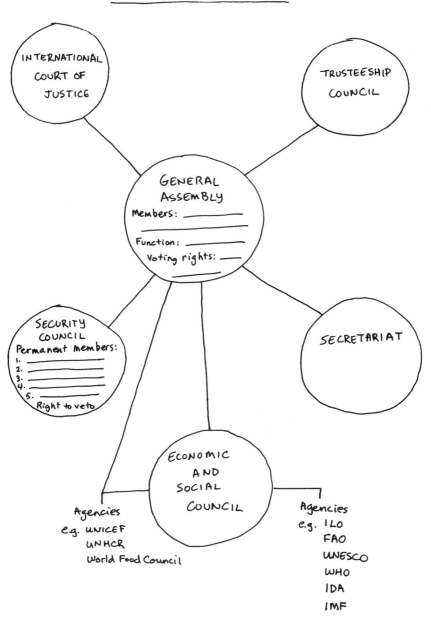

INTERNATIONAL
COURT OF
JUSTICE

TRUSTEESHIP
COUNCIL

GENERAL
ASSEMBLY
Members: _____
_____
Function: _____
Voting rights: ___
_____

SECURITY
COUNCIL
Permanent members:
1. _____
2. _____
3. _____
4. _____
5. _____
Right to veto

SECRETARIAT

ECONOMIC
AND
SOCIAL
COUNCIL

Agencies
e.g. UNICEF
UNHCR
World Food Council

Agencies
e.g. ILO
FAO
UNESCO
WHO
IDA
IMF

You may find it helpful to construct an even simpler diagram to represent the League of Nations. Include descriptive information on it as you did for the UN; this will help you compare the two organizations. Here is the shape you might use—notice how it echoes the information given in the UN diagram:

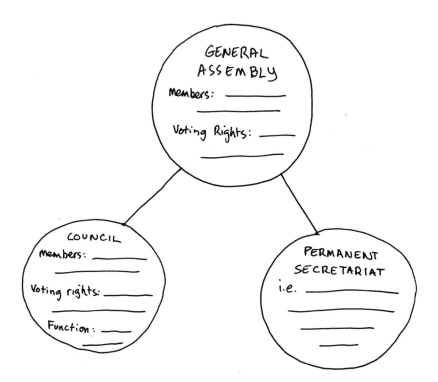

QUOTATIONS   The peacekeeping functions of the UN are described in this selection by means of quotations from the UN Charter. Because the exact wording of the charter is important, it would be worth your while to record these quotations under appropriate headings in your notes or on index cards so that you can refer to and learn them easily. Identify each quotation by its article and chapter number, and supply as much context as is necessary for the words to make sense. For example:

UN Charter—Peacekeeping

Chapter VII "Actions with Respect to Threats to the Peace, Breaches of the Peace, and Acts of Aggression"

Article 39 "_____

_____ "

Article 41 Econ. sanctions, incl. "_____

_____ "

Article 42 When econ. sanctions inadequate, Sec. Council "_____

_____ "

Article 47_____

Article 51 "_____

_____ "

UN Charter—Sovereignty

Article 2 Matters "_____

_____ "

are beyond UN authority. _____

The UN is "_____

_____ "

_____

_____

_____

_____

_____

ESSAY TOPICS   Before drawing up an outline for either of these topics, you will probably find it helpful to reread the selection. Study the topics first, and choose which one you want to focus on. Then, as you read, jot down any points that seem to be relevant; this can be done very briefly, but include a page reference so that you can check the information later if necessary. Next, rearrange your notes to form an essay outline. One is given here for topic 1, so if you decide to work on this topic, make your own outline and then compare it with the one given. If you prefer to work on topic 2, you can use the outline for topic 1 as a model.

1. What problems made the League of Nations ineffective? How did the founders of the United Nations try to prevent the recurrence of these problems?
2. What are the two basic functions of the UN? How successful has it been in performing these functions?

Essay Outline (Topic 1)

I. League of Nations—Problems

1. Structure
Unrealistic representation of relative power of nations
a. Assembly
b. Council

2. Membership
Absence of several Great Powers—esp. USA

3. Consequence
Rivalries, breakdown of collective security, World War II

II. United Nations—Attempts to Resolve

1. Structure
a. Assembly—no veto
b. Security Council—only Great Powers have veto

2. Membership
No potential member-state excluded
All Great Powers on Security Council

3. Consequence
Partial success—no world war so far, some help in local conflicts

**SELECTION
3-4**

Introduction to Anthropology

The title of this selection from a text called *Contemporary Cultural Anthropology* is the same as the title of the course for which it might normally be assigned. The selection is the whole first chapter of a general anthropology textbook—it may seem long to you, but it represents the amount of reading you might well be expected to do during the first week of such a course. You will see that the chapter introduces you to anthropology by giving two main kinds of information: an explanation of certain key concepts and an overview of the various fields of anthropology. The emphasis is on cultural anthropology, but other aspects of the discipline are described as well.

As with the other selections, skim it first to see what questions are addressed, and write those questions down. Begin your skimming by reading the summary at the end of the selection. Then go through the selection from the beginning, looking at the headings, subheadings, italicized words, and at the first or last sentences of some of the paragraphs. Only after you have skimmed the passage and written down questions for yourself should you refer to the questions noted under Questions on the Text. As before, you should finally reread the selection carefully for answers to your questions.

We human beings have probably always thought of ourselves as extraordinary creatures who occupy a unique position in the universe. This attitude is expressed, in one way or another, in most of the world's religions. For example, according to the Judeo-Christian-Islamic tradition, all living things were specially and individually created by God. However, God made humans with a unique property—a soul—by which they were rendered fundamentally different from all other creatures. Another example of the idea of human uniqueness can be seen in Australian Aboriginal religions. While these religions emphasize natural bonds between humans and other animals, humans are assigned a special role—maintenance of the world order through ritual—which makes them superior to other animals.

Modern science, which deals with natural phenomena that are directly or indirectly observable, approaches humans from a different perspective than does religion, ignoring questions of the existence of souls or the role of ritual in sustaining the world order. Even so, until very recently scientists continued the tradition of stressing how the extraordinary and superior attributes of the human animal place it in a special category, apart from other animals. Scientists recognized humans to be animals, but possessing traits and talents that were thought to be fundamentally different from any qualities found among the "lower" forms of life. The lives of nonhuman animals were said to be ruled by *in-*

1

2

stincts—inheritable and unalterable behavioral tendencies to make complex and specific responses to environmental stimuli. Human behavior, on the other hand, was seen as being based on ideas and concepts that are socially learned and transmitted, rather than genetically inherited.

Not long ago anthropologists and other scientists believed that humans were   3
the only tool-using animals, and that only humans possessed the capacity for complex forms of communication. The sophisticated technologies and elaborate systems of communication possessed by humans were made possible by a remarkably large and complex brain. The development of the intellectual capacity of humans, associated with increasingly larger brains, was said to release humans from instinctive behavior and to lay the basis for learned behavior. This capacity also gave humans the means of adapting to almost any environment without undergoing major physical changes. Rather than having to alter our physical characteristics to live in a new environment, we humans use our brains to figure out how to get by, through the use of clothing, shelter, or other means.

While this view is fundamentally valid, today we are discovering that our   4
special qualities are not really as special as we once thought. Many other animals do not behave in response to biologically derived instincts alone; much of their behavior is conditioned by learning. We now know that a number of animals use and make rudimentary tools and that some are even capable of complex forms of communication. We have also learned that we, too, are conditioned by biology in often subtle and complex ways; like the behavior of other animals, our behavior reflects our biological makeup and our adaptation to an environment. We remain a unique species, but what we once believed to be differences in kind between humans and other animals are in many cases turning out to be just differences in degree.

Culture

Perhaps the most important defining characteristic of humans is *culture*. The   5
term *culture* as used here is not limited to operas, symphonies, paintings, and other artistic endeavors. These are seen by anthropologists as examples of culture: Culture itself is *the customary manner in which human groups learn to organize their behavior and thought in relation to their environment*. Defined in this manner, culture has three principal aspects: *behavioral, perceptual,* and *material*. The behavioral component refers to how people act, especially how they interact with each other. In child rearing, for example, parents and children tend to interact in a relatively patterned fashion. Then there is the matter of perception, the views people have of the world. For example, parents have a limited range of ideas about how they should act, and what significance parenthood carries in the scheme of things. Finally, there is the material component of culture—the physical objects that we produce.

Learning

Most of what goes into making up culture is a result of *learning*—modifying behavior in response to experience within an environment. Learning is practically universal among organisms. But no other organism has a greater capacity for learning than a human, or depends as much on learned behavior for its survival. 6

While the survival of most other organisms is to some extent safeguarded by instincts, humans rely heavily on culture for their survival. People must learn how to live in a particular social and physical setting, biology playing but a minimal role. Think of the chances for survival that most urban-dwelling Westerners would have if suddenly stranded in a tropical area or arid desert. Without the help of someone who had learned how to live in the particular setting, the urbanite would probably quickly perish. Culture, in essence, constitutes the shared survival strategies of a group of people transmitted over generations. 7

The ideas and modes of behavior that constitute culture are transmitted largely by a complex system of symbols that includes language. Again, while all organisms can communicate in at least rudimentary fashion, and some, such as porpoises and chimpanzees, have highly developed means of communicating, humans have evolved an extremely complex system of communication that is unique to our species. Without it the creation of human culture as we know it would be impossible. 8

Society

Culture is not created in a vacuum, nor by isolated individuals. It is the product of humans interacting in groups. From their parents and from others around them, humans learn how to act and how to think in ways that are shared by or comprehensible to people in their group. Humans are by nature social animals. From birth to death, humans are biologically conditioned to live not as separate individuals, but as members of groups. Since the beginning of human evolution, our survival has been a cooperative enterprise. Even hermits do not escape the rest of humanity, for everything they think, know, or believe has been conditioned by others. Culture is a group effort and is *socially shared*. 9

We sometimes speak of those who share the same cultural perceptions and modes of behavior as members of a society. *Society* refers to the ways in which interaction among individuals is patterned. It is through their common experiences as members of a society that humans evolve shared cultural attributes. Thus, without society there would be no culture, for there would be no interaction by which people could develop shared knowledge, values, and beliefs. But it is not simply a one-way process. It is culture, by and large, that distinguishes human society from societies of other organisms. Moreover, human society has become highly dependent on culture—it is impossible to visualize one without the other. Without culture there would be only a very limited basis for humans to interpret one another's behavior. It is also through the dimension of culture that human society has attained its unique level of complexity and flexibility. 10

Variations exist within both culture and society. The term *society* can be 11
applied to the total human community, encompassing all of humanity. Alternatively, we may speak of American or Canadian society, or we may restrict ourselves to even smaller geographical or social groupings. We could conceivably speak, for instance, of southern California society or Navajo society. Culture too is something of a Chinese-box concept. Just as there are societies within societies, there are cultures within cultures, the smaller ones often referred to as *subcultures*.

Just as people interact with one another in varying degrees, they share culture to different degrees. For example, most Americans share certain attitudes 12
that are common virtually to all, such as a belief that everyone should have an equal chance to "make good" in life. At the same time, there are certain cultural concepts and practices that are shared by some Americans but not by others. For instance, many black Americans share certain handshaking conventions that are generally not used by whites. Not all black Americans shake hands in the same way, and many nonblacks shake hands in imitation of black patterns. Nevertheless, since a large number of American blacks have shared common experiences and developed similar strategies for living, they have formed something that is recognizable as American black culture. The manner in which many black males shake hands reflects a pattern of male camaraderie that has developed within an environment of discrimination and impoverishment and represents a symbolic demonstration of unity and cultural distinctiveness.

Subcultural variations are not static, for people interact with others outside 13
their subgroup, and they respond to change. In the case of black handshaking, whites adopted this system of gestures through their interaction with blacks. In turn some blacks have abandoned or altered these gestures since they no longer demonstrate cultural distinctiveness, and in time they may cease to be an element of black culture.

Production

Humans do not interact simply because they are so inclined or to develop 14
cultures. One important reason for our coming together and organizing our lives is to produce the material conditions that sustain or improve life. At the most basic level this production is of food and shelter, which are required for our survival. But beyond that is a desire to produce things that lift existence beyond a rudimentary level. Whether it is by gathering wild foods, hunting animals, and making implements to assist in such work or by growing foods and manufacturing the things of industrial society, all human societies devote a considerable amount of attention to production. In fact, it can be said that a society's organization, as well as its people's belief systems and values, will reflect their productive capability and strategy.

One main characteristic of the evolution of human society has been a pro- 15
gressive increase in productive capability. In very general terms, human society has evolved in recent centuries from reliance on the collection of natural foods,

through increasingly complex systems of agriculture, to a greater emphasis on industrial production. This evolutionary process has been closely interrelated with population growth and increased social scale. Human society has evolved from small bands scattered across the globe with limited productive capabilities to something which is millions of times larger, encompassing the entire globe in an ever more integrated fashion, and which is capable of production on a scale that far exceeds that of human society in the not too distant past.

This is not to imply that human society is concerned solely with produc- 16
tion—far from it. There are many other dimensions to human life. Nor is it intended to give the impression that all humans or all human societies share the same concern with production or that they should. It is not intended to attach any absolute value to increased production or to treat it as an evolutionary imperative: increased productive capability is not inevitable nor is it always an absolute benefit. Nevertheless, production is a fundamental part of human life and the demand and desire for increases in productive capabilities is widespread and an important aspect of the evolution of human society.

Although our initial definition of culture referred to customary behavior, 17
implying continuity, we should not ignore the fact that change too is a major feature of human existence: Culture, too, is dynamic. True, continuity often exists—black handshake patterns have persisted for several decades—but things rarely remain the same for long. In our more secure moments we may prefer to emphasize the unchanging nature of our social and physical universe, but change is never very far away.

Environmental Adaptation

The lives of humans, like those of other animals, are influenced by their 18
surroundings, by their *environment*: the *physical environment*, which involves things like climate, rainfall patterns, and terrain; the *biotic environment*—all of the plant and animal life in a given area; and the *social environment*—interaction with other members of our species. A coastal Californian's environment would include the beaches, the almost desertlike terrain and climate, the animals that have survived or thrived with human occupation, and the mixture of humanity that has been drawn to the region.

These different aspects of the environment and humans are interrelated in 19
complex and systematic ways. The study of the relationship between organisms and their physical, biotic, and social environments is called *ecology*. The study of ecology can be approached from a very general, all-encompassing perspective, or from a narrower focus, emphasizing one or a few aspects. The aspect that is of most relevance here is what is commonly termed *cultural ecology*, the study of how human culture and the environment are interrelated.

One of the primary tasks of cultural ecology is the study of human adapta- 20
tion. *Adaptation* is the process by which a population or an individual adjusts to environmental conditions in order to maintain itself and survive, if not prosper.

How an organism, species, or society adapts to its environment is called an *adaptive strategy*: the conscious or unconscious plans of action carried out by a population in response to its environment (Moran 1979: 325). The adaptive strategy of the Arctic-dwelling Inuit,* for example, includes the technologies and techniques Inuit have devised for hunting caribou, seals, and other animals in their environment, the types of clothing and shelter they manufacture or acquire through trade to survive in the harsh climatic conditions, and the ways in which they space themselves across the landscape, distribute food, control sexual relations, and manage interpersonal aggression.

Biological Adaptation

For virtually any species there are both biological and nonbiological aspects   21
of their adaptive strategy. The biological aspects are of three sorts. First, there are relatively short-term adjustments to the environment; for instance, humans sweat as the temperature rises. Then there are nongenetic adaptations. For example, in sedentary American society, exercise—jogging, aerobic dance, lifting weights—can alter an individual's physical attributes and contribute to a greater immunity to diseases and a longer life expectance—changes that will influence that individual's future adaptational capabilities. Finally, there are long-term biological changes that alter the physical characteristics of the population as a whole. These physical changes, which occur over generations, comprise *organic evolution*, the process by which populations adapt either continuously or suddenly at intervals (which one is currently the subject of considerable debate), to the opportunities and limitations of ever-changing environments. It is through the process of organic evolution over the past few million years that humans have come to assume their present characteristics.

The central mechanism of organic evolution is natural selection, which   22
serves to link biological change and the environment. Charles Darwin, the nineteenth-century pioneer in the study of organic evolution, defined *natural selection* as a process whereby the best-adapted members of a population assume genetic dominance, because they are better able to survive and multiply than other members of the same population. It is a key element in the adaptive strategy of most species, as they develop physical peculiarities that allow them to exploit their surroundings better.

Cultural Adaptation

Physical alterations are not necessary for comfortable living in an environ-   23
ment, however. In addition to our biological flexibility, we humans can adjust our activity patterns, clothing, shelter, diet, and so forth, and by so doing create a relatively comfortable microenvironment for ourselves. Through culture we are capable of adapting relatively quickly to almost any earthly envi-

---

* The term "Inuit" is used instead of "Eskimo" throughout the text, the latter being a European term for the native peoples of the Arctic, while the former is an indigenous term currently used for purposes of identification by the indigenous peoples of the Arctic themselves.

ronment. We may not always like the setting within which we find ourselves, and some environments are much easier for us to prosper in than others, but we humans are capable of devising ways to survive almost anywhere.

Freed from many of the biological and environmental constraints facing other organisms, humans have created a great diversity of adaptational strategies. The most significant of these are reviewed in Chapter 5. These strategies are ways that groups of humans have learned to exploit their particular environment to promote their survival or prosperity. *Exploitation* in its most basic sense means to turn to economic account, or to utilize. It is common to think of exploitation in terms of minerals, plants, and animals. But other human beings may serve as resources within the environment as well. The adaptive strategies we adopt in exploiting our surroundings rely primarily on three aspects of culture: technology, social organization, and ideology. For the sake of clarity, it is useful to treat these aspects separately. They are, nonetheless, closely interrelated. 24

Because of its concrete results, the role of *technology*—the skills and knowledge by which people make things or extract resources—is the most obvious part of an adaptive strategy. The indigenous people of the Arctic, the Inuit, devised an array of technical means for meeting their subsistence needs and for achieving a reasonable level of comfort. They used spears, harpoons, hooks, and traps to catch and kill animals. To move across the sea and land they built boats and sleds and made snowshoes. To protect themselves from the elements they produced an array of clothes made from animal skins and built dwellings of ice and skins. All these activities took knowledge of local resources and technical skills passed down until very recently as part of Inuit culture. 25

The ways people organize themselves socially are as important a part of their adaptation as is their technology. One important social dimension of an adaptive strategy is the way labor is divided. In procuring plant and animal resources, traditional Australian Aboriginal foragers divided their labor primarily according to gender: Males hunted larger animals and females gathered plants. We speak of this differentiation of activities within a society as the *division of labor*. In our own society, the division of labor is more complex than that of Aborigines, involving highly specialized activities unheard of in any foraging society. How labor is divided in a society reflects the nature of its adaptive strategy as well as environmental conditions, particularly the resources available. 26

The availability of resources also influences other social aspects of an adaptive strategy, such as the size of groups. In the dry Great Basin area, where Shoshone Indians lived as foragers until the nineteenth century, food resources were too scarce to support large populations on a permanent basis. Accordingly, during the winter months single families went off by themselves, gathering food independent of other families. During the summer, when food resources were a bit more plentiful, the Shoshone formed larger, multifamily groups. 27

The third cultural component of an adaptive strategy is *ideology*—a people's   28
values and beliefs. To many hunters, being able to recite the correct prayers is
as important in hunting as is knowing how to set a trap or stalk an animal. A
person's views of how to go about living in the world are not based solely on
observable facts. How individuals interact with the environment is conditioned
by their society's beliefs concerning the nature of the universe. The religious
beliefs of Australian Aborigines stress harmonious relations with the environment. Through myth and ritual, these beliefs link humans with their natural
environment, space people across the landscape, and promote the well-being of
plant and animal resources. By contrast, miners and industrialists approach the
world aggressively; their allegiance is to the wider industrial society that spans
the globe, rather than to an arid piece of desert.

Studying Cultural Variations

We live in a very complex world inhabited by groups of people pursuing a   29
multitude of different interests and holding very different views about the nature of things in the universe, how they are related, and how the whole thing
works. Each of us is to some degree the product of a specific social setting and
associated cultural tradition. Our views are shaped by these factors in such a
way as to make any universally applicable perception of the world order unlikely. It is difficult for us to see the forests for the trees, for our vision is
blocked or restricted by the limitations of our own circumstances.

It is to this complexity of personal viewpoints and to the tremendous varia-   30
tion present in the human experience that the discipline of anthropology addresses itself. Simply defined, *anthropology* is the scientific study of humanity.
Anthropology is not unique in this regard, since historians, economists, philos-
ophers, medical researchers, psychologists, and theologians—to name but a
few—are also students of the human condition. What is different about anthropology is not so much *what* is studied as *how* it is studied. Anthropology is
distinguishable from other branches of human studies in the emphasis it places
on universalism, holism, integration, and cultural relativism.

Universalism

A fundamental principle of modern anthropology is that all peoples are fully   31
and equally human: whether Bushman, Inuit, or Irish, we are all of one species. There are no races that are "closer to the ape," and none that is more
highly evolved than the others. Since we are all equally human, anthropologists
are as interested in the Bam Buti (or Pygmies) and Australian Aborigines as
they are in people living in the industrial societies of North America and Western Europe. No human group is too small, too remote, too ancient, or too
unusual to merit the anthropologist's attention. *All* human beings—the living
and the dead, the familiar and the exotic—are the subject of anthropological
studies. They all tell us something important about the human condition, about
the potentialities and limitations of the human species.

Holism

Economists study systems of production, exchange, and consumption. Polit-   32
ical scientists study the bases of social order and conflict and the distribution
and dynamics of power and authority. Other scholars in human studies select
other specific facets of human experience for intensive study. Anthropologists,
on the other hand, seek to comprehend *all* aspects of the human condition.
Anthropologists want to understand a society's economy and political organization, but they also want to know about its religion, its rules of marriage and
etiquette, its language, its technology, and how its children are raised. Furthermore, they look at humans as a species of animals. Thus, the holistic orientation in anthropology includes recognition of both the biological and the cultural
aspects of human existence. Attention to all these facets of the human condition
is based on the notion that the parts and the whole are interrelated and, furthermore, that we can only understand the parts to the extent to which we understand the whole and how the various parts fit into it. Anthropologists therefore
study all phenomena in relation to an encompassing whole and are interested in
studying all the parts to further our knowledge of the nature of the totality.
They are careful to point out, however, that the whole is not merely the sum of
its parts—just as a human is more than a collection of cells, organs, blood,
bone, and so on.

Integration

The anthropological concept of holism argues that the various components   33
of human existence are integrated. To the anthropologist, it is not enough to
study, say, Navajo politics, art, religion, kinship, economics, and so on. The
anthropologist views these aspects of Navajo culture as integral and as integrated parts of the larger biological and social environment within which the
Navajo live: the arid lands of Arizona and United States society. Full comprehension of any custom is possible only when we take into account the broader
context within which the custom occurs. Anthropologists are constantly striving
to achieve that more inclusive perspective.

Cultural Relativism

In addition to its scientific goals, anthropology also has the aim of promot-   34
ing understanding among those of different cultural backgrounds. The most
important factor inhibiting our understanding of other peoples is ethnocentrism.
Ethnocentrism is the interpretation of the behavior of others in terms of one's
own cultural values and traditions. In its extreme expressions, ethnocentrism is
cultural chauvinism—the attitude that one's own customs and beliefs are auto-
matically and unquestionably superior to those of others.

Anthropologist I. M. Lewis has remarked that "ethnocentrism is the natural   35
condition of mankind." Every person who is raised in a society is taught from
earliest childhood how to think and act. This thorough indoctrination in the

values of one's own culture is a lifelong process. The basic values and standards of our culture are continuously reinforced in religion, in public ceremonies, on television, at sports events, and at cocktail parties. Wherever we go, we are tutored in what is considered to be true, real, just, desirable, and important. Furthermore, we are not mere recipients of this indoctrination. Each of us is a teacher of others as well as a student. Through the constant give and take of social interaction we come to share beliefs, customs, and behavior patterns with other people and hence create our own culture.

In some respects, the built-in ethnocentrism of all cultures serves as a positive force. It can give a people a sense of pride, well-being, and security. This is the aim of many consciousness-raising movements among ethnic minorities, such as Black Power, Red Power, and Brown Power. But ethnocentrism has a negative side as well. Extreme ethnocentrism is at the heart of all bigotry and discrimination. Oppressors have always justified their empires with an ideology that those they oppress and exploit are "backward," "primitive," or in some other way inferior. As was the case with eighteenth- and nineteenth-century European colonialists, oppressors often proclaim that by forcing their own systems and values on others, they are selflessly providing inferior peoples with the opportunity to improve their lot. But in fact they are often doing little more than destroying these peoples' way of life and seizing their lands.   36

Ethnocentrism does not promote understanding. In order to understand others, it is necessary to adopt a position of cultural relativism. *Cultural relativism* is judging and interpreting the behavior and beliefs of others in terms of *their* traditions and experiences. What is right in one culture is not necessarily right in, or for, another. In many cultures, the killing of infants is an accepted practice. Most Americans would judge infanticide to be morally wrong regardless of the circumstances. But in many societies, there are no safe and effective means of contraception or abortion, so birth control is sometimes carried out after the fact. This practice regulates a proper spacing of births and may, in addition, help to maintain a low density of population in regions where there is a scarcity of basic resources. In such a context, infanticide is a rational way of trying to avoid the problems associated with overpopulation or too rapid a rate of birth.   37

Cultural relativism does not mean that anything a particular people does or thinks must be approved or accepted without criticism. Rather, it means we should evaluate cultural patterns within the context of their occurrence.   38

The Fields of Anthropology

While the discipline of anthropology strives for a complete and systematic picture of humanity, no single individual possibly could command a detailed understanding of every aspect of the lives of all peoples. Consequently, specialization in anthropology is a practical necessity. Most anthropologists select one or two aspects of the human condition for intensive study, yet remain interested   39 in relating their own specialized findings to what workers in other areas are doing. The major subdivisions of anthropology are physical (or biological) anthropology and sociocultural anthropology, each of which has many branches.

Physical Anthropology

Physical anthropology is the study of humanity as a biological phenomenon. Physical anthropologists study specimens both living and dead. Some study *fossils*, traces or remains of once-living organisms. By looking at the fossil remains of our now extinct forebears they can answer questions about when our ancestors began walking upright and at what stage of evolution humans achieved brain sizes of modern proportions. A complete picture of what life was like for our ancestors and how and why we evolved requires that the physical anthropologist enlist the aid of other specialists: paleoanthropologists, who specialize in the study of ancient human and prehuman society and provide data on ancient plant and animal life; geologists, who explain local physical and climatic conditions; and archaeologists, who provide information concerning our ancestors' tools, houses, and other material remains. 40

Other physical anthropologists specialize in investigating the biological diversity of modern populations. Since they are dealing with flesh-and-blood specimens, and not just bones and teeth, they have the opportunity to study such visible characteristics as skin color and hair texture. They can also look at traits that are all but invisible, such as blood types and genes. It is possible for them to study in detail the biological adjustments contemporary humans make to their surroundings as well. 41

A major branch of physical anthropology that scarcely existed before the 1950s is *primatology*, the study of our nearest living relatives—apes, monkeys, and prosimians. Some primatologists focus on the study of primate biology, but more specialize in investigating the social behavior of primates such as chimpanzees, gorillas, and baboons. These studies contribute to our understanding of the behavior of our prehuman ancestors. For example, since primatologist Jane Goodall found that wild chimpanzees make and use crude tools on a fairly consistent basis, many paleoanthropologists have concluded that tool-using behavior among our ancestors is probably much more ancient than previously supposed. 42

Sociocultural Anthropology

Sociocultural anthropology is the study of the social, symbolic, and material lives of humans. While physical anthropology concentrates on the study of the biological basis of the human condition, sociocultural anthropology is concerned with the social inheritance of humankind—all those aspects of human existence which are passed on through social and cultural experience rather than through genes. This endeavor takes three major forms—archaeology, anthropological linguistics, and ethnology, each of which contains numerous specialized branches. 43

Archaeology.   *Archaeology* is the study of the material remains of people.   44
Thus, while the physical anthropologist tries to reconstruct human evolution
through the interpretation of fossils, the archaeologist attempts to reconstruct
extinct societies and their cultures through the interpretation of *artifacts*, objects of human manufacture. For the most part, the archaeologist is limited to
studying those expressions of human culture which are material and which may
be preserved over long periods of time. This means that while the archaeologist
is able to learn a fair amount about tools, weapons, pottery, diets, and house
types of a long-extinct society, he or she will probably learn little about its
nonmaterial culture, such as its kinship system and language unless supplemen-
tary evidence is available (such as early written accounts). But physical evidence can suggest insights about nonmaterial aspects of extinct societies. For
example, the discovery of Neanderthal burial sites containing bones laid out in
a sleeping position and accompanied by tools and the remains of a meal suggests that these early humans must have believed in some kind of afterlife.

One of the major branches of archaeology is *prehistory*, the study of ancient   45
preliterate cultures. In reconstructing the cultural lives of ancient peoples, prehistorians rely not only on material remains but also on the study of contemporary peoples whose life-styles are comparable with those of past societies. By
studying present-day foragers, prehistorians can learn more about the ways in
which our foraging ancestors lived: how they hunted, how they spaced themselves across the land, the nature of their religious beliefs, and so forth.

Another significant branch of archaeology is the field of *historical archaeol-*   46
ogy. While many societies have left written records of their activities, these
records are never a complete reflection of the people's lives. Archaeologists
have become very good at extracting information from the incomplete material
remains of these societies in order to catch every possible clue to what the daily
lives of peoples of the past were like. Archaeological excavations at Pompeii
and in the Nile Valley have provided detailed information on everything from
people's religious practices to their eating habits. Likewise, recent excavations
in California are yielding much new information about the daily operation of
old Spanish missions and helping us to learn more about the early contacts
between Native Americans and Europeans in the New World. These successes
are partly due to the highly refined techniques of excavation and methods of
analysis employed by archaeologists, but credit also goes to other specialists—
such as historians, chemists, and biologists—who contribute their skills to the
archaeological enterprise.

Anthropological Linguistics.   The anthropological study of language, *an-*   47
thropological linguistics, is another major branch of sociocultural anthropology. Language is perhaps the most important single element of culture, because
it is largely through language that we acquire and transmit culture to others. An
entire chapter of this text is devoted to anthropological linguistics (Chapter 4);
for now, we will simply identify its main subfields.

Descriptive linguistics deals with how languages are constructed and how   48
the various parts are interrelated to form coherent systems of communication.
Historical linguistics concerns the evolution of languages (how languages grow
and change). *Sociolinguistics* studies the relationship between language and social factors, such as class, ethnicity, age, and sex. Finally, a general field of
study that is of interest to many anthropological linguists is *language and culture*, the examination of the ways language might affect how we think, or,
conversely, how our beliefs and values might influence our linguistic behavior.

Ethnology. *Ethnology*, the systematic, comparative study of patterns and   49
processes in living and recent cultures, is by far the largest branch of sociocultural anthropology. Historically, and at present, ethnology has been divided
into a number of theoretical perspectives. These will be dealt with at length in
the next chapter.

Ethnologists are divided not only by differing theoretical traditions, but also   50
by other forms of specialization. Ethnology, which concerns understanding
how and why cultures work, is built on a body of descriptive material in which
the vast array of human beliefs, practices, and achievements are laid out. This
process of describing individual cultures—largely through fieldwork—is called
ethnography. The amount of ethnographic information available on all human
cultures is far too vast to be studied in depth by a single individual; most
ethnologists specialize in the ethnography of one or two geographical areas,
such as sub-Saharan Africa or the Amazonian Basin. Usually, an ethnologist
will have done firsthand research among some group in the area, and for purposes of comparison and background will also be informed about other peoples
in the region. In addition to geographic specialization, most ethnologists choose
one or two subject areas, such as religion, politics, kinship, or economics, for
intensive study.

Because ethnology and cultural anthropology are virtually the same thing,   51
we have no need to go into greater detail at this point. Use of the term *cultural
anthropology* is largely a reflection of American academic tradition. In areas of
British influence, *social anthropology* is preferred. The two terms represent
different intellectual orientations and histories, although that is less true now
than in the past. We have sought to blend the terms to ensure that our perspective is as holistic as possible.

A Holistic View of Sociocultural Anthropology

Coherence and direction in offering a holistic view of human culture is   52
achieved by building the synthesis on a few central themes, and looking at how
they are related to people's behaviors, perceptions, and material culture and to
the physical world. These themes are *integration, adaptation, context*, and *dynamism*. All have been discussed to some degree, but let us look more closely
at how they will be used in the chapters that follow.

Regarding integration, we will look at how specific beliefs and practices are   53
related to other aspects of culture and to the encompassing environment. In
trying to understand why people believe or act as they do, the anthropologist
seeks to determine *causal relationships* among various phenomena. By looking
at the various factors that produce a certain pattern of medical treatment, for
example, we are trying to understand *why* that pattern exists and not some
other. Methods of health care in Western industrial societies do not reflect an
absolute medical standard for the treatment of illness; they are the product of a
particular cultural tradition. To understand doctor-patient relations within this
tradition requires looking beyond the physiological manifestations of the patient's illness and investigating such things as the ethnic and class backgrounds
of the patient and doctor, the cultural rules for doctor-patient interaction, and
the views of members of the culture toward the particular disease.

Direct causes are not always easy to determine. It is often more useful to   54
think of *conditioning factors*: the range of interrelated factors that set the stage
for something. This entails delving beyond the immediate to the less apparent
motivating factors. For example, alcoholism among Native Americans is commonly explained as a result of unemployment, the availability of liquor, or the
destruction of their traditional culture. No one would deny that these are con-
tributing factors, but a full understanding of the causes of Native American
alcoholism requires that we look at the conditions in American society that
deny these people a viable place in that society, and that destroyed their traditional way of life.

Our second theme is adaptation. As has already been noted, humans have   55
devised a wide range of strategies for adapting to their environments. While
recognizing this diversity, in this text we will pay special attention to two
fundamental patterns of adaptation that are associated with social scale: small-
scale and large-scale. *Small-scale societies* are characterized by localized social
interaction and the exploitation of local resources. This localized orientation
makes them relatively autonomous. For example, before their incorporation
into Canadian society, the Inuit were largely independent of neighboring people. Although they did maintain relations with these neighbors, the Inuit preferred relations within their own fairly narrow social and spatial boundaries and
relied almost exclusively on local resources for their subsistence needs.

Large-scale societies, by contrast, are much less localized in orientation and   56
much more dependent on extensive and highly specialized interchange of
goods, ideas, and people. Some large-scale societies, such as those of Canada
or India, encompass large and diverse populations and areas. Others, such as
the island nations of Fiji or Tonga, are much smaller and more homogeneous.
In these small nations, there is a high degree of social complexity and an orientation toward social and economic exchange beyond the local level that is not
found in small-scale societies. While traditional Inuit moved about almost exclusively in the Arctic and manufactured most of the things that they needed
from resources close at hand, Fijians maintain significant social and economic
ties with others the world over.

Few small-scale societies are left in the world today, although some societies exhibit vestiges of their more independent pasts. Why this is so relates to our third theme, context. Adaptational strategies exist in relation to an environmental context, and the context within which most people live is one of an increasingly integrated world. One of the givens of this text is that are no known societies in the world today that are completed isolated. An analysis of any society, whether Fijian or Inuit, requires that we look at how that society fits within the context of this world system. This is not to say that local environmental conditions are not important; but the meanings they assume for those living there are strongly influenced by the international system. To most Pacific islanders their immediate physical surroundings are of considerable significance, but primarily in terms of their ability to attract tourists, international fishing fleets, or multinational mining companies and to produce wealth that is recognized in an international context.

The underpinnings of this worldwide social system are found in international trade. The manner in which societies are integrated into this system reflects their place in an international division of labor. As Immanuel Wallerstein (1979: 5) has noted, the defining characteristic of a social system is "the existence within it of a division of labor, such that various sectors or areas within it are dependent upon economic exchange with others for the smooth and continuous provisioning of the needs of the area." In small-scale societies this division of labor may occur within a single family or village. In large-scale societies like the United States there is a division of labor within national boundaries —there are factory workers, teachers, government bureaucrats, and so forth. But this division of labor and, in fact, almost all aspects of life in the United States are influenced by the place this nation has within the encompassing world system. The used-car salesman cannot be understood without reference to international considerations regarding the production and exchange of oil and automobiles. The *world system*, then, is a social system encompassing the entire world and entailing a single division of labor. Throughout the chapters that follow, we will refer to how people's beliefs and practices are related to this world order.

Our final theme is dynamism By *dynamism* we mean that human culture is in a constant state of flux, always changing, always evolving. The present world system did not always exist; there is no assurance that it always will. The roots of this dynamism are in the very nature of human cultural adaptation. Our reliance on culture has provided us with a valuable adaptive mechanism, allowing us tremendous flexibility, but it has left us vulnerable as well. Like other animals, we must reproduce ourselves biologically in order to ensure our continued survival; but, unlike most other animals, we must also seek to reproduce our culture. We must reproduce the knowledge and organizational patterns we have developed to acquire, produce, and distribute what we need or desire. People of the Fly River area of New Guinea traditionally have sought to ensure cultural reproduction by dramatic initiation rites in which youths are instilled with desired values and knowledge. In our society we use schools, television, and so on toward much the same end. However, people are not always able or even willing to reproduce things exactly as they were before. Conditions change, our goals, strategies, and knowledge change, and in the process human culture continues to evolve.

Summary

Like other animals, we humans are influenced both by our biological 60 makeup and by our environment. But we differ greatly from other animals in the degree to which we have developed culture—learned and socially shared ways of behaving and thinking. We also differ from each other; cultural practices vary considerably from one society to the next and even among subgroups of the same society.

For humans, the environment to which our behaviors must be adapted in- 61 cludes social as well as biological factors. Cultural ecology is the study of interrelationships between humans and this multifaceted environment. Some adaptations are physiological changes—short-term, developmental, or passed down over long periods of time through evolutionary processes. Others are cultural strategies involving technology, social organization, and ideology.

Anthropology is the scientific study of humanity's varied behaviors. Anthro- 62 pologists strive for a universal, holistic, integrated, and relativistic approach. Because their topic—all of humanity—is so broad and varied, individual anthropologists explore only pieces of it. Physical anthropologists study biological data on living and ancient humans and primates. Sociocultural anthropologists focus on cultural aspects of human life. One branch, archaeology, studies artifacts and other clues to the lives of ancient peoples, both those who left written records and earlier peoples who did not. Another branch, anthropological linguistics, studies the structure and characteristics of languages for clues to understanding cultures and cultural processes. The third branch of sociocultural anthropology, ethnology, analyzes ethnographic descriptions of recent and living populations for general patterns and processes.

To pull together the piecemeal insights of anthropology, this book follows 63 four themes to see how they are related to the three chief aspects of culture—behaviors, perceptions, and material production. These themes—integration, adaptation, context, and dynamism—can be applied in varying degrees to all societies.

Suggested Readings

These are a few books that introduce the discipline and the people anthropologists study:

Bowen, Elenore Smith. 1964. *Return to laughter*. New York: Doubleday/Anchor. (Africa)

Duvignaud, Jean. 1977. *Change at Shebika*. Austin: University of Texas Press. (North Africa)

Fernea, Elizabeth. 1969. *Guests of the sheik*. New York: Doubleday/Anchor. (Middle East)

Liebow, Elliot. 1967. *Tally's corner*. Boston: Little, Brown. (United States)

Read, Kenneth. 1980. *The high valley*. New York: Columbia Univ. Press. (Papua New Guinea)

Ruesch, Hans. 1950. *Top of the world*. New York: Harper & Row. (Arctic North America)

Service, Elman. 1978. *Profiles in ethnology*. New York: Harper & Row. (brief descriptions of twenty-three different societies)

Siskind, Janet. 1973. *To hunt in the morning*. New York: Oxford. (South America)

Thomas, Elizabeth Marshall. 1959. *The harmelss people*. New York: Vintage. (Southern Africa)

Turnbull, Colin. 1962. *The forest people*. New York: Doubleday/Anchor. (Central Africa)

Wikan, Unni. 1980. *Life among the poor in Cairo*. London: Tavistock. (Urban Egypt)

Wilson, Carter. 1974. *Crazy February*. Berkeley: University of California Press. (Southern Mexico)

from *Contemporary Cultural Anthropology* (1989) by Michael C. Howard

QUESTIONS FROM SKIMMING   In the left-hand column below, wrote down the questions you expect the selection will answer, along with the appropriate page number(s). Reread the selection carefully, and use the right-hand column to record the answers to the questions after you have compared your questions to those of your classmates and to the list of Questions on the Text that follows.

QUESTIONS (put page number after question)	ANSWERS

QUESTIONS (put page number after question)	ANSWERS

Compare your questions to those listed here.

Are human beings different from other animals? In what ways?

How is *culture* defined?

What are the three principal aspects of culture? What examples are there of each?

What is *learning*?

How does learning contribute to culture? How is culture transmitted?

How is *society* defined?

Why does culture depend on society?

Why does society depend on culture?

What examples are there of societies within societies and cultures within cultures?

How do cultures and subcultures change?

Why do human societies devote so much attention to production?

How has human society evolved in terms of production?

What are the three kinds of *environment* that influence human development?

What is meant by *ecology*? What is *cultural ecology*?

What is meant by *adaptation* and *adaptive strategy*?

What are the three kinds of *biological adaptation*? What are examples of each?

What is meant by *organic evolution*?

Why is *natural selection* the central mechanism of organic evolution?

What is *cultural adaptation*? How is it different from biological adaptation?

What are the three aspects of culture that contribute to the adaptive strategies we use to exploit our surroundings?

What is meant by *technology*? What is its role in cultural adaptation?

What are some examples of technology?

What is the relationship between social organization and cultural adaptation?

What is one important social dimension of a society's adaptive strategy? What example is given?

How does the availability of resources affect other aspects of an adaptive strategy? What example is given?

What is meant by ideology? What are some examples?

What is *anthropology*?

How is it different from other branches of human study?

What is meant by *universalism*?

What is meant by *holism*?

What is meant by *integration*?

What is meant by *cultural relativism*?

What is *ethocentrism*?

Why does everybody tend to be ethnocentric?

What are the positive and negative aspects of ethnocentrism?

What example is given of cultural relativism?

What are the fields of anthropology?

What is *physical anthropology*?

What are *fossils*? How are they connected to physical anthropology?

Why do some physical anthropologists specialize in modern populations?

What is *primatology*?

What example is given of a primatologist's work?

What is *sociolcultural anthropology*?

What are the three major forms of sociocultural anthropology?

What is *archaeology*?

What are *artifacts*?

What are archaeologists able to find out about in material terms? in nonmaterial terms? What example is given?

What are the branches of archaeology? What is studied in each of these branches?

What is *anthropological linguistics*?

What are its main subfields?

What is *ethnology*?

How is ethnology divided?

What is *ethnography*?

In what kinds of subjects do ethnologists specialize?

What are the four central themes in this anthropology test?

How do anthropologists try to relate specific facts or phenomena to other aspects of a given culture or environment?

What two types of society will be particularly considered in this book? What will they show? What examples are given of each?

What factor is common between virtually all societies of the world today? What examples are given?

How does human society reproduce itself?

How does it change?

What examples are given?

QUESTIONS BEYOND THE TEXT

1. Can you think of any specific cultural differences between yourself and people you know (perhaps other people in your class)—that is, differences in the way the groups to which you belong organize their behavior and thought in relation to their environment? Think, for example, of cooking and eating habits or of child-rearing methods.

2. Have you observed a child learning your own culture? Think about any instances you may have seen of children being taught particular patterns of behavior (for example, table manners) which would be different in another culture.

3. How would you identify the society, and the societies within that society, to which you belong? What are the symbolic ways of demonstrating your membership in those societies?

4. In what different physical environments have you or your friends lived? How did you or they adapt to those environments? Were these biological or cultural adaptations?

5. In what respects do the values of your own culture differ radically from those of another culture with which you have come in contact? Why do you think these differences in values exist?

OUTLINE NOTES   The only part of this selection that lends itself to outlining are paragraphs
                          39–59. Here is a partial outline; you are asked to complete it.

The Fields of Anthropology

I. Physical Anthropology

    1. Study of Human Evolution
       Evidence from fossil remains
       Collaboration with other specialists:

         a. _____

         b. _____

         c. _____

    2. Study of Modern Populations
       a. Human populations

       _____

       b. Primatology

       _____

II. Sociocultural Anthropology

    1. Archaeology
       Definition:

       _____

       Branches:
       a. Prehistory

       _____

         b. _____

       _____

    2. Anthropological Linguistics
       Definition:

       _____

       Branches:

         a. _____

       _____

         b. _____

       _____

         c. _____

       _____

        d. _____

        _____

  3. _____

        Based on _____
        Divided by:

        a. _____

        b. _____

        c. _____

VOCABULARY NOTES

The first part of this selection (paragraphs 5–37) is devoted to laying out some basic ideas and defining the terms used in the book. Some of these terms will be new words to you; others won't be new in themselves, but the definitions probably will be. You need to understand these terms in order to understand the selection, and so you should record them and their definitions. The terms that the writer thinks are important are either printed in *italics*, or used as subheadings: find them, make an alphabetized list (including paragraph references), and compare it with the list below. Then look up the paragraph references and write the definition beside each word; because precision is important here, it may be best to quote the definition from the text, but if you do so, be sure to enclose the definition in quotation marks and record the bibliographic information (the name of the author, the date of publication, and the page number).

    adaptation (paragraph 20)
    adaptive strategy (paragraph 20)
    anthropology (paragraph 30)
    culture (paragraph 5)
    cultural relativism (paragraph 37)
    division of labor (paragraph 26)
    ecology (paragraph 19)
    environment (paragraph 18)
        physical environment
        biotic environment
        social environment
    ethnocentrism (paragraph 34)
    exploitation (paragraph 24)
    holism (paragraph 32)
    ideology (paragraph 28)
    instincts (paragraph 2)
    integration (paragraph 33)
    learning (paragraph 6)

natural selection (paragraph 22)
organic evolution (paragraph 21)
society (paragraph 10)
subcultures (paragraph 11)
technology (paragraph 25)
universalism (paragraph 31)

PERSONAL INDEX   If you have learned all these terms, you probably will not need notes of the general principles described in paragraphs 5–37, for they will be fairly easy to remember. The examples, however, will not, for they involve unfamiliar peoples whose names may be new to you. Furthermore, you can expect many more such examples to come up in a course in anthropology. To help you keep such examples sorted out in your mind, you may want to record them on index cards as you read them in the text, using the names of the different peoples as titles for the cards. Then when one of the same peoples is mentioned in a different place, add the new information to the appropriate card. Here is what one such card might look like; the information on it is taken from paragraphs 20, 25, and 55 of the selection, but the page references shown here are to the original book. Because all the information on this card comes from the same book, the name of the author and date of publication is given only once, at the top; but a page reference is given for each point.

INUIT (Howard 1989)

People of the Arctic, also called "Eskimos" (8)
Adaptive strategy: hunting caribou, seal, etc.; clothes and buildings
    for cold climate (9–10)
Technology: spears, harpoons, hooks, traps; boats, sleds,
    snowshoes; use of skins (10–11)
Traditionally small-scale societies—relations within narrow social
    and spatial boundaries; needs supplied only from local resources
    (18)

Try making similar cards for the following:

Australian Aborigines
Shoshone Indians

What other peoples mentioned in the selection could you make cards for?
    You could also make cards for the names of individual scholars, such as
Charles Darwin.

ESSAY TOPICS   You will almost certainly want to read the selection again before you write an essay on either of the following topics. But think about the topic you plan to write about before you reread, and write down any points that come to mind. As you reread, make additional rough notes about the topic. Finally, sort your notes by rewriting them in outline form. It should then be relatively easy to write the essay.

As with other selections, a sample outline for an essay on one of the topics follows. If you decide to focus on topic 1, construct your own outline before looking at the one given here.

1. What are anthropologists interested in studying? What principles guide their approach to the subject, and what kinds of evidence do they draw on?

2. Human beings live in a wide variety of physical environments. Explain how they are able to adapt to such different conditions.

Essay Outline (Topic 1)

I. Anthropologists Study Human Beings as a Species
  1. Physical characteristics
     a. Evolution
     b. Relationship with other primates
     c. Biological differences among different groups of humans
  2. Cultural Characteristics
     a. Prehistory
     b. Variety of modern cultures
II. Principles
  1. Universalism
  2. Holism
  3. Integration
III. Evidence
  1. Physical Anthropology
     a. Fossil remains
     b. Observations of modern primates
     c. Biological data from modern peoples
  2. Cultural Anthropology
     a. Material artifacts recovered by archaeology
     b. Ethnographic data from modern peoples

Mendel's Principles of Genetics

This selection is from *Principles of Genetics*, an introductory book on the branch of biology that deals with how hereditary characteristics are transmitted from one generation to another. As such, it is a bit more specialized than the other selections, and if you do not have much background in biology, you may find it more difficult. It does, however, explain its topic clearly, and because the topic itself is important for understanding the natural world, it is well worth investing some time and effort in it.

Treat the selection in the same way you have the others: skim it first and list the questions that it seems to be answering. You may find, however, that the material is so unfamiliar that you cannot tell what it is about by merely skimming—that you must read most of it in order to come up with the questions. That is fine, and it illustrates one of the key points of this book—namely, that the most appropriate strategy for reading a text depends on the material that you're working with as well as on why you are reading it. Try, however, to read the material this first time as fast as you can, and don't worry if you don't understand everything yet.

Once you have a list of questions, use them together with those listed under Questions on the Text as a guide for your second reading. Try to find an answer to each one, and then think about and discuss the Questions beyond the Text. If you are working on your own, write down the answers to both types of questions.

1 Both this book and the subject of genetics are concerned with understanding the mechanisms and controls of the process by which genes are transmitted, are expressed, direct the formation of the individual, and are affected in the course of evolution. In this section of the book we are concerned with the rules of transmission of genes, the units that control and determine the processes of development and the ultimate appearance of individuals. Gregor Mendel discovered these rules of inheritance—we derive and expand upon his rules in this chapter.

2 In 1900 three botanists, Carl Correns of Germany, Erich von Tschermak of Austria, and Hugo DeVries of Holland, simultaneously and independently rediscovered the rules governing the transmission of traits from parent to offspring. These rules had been previously published in 1866 by an obscure Austrian monk named Gregor Mendel. Although his work was widely available after 1866, it was not until the turn of the century that the scientific community was ready to appreciate Mendel's great contribution. There were at least four reasons for this lapse of 34 years.

3 First, before Mendel's experiments, biologists were primarily concerned with explaining the transmission of characteristics that could be measured on a

continuous scale such as height, cranium size, and longevity. They were looking for rules of inheritance that would explain such **continuous variations**,
especially after Darwin's theory of evolution was put forth in 1859. Mendel,
however, suggested that inherited characteristics were discrete and constant
(**discontinuous**): Peas were either yellow or green. Evolutionists were looking
for small changes in traits with continuous variation, whereas Mendel presented
them with rules for discontinuous variation. His principles did not seem to
cover the type of variation that biologists thought prevailed. Second, there was
no physical element with which Mendel's inherited particles could be identified. One could not say, upon reading Mendel's work, that a certain subunit of
the cell followed Mendel's rules. Third, Mendel worked with large numbers of
offspring and converted these numbers to ratios of observed classes. Biologists,
practitioners of a very descriptive science at the time, were not well trained in
mathematical tools. And last, Mendel was not well known and did not perse-
vere in his attempts to convince the academic community.

Between 1865 and 1900, two major changes took place in biological sci-   4
ence. First, by the turn of the century, not only had scientists discovered chro-
mosomes, but also they had learned to understand their movement during cell
division. Second, biologists were more prepared to handle mathematics by the
turn of the century than they were during Mendel's time.

Mendel's Experiments

Gregor Mendel was an Austrian monk (of Brünn, Austria, which is now   5
Brno, Czechoslovakia). The essence of his experiments was to **crossbreed**
plants that had discrete, nonoverlapping characteristics and then to observe the
distribution of these characteristics in the next several generations. Mendel
worked with the common garden pea plant, *Pisum sativum*. He chose the pea
plant for several reasons. (1) The garden pea was an ideal plant with which to
work because of its ease in cultivation and relatively short life cycle. (2) The
plant had discontinuous characteristics such as flower color and pea texture. (3)
In part because of its anatomy, pollination of the plant could be easily controlled—foreign pollen could be kept out, and **cross-fertilization** could be arti-
ficially accomplished.

Figure 1-1 shows a cross section of the pea flower and indicates the keel in   6
which the anthers and stigma develop. Normally, **self-fertilization** occurs when
pollen falls onto the stigma before the bud opens. Mendel cross-fertilized the
plants by opening the keep of a flower before the anthers matured and by
placing pollen from another plant on the stigma. In more than 10,000 plants
examined by Mendel, only a very few were fertilized other than the way he had
intended them to be (either self- or cross-pollinated).

Mendel used plants that had been obtained from suppliers and grew them for   7
two years to ascertain that they were homogeneous, or true-breeding, for the
particular characteristic under study. He chose for study the seven characteris-

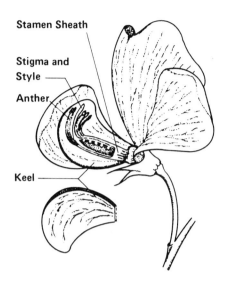

Figure 1-1 Anatomy of the Garden Pea Plant Flower

tics shown in Figure 1-2. Take as an example the characteristic of plant height. While height is often continuously distributed, Mendel used plants that showed only two alternatives: very tall or dwarf. He made the crosses shown in Figure 1-3. In the parental, or P_1, generation, tall plants were pollinated by dwarf plants, and in a **reciprocal cross** dwarf plants were pollinated by tall ones to determine whether the results were independent of the parents' sex. As we will see later on, some traits have inheritance patterns related to the sex of the parents carrying the traits. In these cases reciprocal crosses give different results; with Mendel's tall and dwarf pea plants, the results were the same.

Offspring of the cross of P_1, individuals are referred to as the first **filial generation**, F_1. Mendel also referred to them as **hybrids** because they were the offspring of unlike parents (tall and dwarf). We will specifically refer to the offspring of tall and dwarf peas as **monohybrids** because they are hybrid for only one characteristic (height). Since all the F_1 offspring plants were tall, Mendel referred to tallness as the **dominant** trait. The alternative, dwarfness, he referred to as **recessive**. When the F_1 offspring were self-fertilized to form the F_2 generation, both tall and dwarf offspring occurred; the dwarf characteristic reappeared. Among the F_2 offspring Mendel observed 787 tall and 277 dwarf plants for a ratio of 2.84 to 1. It is an indication of Mendel's insight that he recognized in these numbers an approximation to a 3:1 ratio, a ratio that suggested to him the mechanism of the inheritance of height.

ALTERNATE FORMS

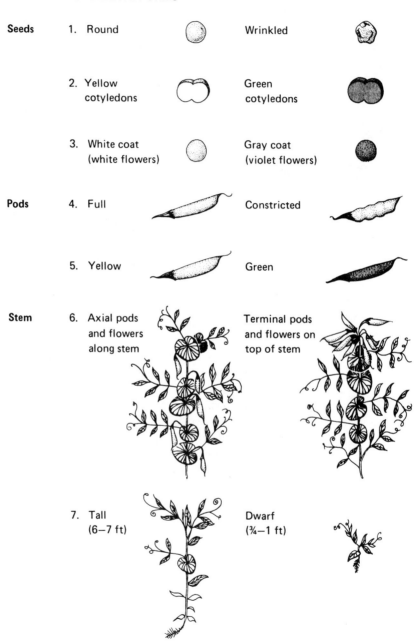

Seeds   1. Round   Wrinkled

2. Yellow   Green
   cotyledons   cotyledons

3. White coat   Gray coat
   (white flowers)   (violet flowers)

Pods   4. Full   Constricted

5. Yellow   Green

Stem   6. Axial pods   Terminal pods
   and flowers   and flowers on
   along stem   top of stem

7. Tall   Dwarf
   (6–7 ft)   (¾–1 ft)

Figure 1-2 Seven Characteristics Observed by Mendel in Peas

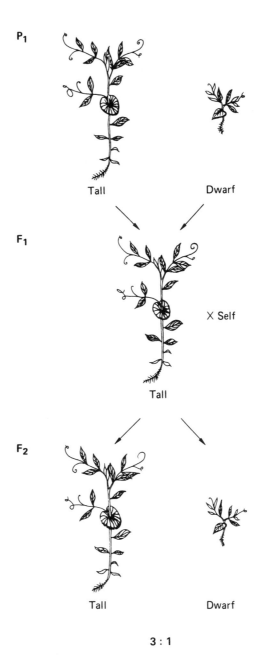

P₁

Tall   Dwarf

F₁

X Self

Tall

F₂

Tall   Dwarf

3 : 1

Figure 1-3 First Two Offspring Generations from the Cross of Tall Plants with
Dwarf Plants

Rule of Segregation

Mendel assumed that each plant contained two determinants (which we now   9
call **genes**) for the characteristic of height. Different forms of a gene exist
within a population and are termed **alleles**. For example, a heterozygous pea
plant possesses the *dominant tall allele* and the *recessive dwarf allele* for the
gene that determines plant height. A homozygous pair of dwarf alleles is required to develop the recessive phenotype. Only one of these alleles is passed
into a single gamete, and the union of two gametes to form a zygote restores
the double complement of alleles. The fact that the recessive trait reappears in
the F_2 generation shows that the allele controlling it was unaffected by being
hidden in the F_1 individual. This explanation of the passage of these discrete
trait determinants, the genes, is referred to as Mendel's first principle, the **rule
of segregration**. The rule of segregation can be summarized as follows: A
gamete receives only one allele from the pair of alleles possessed by an organism: fertilization (the union of two gametes) reestablishes the double number.
We can visualize this process by redrawing Figure 1-3 using letters to denote
the alleles. Mendel used capital letters to denote alleles that controlled dominant traits and lowercase letters for alleles that controlled recessive traits. Following this notation, *T* will be used for tall and *t* for short (dwarf). From Figure
1-4 we can see that Mendel's rule of segregation explains the homogeneity of
the F_1, (all tall) generation and the 3:1 ratio of tall to dwarf in the F_2 generation.

Let us define some terms. The **genotype** of an organism is the genes it   10
possesses. In Figure 1-4 the genotype of the parental tall plant is *TT*; that of the
F_1 tall plant is *Tt*. **Phenotype** refers to the observable attributes of an organism.
Plants with either of the above two genotypes, *TT* and *Tt*, are phenotypically
tall. Genotypes come in two general classes: **homozygotes**, in which both alleles are the same, as in *TT* or *tt*, and **heterozygotes**, in which the two alleles
are different, as in *Tt*. These last two terms were coined by William Bateson in
1901. The word **gene** was first used by the Danish botanist Wilhelm Johannsen
in 1909.

If we look at Figure 1-4, we can see that the *TT* homozygote can produce   11
only one type of gamete, the *T*-bearing kind, and likewise, the *tt* homozygote
can produce only *t*-bearing gametes. Thus, the F_1 individuals are uniformly
heterozygous *Tt*, and each F_1 individual can produce two kinds of gametes in
equal frequencies. *T*- or *t*-bearing. In producing the F_2 generation, these two
types of gametes randomly pair during the process of fertilization. Figure 1-5
shows three ways of picturing this process.

Testing the Rule of Segregation.   We can see from Figure 1-5 that the F_2 12
generation has a phenotypic ratio of 3:1, the classic Mendelian ratio. However,
there is also a genotypic ratio of 1:2:1 for homozygote-dominant:heterozygote:
homozygote-recessive. Demonstrating this genotypic ratio provides a good test
of Mendel's hypothesis of segregation.

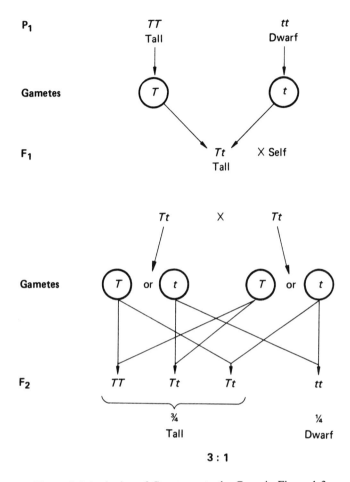

Figure 1-4 Assigning of Genotypes to the Cross in Figure 1-3

The simplest way to test the hypothesis is by **progeny testing**—that is, by   13
self-fertilizing F_2 individuals to produce an F_3 generation, which is what Mendel did. From his hypothesis it is possible to predict the frequencies of the
phenotypic classes that would result. The dwarf F_2 plants were homozygous
recessive, and so, when **selfed** (self-fertilized), they should have produced only
t-bearing gametes and had only dwarf F_3 offspring. The tall F_2 plants, however, were a heterogeneous group of which 1/3 should have been homozygous
TT and 2/3 should have been heterozygous Tt. The tall homozygotes, when
selfed, should have produced only tall F_3 offspring (genotypically TT). However, the F_2 heterozygotes when selfed should have produced tall and dwarf
offspring in a ratio identical to that produced by the selfed F_1 plants: 3 tall:1
dwarf. Mendel's data are presented in Figure 1-6. As you can see, all the dwarf

Schematic Tt ✕ Tt

(as in Figure 1–6)

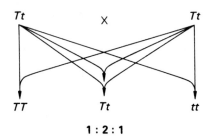

Tt ✕ Tt

TT Tt tt

1 : 2 : 1

Diagrammatic   (Punnett Square)

Pollen

	T	t
T	TT	Tt
t	Tt	tt

Ovules

$TT : Tt : tt$
1 : 2 : 1

Probabilistic   (Multiply; see rule 2, Chapter 3.)

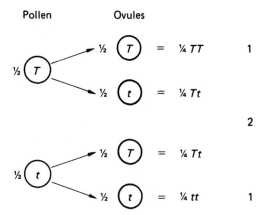

Pollen   Ovules

½ T ⟶ ½ T = ¼ TT 1

              ⟶ ½ t = ¼ Tt

                                                      2

½ t ⟶ ½ T = ¼ Tt

              ⟶ ½ t = ¼ tt 1

Figure 1-5 Methods of Determining F_2 Genotypic Combinations in a Self-Fertilized
      Monohybrid

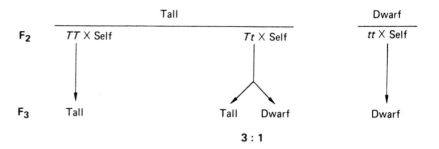

Figure 1-6 Mendel Self-Fertilized F_2 Tall and Dwarf Plants

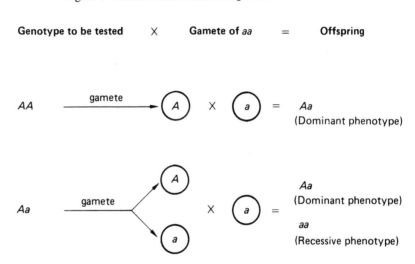

Figure 1-7 Testcross

(homozygous) F_2 bred true as predicted. Among the tall, 28 percent (28/100) bred true and 72 percent (72/100) segregated tall and dwarf phenotypes. The prediction was 1/3 (33.3 percent) and 2/3 (66.7 percent) respectively. Mendel's observed values are well within the experimental error expected from this type of experiment. We thus conclude that Mendel's progeny testing experiment confirmed his hypothesis.

Another way to test the segregation hypothesis is with the extremely useful method of the **testcross**—that is, a cross of any organism with a recessive homozygote. (Another type of cross, a **backcross**, is the cross of a progeny with an individual that has a parental genotype. Hence a testcross can often be a backcross.) Since the gametes of the recessive homozygote contain only recessive alleles, the alleles carried by the gametes of the other parent will determine the phenotypes of the offspring. If a gamete from the organism being

Tall (2 classes)
$TT \times tt$ = all Tt
$Tt \times tt = Tt : tt$
1 : 1

Figure 1-8 Testcrossing the Dominant Phenotype of F_2 from Figure 1-3

tested contains a dominant, the F_1 phenotype will be dominant. Thus, in using a testcross, the genotypes of the gametes from the organism tested determine the phenotypes of the offspring (Figure 1-7). A testcross of the tall F_2 in Figure 1-4 would produce the results shown in Figure 1-8. These results are a further confirmation of Mendel's rule of segregation.

From *Principles of Genetics* (1985) by Robert H. Tamarin

**QUESTIONS
FROM SKIMMING**

In the left-hand column below, write down the questions you expect the selection will answer, along with the appropriate page number(s). Reread the selection carefully, and use the right-hand column to record the answers to the questions after you have compared your questions to those of your classmates and to the list of Questions on the Text that follows.

QUESTIONS (put page number after question)	ANSWERS

**QUESTIONS
ON THE TEXT**

Compare your questions to those listed here.

What are Mendel's principles?

What is the subject of genetics concerned with?

Why was Mendel's contribution to genetics not appreciated at first?

What changes in biological science led to Mendel's recognition?

What were Mendel's experiments?

Why did he work with pea plants?

How is a pea plant fertilized?

What is *self-fertilization*?

What is *cross-fertilization*?

What characteristics of pea plants did Mendel study?

What happened when Mendel cross-fertilized plants of different heights?

What happened when the resulting offspring were self-fertilized?

What is Mendel's rule of segregation?

What is a *gene*?

What is an *allele*?

What is a *genotype*?

What is a *phenotype*?

What are *homozygotes*?

What are *heterozygotes*?

How can Mendel's hypothesis of segregation be tested?

What is *progeny-testing*?

What is a *testcross*?

**QUESTIONS
BEYOND
THE TEXT**

1. What easily visible examples of discontinuous variation are there in humans? Can you think of individual examples of such variation?

2. Do you know of a family whose members have different colored eyes? Of what colors are the parents' eyes? Of what colors are the children's? Which eye color seems to be the dominant trait?

3. Have you heard of any diseases that are carried genetically? How could apparently healthy parents have children who suffer from such a disease? Do you know of any actual instances of that happening?

VOCABULARY NOTES

This is complex material, made all the more difficult by the use of many technical terms. Most of them in this text are identified by being printed in **bold**: pick them out, write each of them on a separate index card, and if you can't immediately say what it means, look for an explanation in the text and write it beside the word.

You may find a few terms that are new to you although they are not printed in bold nor explained in the text; make cards for these too, and consult a dictionary in order to write down their meaning. Then check your set of cards against the list given below, and make cards for any words you have left out. The words and phrases in the list are alphabetized, except for those that have been grouped under a general heading in order to make their meaning clearer. The ones that are not explained in the text have the word *dictionary* in parentheses after the paragraph number.

alleles (paragraph 10)
crossbreed (verb) (paragraph 5)
   backcross (paragraph 15)
   reciprocal cross (paragraph 8)
   testcross (paragraph 15)
dominant trait (paragraph 9)
fertilization (paragraph 6) (dictionary)
   cross-fertilization (paragraph 6)
   self-fertilization (paragraph 7)
filial generation (paragraph 9)
gamete (paragraph 12) (dictionary)
genes (paragraph 10) (dictionary)
genotype (paragraph 11)
heterozygotes (paragraph 11)
homozygotes (paragraph 11)
hybrids (paragraph 9)
   monohybrids (paragraph 9)
phenotype (paragraph 11)
progeny testing (paragraph 14)
recessive trait (paragraph 9)
variations (paragraph 3)
   continuous variations (paragraph 3)
   discontinuous variations (paragraph 3)
zygote (paragraph 11) (dictionary)

DIAGRAMS

Probably the most effective way of learning the information given here is to concentrate on the diagrams. It would be particularly helpful to copy Figures 1-3 and 1-4 and then explain them to yourself or somebody else; you could also try to write out the explanation.

OUTLINE NOTES

If you want to outline this selection, you may find it helpful to use your own headings and rearrange the material. Here is an example of such a rearrangement. You are asked to complete it by writing an explanation of each subheading in the blank beneath it.

Mendel's Experiments

I. Original Experiments

   1. Question

     _____

   2. Materials

     _____

   3. Method
     a. Cross-fertilization of parental generation (P^1)

     _____

     b. Self-fertilization of first filial generation (F^1)

     _____

   4. Results
     a. Characteristics of F^1

     _____

     b. Characteristics of F^2

     _____

   5. Conclusion
     Rule of segregation

     _____

II. Testing the Rule of Segregation

   1. Methods
     a. Progeny testing

     _____

     b. Testcross

     _____

ESSAY TOPICS   Read the topics given below, and decide which one you would like to focus on. Then reread the selection, noting the points that you think should be included in an essay on the topic. Discuss the points with your classmates, if you can, and outline them in the order in which you think they should be presented. If you choose topic 2, you will find a suggested essay outline below: compare your own outline with it before you write the essay. In fact, if you are finding the material difficult, you may want to use this outline directly as a guide for your writing, but if you do that, make your own outline for topic 1 as well.

1. Describe Gregor Mendel's experiments, and explain their significance.
2. What is the principle of segregation, and how can it be proved?

Essay Outline (Topic 2)

1. Principle of Segregation
   Two genes for each characteristic in each individual
   Different forms of gene for any particular characteristic, called alleles
       e.g.,height in peas
           color of eyes in humans
   Dominant and recessive alleles
       e.g.,——————————————————————————————————
       ——————————————————————————————————
   Recessive characteristics only appearing in homozygotes
   Recessive characteristics carried by heterozygotes
   → Reappearance of recessive characteristics in subsequent generations
2. Proof
   Mendel's experiments
   a. Parent generation
       Characteristics
       Cross-fertilization
       Results
   b. First filial generation
       Characteristics
       Self-fertilization
       Results
   c. Second filial generation
       Characteristics
       Self-fertilization
       Results
   Testcross:
       i.e., Cross organisms with recessive homozygotes
           Results must be determined by alleles of organisms being tested

Reading for

CHAPTER FOUR

Insight

Many writers write, not for the purpose of giving information, nor yet to entertain other people, but rather to work out their own thoughts. Once they have worked them out on paper they may publish what they have written, and so they give other people a chance to share in their thoughts, and thus to develop insights of their own.

The selections in this chapter are intended to represent writing of this sort. All of them deal with basic facts about being human—facts that, because you are human, you know already. The purpose of reading these selections is to see these facts in a new light, to question whether they are indeed facts or merely prejudices, and to make new connections between them.

Dealing with References

Several of the writers who are represented in this section refer a great deal to other writers: in their conversation with you, the reader, they include the ideas of people who wrote in other places at other times. Often you will know nothing about the writers referred to, but that should not prevent your taking part in the conversation, for you can still see what the writer of the particular selection is saying, and you can tell from the fact that the reference is made that he or she is establishing a link with a literary tradition. If you do know anything about that tradition, you should think about that knowledge and share it with your classmates; however, not being familiar with particular

243

references will not prevent you from making your own interpretation of the selection.

Connecting the Selections with One Another

While you can read any of these selections individually and get a great deal out of it, you may find it interesting to think about how they relate to one another—for they deal with many of the same fundamental issues. The following questions may give you some ideas about what to look for:

1. What do Aristotle (Selection 4-1) and Henry David Thoreau (Selection 4-2) have to say about people living in isolation from other people? How do you account for the differences between their views? Can these views be reconciled in any way, or do you think that one or the other of them is wrong?
2. What does Jorge Luis Borges (Selection 4-3) seem to have in common with either Aristotle or Thoreau? In what ways is he different from each of them?
3. Both Aristotle and C. S. Lewis (Selection 4-4) are concerned with the question of what justice, or morality, is. What answer does each give to the question? Are their answers the same or different?
4. How do you think C. S. Lewis (a European) would respond to the political suggestion made by Borges (a South American) in his second to last paragraph? (Consider what Lewis has to say about Nazi Germany, and also about the general condition of human beings with regard to the Law of Nature.)
5. The first four selections are written by men. Does anything about what they say, or how they say it, bear out what Simone de Beauvoir says in Selection 4-5 about male attitudes toward women? Does anything in what she says suggest grounds on which you might question the statements and arguments of the others?

Using the Reading Selections and Exercises

Because the main purpose in reading these selections is to develop your own thinking (rather than simply learning what someone else thinks), you are asked, before you read each selection, to explore your own ideas. This is best done through discussion with your friends and classmates; specific questions are provided under the heading Prereading to help you focus on the topic that the selection addresses. (You might also write down your thoughts about these questions.)

After you have clarified your own assumptions—and have discovered, perhaps, some differences of opinion—consider the selection itself. Read it slowly and carefully (perhaps your instructor will read it aloud to you), and be prepared to go back a few sentences, or even a whole paragraph, if you lose track of the connections between the ideas. If you are reading on your own, you may want to read it two or three times before you can say confidently what you think the writer is getting at.

Following each selection is an exercise called Quotations to Think About, in which you are asked to think about what certain significant statements in the text mean and to consider whether they are true. To work out the meaning, you will certainly have to go back to the relevant section of the text and think about each quotation in context; but you should also think of what, in your own experience, the quotation could be referring to. Having related it to your own experience, you will then be able to say whether, or to what extent, you think the statement is true. Remember there are no "right" answers to these questions, and be prepared to disagree with your classmates and your instructor if either the text, or your own experience, suggests a different interpretation from theirs.

The Making Connections exercises are meant to help you see each selection as a whole. You will need to go through the whole text of the selection again to see how the main ideas are connected and how certain key words are used throughout. Once you have done this you will have a much clearer idea of what the text says to you and also of what you think about it.

All the questions in this section are designed primarily as a basis for class discussion. They can, however, be treated as essay topics. Your instructor may spend a class period discussing one and then, as an assignment, ask you to write your response to another question about the same selection.

SELECTION
4-1

from *Politics*

Aristotle

Writing in the fourth century B.C., the Greek philosopher Aristotle attempted to bring order to a number of fields of knowledge. The following selection from his famous work on political theory discusses how human beings organize themselves into groups and how they benefit from such organizations.

PREREADING

Before reading the passage, think about these questions:

1. Which communities do you belong to? Which of them is the most important to you? Why?

2. Do you know of, or can you imagine, anyone who does not belong to a community? What do you think such a person must be like?

The Political Association

We must . . . consider analytically the elements of which a polis [or state] is composed. . . . If . . . we begin at the beginning, and consider things in the process of their growth, we shall best be able, in this as in other fields, to attain scientific conclusions. . . .

First of all, there must necessarily be a union or pairing of those who cannot   5
exist without one another. Male and female must unite for the reproduction of the species—not from deliberate intention, but from the natural impulse, which exists in animals generally as it also exists in plants, to leave behind them something of the same nature as themselves. . . . The first form of association naturally instituted for the satisfaction of daily recurrent needs is thus the fam-   10
ily; and the members of the family are accordingly termed by Charondas "associates of the breadchest." . . .

The next form of association—which is also the *first* to be formed from more households than one, and for the satisfaction of something more than daily recurrent needs—is the village. The most natural form of the village   15
appears to be that of a colony or offshoot from a family; and some have thus called the members of the village by the name of "sucklings of the same milk," or, again, of "sons and the sons of sons." . . .

When we come to the final and perfect association, formed from a number of villages, we have already reached the polis—an association which may be   20
said to have reached the height of full self-sufficiency; or rather [to speak more exactly] we may say that while it *grows* for the sake of mere life [and is so far,

and at that stage, still short of full self-sufficiency], it *exists* [when once it is fully grown] for the sake of a good life [and is therefore fully self-sufficient]. . . .   25

From these considerations it is evident that the polis belongs to the class of things that exist by nature, and that man is by nature an animal intended to live in a polis. He who is without a polis, by reason of his own nature and not of some accident, is either a poor sort of being, or a being higher than man: he is like the man of whom Homer wrote in denunciation: "Clanless and lawless and 30 hearthless is he." The man who is such by nature [i.e., unable to join in the society of a polis] at once plunges into a passion for war; he is in the position of a solitary advanced piece in a game of draughts.

The reason why man is a being meant for political association, in a higher degree than bees or other gregarious animals can ever associate, is evident. 35 Nature, according to our theory, makes nothing in vain; and man alone of the animals is furnished with the faculty of language. The mere making of sound serves to indicate pleasure and pain, and is thus a faculty that belongs to animals in general: their nature enables them to attain the point at which they have perceptions of pleasure and pain, and can signify those perceptions to one an- 40 other. But language serves to declare what is advantageous and what is the reverse, and it therefore serves to declare what is just and what is unjust. It is the peculiarity of man, in comparison with the rest of the animal world, that he alone possesses a perception of good and evil, of the just and the unjust, and of other similar qualities; and it is association in [a common perception of] these 45 things which makes a family and a polis. . . .

We thus see that the polis exists by nature and that it is prior to the individual. [The proof of both propositions is the fact that the polis is a whole, and that individuals are simply its parts.] Not being self-sufficient when they are isolated, all individuals are so many parts all equally depending on the whole 50 [which alone can bring about self-sufficiency]. The man who is isolated—who is unable to share in the benefits of political association, or has no need to share because he is already self-sufficient—is no part of the polis, and must therefore be either a beast or a god. [Man is thus intended by nature to be a part of a political whole, and] there is therefore an immanent impulse in all men towards 55 an association of this order. But the man who first *constructed* such an association was none the less the greatest of benefactors. Man, when perfected, is the best of animals; but if he be isolated from law and justice he is the worst of all.

Injustice is all the graver when it is armed injustice; and man is furnished from birth with arms [such as, for instance, language] which are intended to 60 serve the purposes of moral prudence and virtue, but which may be used in preference for opposite ends. That is why, if he be without virtue, he is a most unholy and savage being, and worse than all others in the indulgence of lust and gluttony. Justice [which is his salvation] belongs to the polis; for justice, which is the determination of what is just, is an ordering of the political asso- 65 ciation.

1. ". . .while [the polis] *grows* for the sake of mere life, it *exists* for the sake of a good life . . ." (lines 22–24). How do you think the Greek polis could have enriched the lives of its citizens? Do you think that a modern state does so?

2. ". . . It is evident that the polis belongs to the class of things that exist by nature, and that man is by nature an animal intended to live in a polis" (lines 26–28). Why does Aristotle think that the state is a *natural* phenomenon? Do you think that it is? Why, or why not?

3. "The man who is isolated—who is unable to share in the benefits of political association, or has no need to share because he is already self-sufficient—is no part of a polis, and must therefore be either a beast or a god" (lines 51–54). Why, according to Aristotle, does a person have to belong to a state in order to be human? Do you think he is right?

4. "Justice belongs to the polis; for justice, which is the determination of what is just, is an ordering of the political association" (lines 64–66). What does this suggest about people whose political community has broken down? What also does it suggest about relationships between states?

1. Make a list of the different forms of association that Aristotle considers in this passage. How has he arranged his discussion of them? What principle is he following?

2. At eight points Aristotle refers to animals. Underline each of these references, or copy them onto a separate sheet of paper. What, in each case, does he suggest about the relationship between animals and human beings?

3. Underline, or write on a separate sheet, every sentence in which Aristotle uses the words *just, unjust, justice,* or *injustice.* With what does he associate justice and its opposite, injustice?

from *Walden, or Life in the Woods*
Henry David Thoreau

Henry David Thoreau, the nineteenth-century American writer, concentrated much of his work on the relationship of the individual to society. In the following selection from his book *Walden,* Thoreau discusses his reasons for living apart from the society of others.

PREREADING

Before reading the passage, think about the following words:

    a. society, sociable, company, companion, companionable

    b. solitude, solitary, alone, lonely, lonesome

What value do you give to each of these words—that is do you associate them with good, bad, or neutral feelings? How do the two sets compare with each other?

Solitude

We are the subjects of an experiment which is not a little interesting to me. Can we not do without the society of our gossips a little while under these circumstances—have our own thoughts to cheer us? Confucius says truly, "Virtue does not remain as an abandoned orphan; it must of necessity have neighbors."   5

With thinking we may be beside ourselves in a sane sense. By a conscious effort of the mind we can stand aloof from actions and their consequences; and all things, good and bad, go by us like a torrent. We are not wholly involved in Nature. I may be either the driftwood in the stream, or Indra in the sky looking down on it. I *may* be affected by a theatrical exhibition; on the other hand, I   10 *may not be* affected by an actual event which appears to concern me much more. I only know myself as a human entity; the scene, so to speak, of thoughts and affections; and am sensible of a certain doubleness by which I can stand as remote from myself as from another. However intense my experience, I am conscious of the presence and criticism of a part of me, which, as it were,   15 is not a part of me, but a spectator, sharing no experience, but taking note of it, and that is no more I than it is you. When the play, it may be the tragedy, of life is over, the spectator goes his way. It was a kind of fiction, a work of the imagination only, so far as he was concerned. This doubleness may easily make us poor neighbors and friends sometimes.   20

I find it wholesome to be alone the greater part of the time. To be in company, even with the best, is soon wearisome and dissipating. I love to be alone. I never found the companion that was so companionable as solitude. We are for the most part more lonely when we go abroad among men than when we stay in our chambers. A man thinking or working is always alone, let him be where he will. Solitude is not measured by the miles of space that intervene between a man and his fellows. The really diligent student in one of the crowded hives of Cambridge College is as solitary as a dervis in the desert. The farmer can work alone in the field or the woods all day, hoeing or chopping, and not feel lonesome, because he is employed; but when he comes home at night he cannot sit down in a room alone, at the mercy of his thoughts, but must be where he can "see the folks," and recreate, and, as he thinks, remunerate himself for his day's solitude; and hence he wonders how the student can sit alone in the house all night and most of the day without ennui and "the blues"; but he does not realize that the student, though in the house, is still at work in *his* field, and chopping in *his* woods, as the farmer in his, and in turn seeks the same recreation and society that the latter does, though it may be a more condensed form of it.

Society is commonly too cheap. We meet at very short intervals, not having had time to acquire any new value for each other. We meet at meals three times a day, and give each other a new taste of that old musty cheese that we are. We have had to agree on a certain set of rules, called etiquette and politeness, to make this frequent meeting tolerable and that we need not come to open war. We meet at the post-office, and at the sociable, and about the fireside every night; we live thick and are in each other's way, and stumble over one another, and I think that we thus lose some respect for one another. Certainly less frequency would suffice for all important and hearty communications. Consider the girls in a factory,—never alone, hardly in their dreams. It would be better if there were but one inhabitant to a square mile, as where I live. The value of a man is not in his skin, that we should touch him.

I have heard of a man lost in the woods and dying of famine and exhaustion at the foot of a tree, whose loneliness was relieved by the grotesque visions with which, owing to bodily weakness, his diseased imagination surrounded him, and which he believed to be real. So also, owing to bodily and mental health and strength, we may be continually cheered by a like but more normal and natural society, and come to know that we are never alone.

I have a great deal of company in my house; especially in the morning, when nobody calls. Let me suggest a few comparisons, that some one may convey an idea of my situation. I am no more lonely than the loon in the pond that laughs so loud, or than Walden Pond itself. What company has that lonely lake, I pray? And yet it has not the blue devils, but the blue angels in it, in the azure tint of its waters. The sun is alone, except in thick weather, when there sometimes appear to be two, but one is a mock sun. God is alone—but the devil, he is far from being alone; he sees a great deal of company; he is legion.

I am no more lonely than a single mullein or dandelion in a pasture, or a bean   65
leaf, or sorrel, or a horse-fly, or a bumblebee. I am no more lonely than the
Mill Brook, or a weathercock, or the north star, or the south wind, or an April
shower, or a January thaw, or the first spider in a new house.

QUOTATIONS TO THINK ABOUT

1. "We are subjects of an experiment which is not a little interesting to me" (line 1). What do you think this experiment is? (Note that shortly before this excerpt appears this sentence: "*Next* to us is not the workman whom we have hired with whom we love so well to talk, but the workman whose work we are.")

2. "'Virtue does not remain as an abandoned orphan; it must of necessity have neighbors'" (lines 3–5). Who or what do you think are virtue's neighbors?

3. What does Thoreau mean when he says "With thinking we may be beside ourselves in a sane sense" (line 6)?

4. "This doubleness may easily make us poor neighbors and friends sometimes" (lines 19–20) Why do you think this should be so?

5. What reasons does Thoreau give for suggesting that it is "wholesome to be alone the greater part of the time" (line 21)? Do you think he is right?

6. "Solitude is not measured by the miles of space that intervene between a man and his fellows" (lines 26–27). What is it measured by?

7. "Society is commonly too cheap" (line 39). What does this mean? Do you agree?

8. ". . . we may . . . come to know that we are never alone" (lines 55–56). How can we do this?

MAKING CONNECTIONS

1. In both paragraph 2 and paragraph 5, Thoreau refers, more or less directly, to insanity. Underline or copy out exactly what he says about it in each place. Is he saying the same thing in both of them? If not, what is the difference?

2. In paragraph 4 and paragraph 5, Thoreau uses the phrase *never alone*. Find the phrase in each of these places and underline or write out the sentence in which it appears. What does he use it to mean in each of these sentences? Is there any difference between the two meanings?

3. Think again about the two sets of words you considered before reading the passage:
   a. society, sociable, company, companion, companionable
   b. solitude, solitary, alone, lonely, lonesome

What value did you put on each of them? Now identify each place where Thoreau uses the words, and write down on cards or slips of paper the sentences in which they appear. Group these sentences according to whether the word in question belongs to set a or set b. Now look at your two sets of sentences. In his use of the words, what ideas does Thoreau associate with each set? What does this suggest about the relative values he puts on society and on solitude? Does this agree with your own sense of values, or with other people's?

SELECTION
4-3

from *Other Inquisitions*

Jorge Luis Borges

Jorge Luis Borges, an author from Argentina, was one of the foremost writers of the twentieth century. He published the book from which the following selection is taken shortly after World War II. In this selection, he contrasts Argentines' concept of the state with that of Europeans and North Americans.

PREREADING

Before reading the passage, think about these questions:

1. In what ways do you personally come into contact with the state—that is, the government? On thinking about such contacts, how would you describe your relationship with the state—is it your friend or your enemy?

2. How would you define patriotism? Would you describe yourself as patriotic? Why, or why not?

3. Do you know of any story (it could be a news story, a novel, or a movie) in which one or more individuals is in opposition to official authorities? With which side do you sympathize in this story? Why?

4. What do the words *communism* and *fascism* mean to you? Can you give examples of each of these political systems? What do you know of what life is or was like for ordinary people in the case of each of your examples?

Our Poor Individualism

The illusions of patriotism are limitless. In the first century of our era Plutarch ridiculed those who declared that the moon of Athens was better than the moon of Corinth; in the seventeenth century Milton observed that God usually revealed Himself first to His Englishmen; at the beginning of the nineteenth, Fichte declared that to have character and to be German were, obviously, the same thing. Here in Argentina, nationalists are much in evidence; they tell us they are motivated by the worthy or innocent desire to foment the best Argentine traits. But they do not really know the Argentine people; in speeches they prefer to define them in terms of some external fact—the Spanish *conquistadores*, say, or an imaginary Catholic tradition or "Saxon imperialism."

Unlike North Americans and almost all Europeans, the Argentine does not identify himself with the State. That can be explained by the fact that, in this country, the governments are usually exceedingly bad, or the State is an incon-

5

10

ceivable abstraction;[1] the truth is that the Argentine is an individual, not a citizen. Aphorisms like Hegel's—"The State is the reality of the moral idea"— seem like a vicious joke. Films made in Hollywood repeatedly portray as admirable the man (generally a reporter) who tries to make friends with a criminal so he can turn him over to the police later; the Argentine, for whom friendship is a passion and the police something like a *mafia*, feels that this "hero" is an incomprehensible cad. He agrees with Don Quixote that "no one is without sin" and that "good men should not be the executioners of the others" (*Don Quixote*, I, XXII). More than once, as I confronted the vain symmetries of Spanish style, I have suspected that we differ irrevocably from Spain; but those two lines from the *Quixote* have sufficed to convince me of my error; they are like the calm and secret symbol of our affinity. One night of Argentine literature is enough to confirm this: that desperate night when a rural police sergeant, shouting that he would not condone the crime of killing a brave man, began to fight on the side of the deserter Martin Fierro against his own men.

For the European the world is a cosmos where each person corresponds intimately to the function he performs; for the Argentine it is a chaos. The European and the North American believe that a book which has been awarded any sort of prize must be good; the Argentine acknowledges the possibility that it may not be bad, in spite of the prize. In general, the Argentine is a skeptic. He may not know about the fable that says humanity always includes thirty-six just men—the Lamed Vovniks—who do not know each other but who secretly sustain the universe; if he hears that fable, he will not be surprised that those worthies are obscure and anonymous. His popular hero is the man who fights the multitude alone, either in action (Fierro, Moreira, Hormiga Negra), or in the mind or the past (Segundo Sombra). Other literatures do not record anything quite like that. For example, consider the case of two great European writers, Kipling and Franz Kafka. At first glance the two have nothing in common, but the principal theme of one is the vindication of order—of one order (the highway is *Kim*, the bridge in *The Bridge Builders*, the Roman wall in *Puck of Pook's Hill*); the principal theme of the other is the insupportable and tragic solitude of the person who lacks a place, even a most humble one, in the order of the universe.

Perhaps someone will say that the qualities I have mentioned are merely negative or anarchical ones, and will add that they are not capable of political application. I venture to suggest that the opposite is true. The most urgent problem of our time (already proclaimed with prophetical clarity by the almost forgotten Spencer) is the gradual interference of the State in the acts of the individual; in the struggle against this evil—called communism and fascism— Argentine individualism, which has perhaps been useless or even harmful up to now, would find justification and positive value.

---

[1] The State is impersonal; the Argentine can think only in terms of a personal relationship. Therefore, he does not consider stealing public funds a crime. I am simply stating a fact; I do not justify or condone it.

Without hope and with nostalgia, I think of the abstract possibility of a   55
political party that has some affinity with the Argentine character; a party that
would promise us, say, a rigorous minimum of government.

Nationalism seeks to charm us, but the vision it presents is that of an infi-
nitely importunate State; if that utopia were established on earth, it would have
the providential virtue of making everyone desire, and finally achieve, its an-   60
tithesis.

QUOTATIONS TO THINK ABOUT

1. "The illusions of patriotism are limitless" (line 1). What does Borges suggest are the particular illusions of Argentine patriotism? Can you identify any illusions in the patriotism of your own country?

2. ". . . the truth is that the Argentine is an individual, not a citizen" (lines 14–15). If this is indeed the truth, what must be the practical consequences for life in Argentina? Can you think of any other nationality or community of which this might be said?

3. "For the European the world is a cosmos where each person corresponds intimately to the function he performs; for the Argentine it is a chaos" (lines 29–30). How does Borges develop this contrast between the European and Argentine view? Can you think of any examples that illustrate the European view?

4. "The most urgent problem of our time . . . is the gradual interference of the State in the acts of the individual . . . " (lines 49–52). How does the state interfere in individual lives? Do you agree that it is an urgent problem?

MAKING CONNECTIONS

1. Find and underline all the places in the selection where Borges refers to Europe and European writers. What do these references suggest about the relationship between Europe and Argentina, and about Borges's own attitude to European culture and traditions?

2. Borges uses the word *government* twice (lines 13 and 57). What seems to be his opinion of the Argentine government in particular, and of governments in general? Why do you suppose he holds these opinions?

3. How are the two quotations from *Don Quixote* (lines 20–21) connected with what Borges calls "the most urgent problem of our time" (lines 49–50)?

**SELECTION
4-4**

from *Mere Christianity*

C. S. Lewis

C. S. Lewis (1898–1963) was a British critic and novelist who also wrote many books about Christianity. In the following selection, however, he considers how people respond to each other in terms of a general code of morality, not just a Christian one.

PREREADING

1. Make two columns on a sheet of paper and write as headings *Right* and *Wrong*. Then, under each heading, write down corresponding patterns of behavior. For example:

   | *Right* | *Wrong* |
   | Telling the Truth | Telling lies |

   Try to list points that to you seem to be the most important principles. Then compare your list with those of your classmates. In what ways do the lists correspond? In what ways do they differ?

2. How did you know what to write in each column? In other words, where do your ideas of right and wrong come from?

The Law of Human Nature

Every one has heard people quarrelling. Sometimes it sounds funny and ¶1 sometimes it sounds merely unpleasant; but however it sounds, I believe we can learn something very important from listening to the kind of things they say. They say things like this: "How'd you like it if anyone did the same to you?"—"That's my seat, I was there first"—"Leave him alone, he isn't doing L5 you any harm"—"Why should you shove in first?"—"Give me a bit of your orange, I gave you a bit of mine"—"Come on, you promised." People say things like that every day, educated people as well as uneducated, and children as well as grown-ups.

Now what interests me about all these remarks is that the man who makes ¶2 them is not merely saying that the other man's behaviour does not happen to please him. He is appealing to some kind of standard of behaviour which he expects the other man to know about. And the other man very seldom replies: "To hell with your standard." Nearly always he tries to make out that what he has been doing does not really go against the standard, or that if it does there is L15 some special excuse. He pretends there is some special reason in this particular case why the person who took the seat first should not keep it, or that things were quite different when he was given the bit of orange, or that something has turned up which lets him off keeping his promise. It looks, in fact, very much as if both parties had in mind some kind of Law or Rule of fair play or decent behaviour or morality or whatever you like to call it, about which they really agreed. And they have. If they had not, they might, of course, fight like animals, but they could not quarrel in the human sense of the word. Quarrelling means trying to show that the other man is in the wrong. And there would be no sense in trying to do that unless you and he had some sort of agreement as to what Right and Wrong are; just as there would be no sense in saying that a footballer had committed a foul unless there was some agreement about the rules of football.

Now this Law or Rule about Right and Wrong used to be called the Law of Nature. Nowadays, when we talk of the "laws of nature" we usually mean things like gravitation, or heredity, or the laws of chemistry. But when the older thinkers called the Law of Right and Wrong "the Law of Nature," they really meant the Law of Human Nature. The idea was that, just as all bodies are governed by the law of gravitation, and organisms by biological laws, so the creature called man also had his law—with this great difference, that a body could not choose whether it obeyed the law of gravitation or not, but a man could choose either to obey the Law of Human Nature or to disobey it.

We may put this in another way. Each man is at every moment subjected to several different sets of law but there is only one of these which he is free to disobey. As a body, he is subjected to gravitation and cannot disobey it; if you leave him unsupported in mid-air, he has no more choice about falling than a stone has. As an organism, he is subjected to various biological laws which he cannot disobey any more than an animal can. That is, he cannot disobey those laws which he shares with other things; but the law which is peculiar to his human nature, the law he does not share with animals or vegetables or inorganic things, is the one he can disobey if he chooses.

This law was called the Law of Nature because people thought that every one knew it by nature and did not need to be taught it. They did not mean, of course, that you might not find an odd individual here and there who did not know it, just as you find a few people who are colorblind or have no ear for a tune. But taking the race as a whole, they thought that the human idea of decent behavior was obvious to every one. And I believe they were right. If they were not, then all the things we said about the war were nonsense. What was the sense in saying the enemy were in the wrong unless Right is a real thing which the Nazis at bottom knew as well as we did and ought to have practiced? If they had had no notion of what we mean by right, then, though we might still have had to fight them, we could no more have blamed them for that than for the color of their hair.

I know that some people say the idea of a Law of Nature or decent behaviour known to all men is unsound, because different civilizations and different ages have had quite different moralities.

But this is not true. There have been differences between their moralities, ¶7
but these have never amounted to anything like a total difference. If anyone
will take the trouble to compare the moral teaching of, say, the ancient Egyp-
tians, Babylonians, Hindus, Chinese, Greeks and Romans, what will really L65
strike him will be how very like they are to each other and to our own. Some of
the evidence for this I have put together in the appendix of another book called
The Abolition of Man; but for our present purpose I need only ask the reader to
think what a totally different morality would mean. Think of a country where
people were admired for running away in battle, or where a man felt proud of L70
double-crossing all the people who had been kindest to him. You might just as
well try to imagine a country where two and two made five. Men have differed
as regards what people you ought to be unselfish to—whether it was only your
own family, or your fellow countrymen, or every one. But they have always
agreed that you ought not to put yourself first. Selfishness has never been L75
admired. Men have differed as to whether you should have one wife or four.
But they have always agreed that you must not simply have any woman you
liked.

But the most remarkable thing is this. Whenever you find a man who says ¶8
he does not believe in a real Right and Wrong, you will find the same man L80
going back on this a moment later. He may break his promise to you, but if you
try breaking one to him he will be complaining "It's not fair" before you can
say Jack Robinson. A nation may say treaties do not matter; but then, next
minute, they spoil their case by saying that the particular treaty they want to
break was an unfair one. But if treaties do not matter, and if there is no such L85
thing as Right and Wrong—in other words, if there is no Law of Nature—what
is the difference between a fair treaty and an unfair one? Have they not let the
cat out of the bag and shown that, whatever they say, they really know the Law
of Nature just like anyone else?

It seems, then, we are forced to believe in a real Right and Wrong. People ¶9
may be sometimes mistaken about them, just as people sometimes get their
sums wrong; but they are not a matter of mere taste and opinion any more than
the multiplication table. Now if we are agreed about that, I go on to my next
point, which is this. None of us are really keeping the Law of Nature. If there
are any exceptions among you, I apologise to them. They had much better read L95
some other book, for nothing I am going to say concerns them. And now,
turning to the ordinary human beings who are left:

I hope you will not misunderstand what I am going to say. I am not preach- ¶10
ing, and Heaven knows I do not pretend to be better than anyone else. I am
only trying to call attention to a fact; the fact that this year, or this month, or, L100
more likely, this very day, we have failed to practise ourselves the kind of
behaviour we expect from other people. There may be all sorts of excuses for
us. That time you were so unfair to the children was when you were very tired.
That slightly shady business about the money—the one you have almost forgotten—came when you were very hard up. And what you promised to do for old L105
So-and-so and have never done—well, you never would have promised if you

had known how frightfully busy you were going to be. And as for your behaviour to your wife (or husband) or sister (or brother) if I knew how irritating they could be, I would not wonder at it—and who the dickens am I, anyway? I am just the same. That is to say, I do not succeed in keeping the Law of Nature ⎸L110 very well, and the moment anyone tells me I am not keeping it, there starts up in my mind a string of excuses as long as your arm. The question at the moment is not whether they are good excuses. The point is that they are one more proof of how deeply, whether we like it or not, we believe in the Law of Nature. If we do not believe in decent behaviour, why should we be so anxious ⎸L115 to make excuses for not having behaved decently? The truth is, we believe in decency so much—we feel the Rule or Law pressing on us so—that we cannot bear to face the fact that we are breaking it, and consequently we try to shift the responsibility. For you notice that it is only for our bad behaviour that we find all these explanations. It is only our bad temper that we put down to being tired ⎸L120 or worried or hungry; we put our good temper down to ourselves.

These, then, are the two points I wanted to make. First, that human beings, ⎸¶11 all over the earth, have this curious idea that they ought to behave in a certain way, and cannot really get rid of it. Secondly, that they do not in fact behave in that way. They know the Law of Nature; they break it. These two facts are the ⎸L125 foundation of all clear thinking about ourselves and the universe we live in.

QUOTATIONS TO THINK ABOUT

1. "Quarrelling means trying to show that the other man is in the wrong" (lines 23–24). Think about a quarrel that you have recently witnessed or participated in. What did those involved say? Do you think that Lewis's characterization of quarrelling is correct?

2. ". . . [man] cannot disobey those laws which he shares with other things; but the law which is peculiar to his human nature, the law he does not share with animals or vegetables or inorganic things, is the one he can disobey if he chooses" (lines 43–46). Which laws are you subject to? Which of them can you choose to disobey? Is it true that the ones you have no choice about you share with nonhuman creatures and things, and that the ones you have some choice about are unique to humans?

3. ". . . some people say the idea of a Law of Nature or decent behaviour known to all men is unsound, because different civilisations and different ages have had quite different moralities.
   But this is not true. There have been differences between their moralities, but these have never amounted to anything like a total difference" (lines 59–63). What differences can you think of in the moralities of groups of people who represent different cultures and times? (Think of some contentious issues such as abortion, slavery, or the rights of women.) Do you think Lewis is right in saying that the fundamental idea of right and wrong is the same in all cases?

4. "None of us are really keeping the Law of Nature" (line 94). Do you think this is true? Why, or why not?

MAKING CONNECTIONS

Each of the sentences below (labeled A to K) summarizes one paragraph of the selection, but they are placed in a jumbled order.

1. In the blank at the *end* of each sentence, write the number of the paragraph the sentence corresponds to.

2. Use connectives (words such as *also, however*, or *therefore*, or phrases such as *it is true that* or *that is*) to connect the sentences to one another. (See Chapter 1 for more connectives.) Write the connective in the space provided on the left of the sentence you would put it in.

_____ A. People appeal to a common idea of what is right. ____

_____ B. There is a common element in the moralities of different cultures. ____

_____ C. The law of human nature is different from other natural laws because humans can disobey it. ____

_____ D. Quarrels always run on similar lines. ____

_____ E. The idea of right and wrong used to be called the law of nature. ____

_____ F. People say that different civilizations have different moralities. ____

_____ G. Everyone knows what is right, but no one keeps to it. ____

_____ H. People know the law of human nature naturally. ____

_____ I. We have to believe in a real right and wrong—and we have to acknowledge that everyone regularly does wrong. ____

_____ J. Appeals are made to the law of nature even by people who say they don't believe it. ____

_____ K. People always make excuses, showing that they know they are breaking the law of nature. ____

3. Write out or read aloud to your classmates the rearranged sentences, with the connectives, as a continuous passage. You may want to alter the wording and punctuation of the sentences slightly in order to make the passage less clumsy, and in some places you may want to make the connection between sentences by inserting a whole clause instead of just a word or phrase.

SELECTION
4-5

from *The Second Sex*

Simone de Beauvoir

Published in 1949, Simone de Beauvoir's *The Second Sex* has become an important statement regarding the status of women in the late twentieth century. In the selection that follows, the introduction to the whole work, de Beauvoir sets out some fundamental points of analysis.

PREREADING

1. Make two columns on a sheet of paper and write the headings *Masculine* and *Feminine*. Then list as many characteristics as you can think of under each heading.

2. When you have made your lists, compare them with those of your classmates. Then discuss these questions: Why are these characteristics considered masculine and feminine respectively? What do they have to do with actual men and women?

Introduction

For a long time I have hesitated to write a book on woman. The subject is irritating, especially to women; and it is not new. Enough ink has been spilled in quarrelling over feminism, and perhaps we should say no more about it. It is still talked about, however, for the voluminous nonsense uttered during the last century seems to have done little to illuminate the problem. After all, is there a 5 problem? And if so, what is it? Are there women, really? Most assuredly the theory of the eternal feminine still has its adherents who will whisper in your ear: "Even in Russia women still are *women*"; and other erudite persons—sometimes the very same—say with a sigh: "Woman is losing her way, woman is lost." One wonders if women still exist, if they will always exist, whether or 10 not it is desirable that they should, what place they occupy in this world, what their place should be. "What has become of women?" was asked recently in an ephemeral magazine.

But first we must ask: what is a woman? "*Tota mulier in utero*," says one, "woman is a womb." But in speaking of certain women, connoisseurs declare 15 that they are not women, although they are equipped with a uterus like the rest. All agree in recognizing the fact that females exist in the human species; today as always they make up about one half of humanity. And yet we are told that feminity is in danger; we are exhorted to be women, remain women, become women. It would appear, then, that every female human being is not neces- 20 sarily a woman; to be so considered she must share in that mysterious and

threatened reality known as femininity. Is this attribute something secreted by the
ovaries? Or is it a Platonic essence, a product of the philosophic imagination? Is a
rustling petticoat enough to bring it down to earth? Although some women try
zealously to incarnate this essence, it is hardly patentable. It is frequently de-   25
scribed in vague and dazzling terms that seem to have been borrowed from the
vocabulary of the seers, and indeed in the times of St. Thomas it was considered
an essence as certainly defined as the somniferous virtue of the poppy.

But conceptualism has lost ground. The biological and social sciences no   30
longer admit the existence of unchangeably fixed entities that determine given
characteristics, such as those ascribed to woman, the Jew, or the Negro. Science regards any characteristic as a reaction dependent in part upon a *situation*.
If today femininity no longer exists, then it never existed. But does the word
woman, then, have no specific content? This is stoutly affirmed by those who   35
hold to the philosophy of the enlightenment, of rationalism, of nominalism;
women, to them, are merely the human beings arbitrarily designated by the
word *woman*. Many American women particularly are prepared to think that
there is no longer any place for woman as such; if a backward individual still
takes herself for a woman, her friends advise her to be psychoanalyzed and thus   40
get rid of this obsession. In regard to a work, *Modern Woman: The Lost Sex*,
which in other respects has its irritating features, Dorothy Parker has written: "I
cannot be just to books which treat of woman as woman . . . My idea is that all
of us, men as well as women, should be regarded as human beings." But
nominalism is a rather inadequate doctrine, and the anti-feminists have had no   45
trouble in showing that women simply *are not* men. Surely woman is, like
man, a human being; but such a declaration is abstract. The fact is that every
concrete human being is always a singular, separate individual. To decline to
accept such notions as the eternal feminine, the black soul, the Jewish character, is not to deny that Jews, Negroes, women exist today—this denial does not   50
represent a liberation for those concerned, but rather a flight from reality. Some
years ago a well-known woman writer refused to permit her portrait to appear
in a series of photographs especially devoted to women writers; she wished to
be counted among the men. But in order to gain this privilege she made use of
her husband's influence! Women who assert that they are men lay claim none   55
the less to masculine consideration and respect. I recall also a young Trotskyite
standing on a platform at a boisterous meeting and getting ready to use her
fists, in spite of her evident fragility. She was denying her feminine weakness;
but it was for love of a militant male whose equal she wished to be. The
attitude of defiance of many American women proves that they are haunted by   60
a sense of their femininity. In truth, to go for a walk with one's eyes open is
enough to demonstrate that humanity is divided into two classes of individuals
whose clothes, faces, bodies, smiles, gaits, interests, and occupations are mani-
festly different. Perhaps these differences are superficial, perhaps they are des-
tined to disappear. What is certain is that they do most obviously exist.   65

If her functioning as a female is not enough to define woman, if we decline
also to explain her though "the eternal feminine", and if nevertheless we admit,

provisionally, that women do exist, then we must face the question: what is a woman?

To state the question is, to me, to suggest, at once, a preliminary answer. The fact that I ask it is in itself significant. A man would never set out to write a book on the peculiar situation of the human male. But if I wish to define myself, I must first of all say: "I am a woman"; on this truth must be based all further discussion. A man never begins by presenting himself as an individual of a certain sex; it goes without saying that he is a man. The terms *masculine* and *feminine* are used symmetrically only as a matter of form, as on legal papers. In actuality the relation of the two sexes is not quite like that of two electrical poles, for man represents both the positive and the neutral, as is indicated by the common use of *man* to designate human beings in general; whereas woman represents only the negative, defined by limiting criteria, without reciprocity. In the midst of an abstract discussion it is vexing to hear a man say: "You think thus and so because you are a woman"; but I know that my only defence is to reply: "I think thus and so because it is true," thereby removing my subjective self from the argument. It would be out of the question to reply: "And you think the contrary because you are a man", for it is understood that the fact of being a man is no peculiarity. A man is in the right in being a man; it is the woman who is in the wrong. It amounts to this: just as for the ancients there was an absolute vertical with reference to which the oblique was defined, so there is an absolute human type, the masculine. Woman has ovaries, a uterus: these peculiarities imprison her in her subjectivity, circumscribe her within the limits of her own nature. It is often said that she thinks with her glands. Man superbly ignores the fact that his anatomy also includes glands, such as the testicles, and that they secrete hormones. He thinks of his body as a direct and normal connection with the world, which he believes he apprehends objectively, whereas he regards the body of woman as a hindrance, a prison, weighed down by everything peculiar to it. "The female is a female by virtue of a certain *lack* of qualities," said Aristotle; "we should regard the female nature as afflicted with a natural defectiveness." And St. Thomas for his part pronounced woman to be an "imperfect man," an "incidental" being. This is symbolized in Genesis where Eve is depicted as made from what Bossuet called "a supernumerary bone" of Adam.

Thus humanity is male and man defines woman not in herself but as relative to him; she is not regarded as an autonomous being. Michelet writes: "Woman, the relative being . . . " And Benda is most positive in his *Rapport d'Uriel*: "The body of man makes sense in itself quite apart from that of woman, whereas the latter seems wanting in significance by itself . . . Man can think of himself without woman. She cannot think of herself without man." And she is simply what man decrees; thus she is called "the sex," by which is meant that she appears essentially to the male as a sexual being. For him she is sex—absolute sex, no less. She is defined and differentiated with reference to man and not he with reference to her; she is the incidental, the inessential as opposed to the essential. He is the Subject, he is the Absolute—she is the Other.

QUOTATIONS TO
THINK ABOUT

1. "One wonders if women still exist, if they will always exist, whether or not it is desirable that they should, what place they occupy in this world, what their place should be" (lines 10–12). Are any of these questions real questions to you? If so, why? If not, why not?

2. "The fact is that every concrete human being is always a singular, separate individual. To decline to accept such notions as the eternal feminine, the black soul, the Jewish character, is not to deny that Jews, Negroes, women exist today—this denial does not represent a liberation for those concerned, but rather a flight from reality" (lines 47–51). What does it mean to describe someone as a Jew, a Negro (the modern word would be Black or maybe African or African-American) or a woman? Would it be better not to use these categories?

3. "A man is in the right in being a man; it is the woman who is in the wrong" (lines 86–87). Considering how words and sayings that suggest masculinity or feminity are used, do you think this is an accurate statement of popular belief?

4. "Thus humanity is male and man defines woman not in herself but as relative to him; she is not regarded as an autonomous being" (lines 102–103). Do you think that men as individuals can be regarded as more autonomous, or freer to act on their own, than women? If not, does this statement have any justification?

MAKING
CONNECTIONS

1. Underline the three different definitions of *woman* that Simone de Beauvoir cites (lines 14–15, 37–38, and 98–99). What is her own attitude to each of these definitions?

2. This passage includes a number of direct questions. What are these questions? Write them down (with line references) on the left-hand side of a sheet of paper; then on the right-hand side, write whatever answer de Beauvoir gives to the question; or if she gives none, write down the answer you think she implies. Be prepared to say why you think this is her answer. Do you think any of these questions are genuine ones for the author—that is, ones to which she cannot give an answer?

CHAPTER FIVE

Reading for

Testing

You have probably had to take standardized reading tests a number of times during your education, and you may have more such tests ahead. As you know, these tests do not look much like anything else you read, for they consist of a number of short, unrelated passages, each accompanied by multiple-choice items. By now you will probably also have realized that they call for a different kind of reading from any of the kinds of reading practiced so far in this book. Specifically, to be successful in a typical standardized reading test, you should try to develop the following strategies:

1. Focus exclusively on the information provided in each passage. Don't try to think of it in light of what you know already about the subject. (Notice that this is the opposite of what you are asked to do when studying.)

2. Consider each passage separately. Don't allow your interpretation of one passage to affect your interpretation of another, even if they seem to you to be linked. (Again, contrast this with the treatment of the passages in Chapter 4, Reading for Insight.)

3. Pay careful attention to all the words on the page. Even if they don't seem to make sense, always assume that each word is meant to be there and is meant to be taken seriously. (Test makers, unlike novelists or journalists, never make jokes.)

4. Don't spend time puzzling about an item that you can't immediately answer. Leave it and come back to it later. If you run out

of time, and if the test is one in which you lose no more by putting a wrong answer than you do by leaving a blank (your instructor will inform you on this point), fill it in by guessing. You can usually, by a process of elimination, reduce the possible answers to two, so that if you then make a guess you have a 50-percent chance of getting it right.

5. If time is called before you have finished a test, complete the remaining items at random—but again only on those tests where you are not penalized for putting wrong answers rather than leaving blanks. Remember that you have a 25-percent chance of getting a multiple-choice item right, even if you don't read the passage that it is based on at all.

Types of Test Item

Standardized test items nearly always follow the same format: each consists of a stem—usually the first part of a sentence, but sometimes a question—and four different ways of finishing the sentence or answering the question (usually lettered *a, b, c, d*). It is important to look particularly carefully at the stem, because it tells you what kind of item you are dealing with and therefore how you should approach it. Five types of items are customarily used in standardized tests: *main idea, detail, vocabulary, inference,* and *tone.* These types are discussed in this chapter and are illustrated by items based on the following passage. Please read the passage carefully:

One hundred miles of water, more or less, divide the peninsula called Baja, or Lower, California from the rest of Mexico, and flying into La Paz on a clear day, you can see mountains along the west coast of Sinaloa rising dreamlike through the haze above the Sea of Cortés.

This body of water is also known as the Gulf of California, although most native *peninsulares* prefer the more evocative Mar de Cortés, for Hernan Cortés, the conqueror of Mexico, who came here hunting pearls in 1535 and claimed the peninsula for Spain. Judging by maps from this period, Cortés may have called the gulf the Vermilion Sea, perhaps after watching its surface turn blood red, as it often does in the hour between sunset and dark.

By whatever name, the gulf has isolated Baja California and many of its islands since they tore free of the mainland some five million years ago along the San Andreas Fault system, which zigzags up the gulf before rising from the mud flats of the Colorado Delta to menace citizens of the other California.

Main Idea

The stem of a main idea item is usually worded something like these examples:

The main idea of this passage is . . .
A suitable title for this passage is . . .
The purpose of this passage is . . .
The best summary of this passage is . . .

The correct alternative is the one that covers everything that is said in the passage, and if there are two likely choices, the one that is more specific. Frequently, you will find that the main idea appears in a topic sentence (see Chapter 1) towards the beginning of the passage and is also repeated at the end. Here is an example of a main idea item, based on the passage above:

The main idea of this passage is that
a). the Sea of Cortés has many names.
b). Baja Calfornia is an isolated region.
c). Mexico includes some interesting places.
d). the San Andreas Fault is dangerous.

Of these alternatives, (a) is not the correct one, for although the passage does say that the Sea of Cortés has many names, it only does so in paragraph 2; the alternative does not cover paragraphs 1 and 3. Similarly, (d) is not correct because the San Andreas Fault is mentioned only in paragraph 3, not in paragraphs 1 and 2, although the passage does indeed suggest, by the use of the word *menace*, that the fault is dangerous. As for (c), the passage does imply that Baja California is interesting, and it definitely states that the area is in Mexico; but it does not tell about any other interesting places in Mexico, which makes this alternative too general. That leaves (b) as your answer. By selecting it, you form this statement:

The main idea of this passage is that Baja California is an isolated region.

Compare it with this sentence from paragraph 1:

One hundred miles of water, more or less, *divide* the peninsula called Baja, or Lower, California from the rest of Mexico . . .

and with this one from paragraph 3:

By whatever name, the gulf has *isolated* Baja California and many of its islands since they tore free of the mainland some five million years ago . . .

As for paragraph 2, the words *By whatever name*, which introduce paragraph 3, show that all the information about names is an incidental point to be considered less important than the one about isolation.

Detail

Items on detail simply pick up some point made in the passage and ask you to recycle it by selecting an alternative way of saying the same thing. They are usually the easiest items to get right, but they can be tricky, either because the point you are asked to recycle is unimportant to the passage as a whole—it is sometimes even contrary to the main idea—or because the stem itself is a tricky one. Examples of such stems are:

> All of the following are true *except* . . .
> The author does *not* mention . . .

The clearest signal that an item is asking for a particular detail, rather than a main idea or an inference, are the words *According to the passage* used in the stem. But quite often, items on detail are simply presented as statements of fact. Just remember that the test is asking for facts as given in the passage, not as you yourself know them.

Here is a detail item on the above passage:

> The Vermilion Sea is another name for
> a). La Paz.
> b). Sinaloa.
> c). the Gulf of California.
> d). the San Andreas Fault.

To find the correct alternative you have first to locate the words *the Vermilion Sea* in the passage. They are in paragraph 2:

> Cortés may have called the gulf the Vermilion Sea . . .

You then have to decide which gulf is referred to—which is easy, because it is named in the previous sentence as *the Gulf of California*. Notice also that none of the others could be right because none of them is a sea. You will thus choose (c) as your answer, producing this statement:

> The Vermilion Sea is another name for the Gulf of California.

Vocabulary

Items on vocabulary target particular words in the passage. In these items, you are asked to say what certain words mean in that context. The word in question is usually given in the stem, and the correct alternative is a synonym. Do not, however, look simply for a synonym, because the word may be being used in an unusual sense; instead, locate the stem word in the passage and then see which of the alternatives could best fit in its place. The word may be one you don't know, in which case you must infer its meaning from its relationship with other words in the passage. (See the advice on vocabulary in Chapter 1.)

Vocabulary items are easy to recognize because the word *word* is usually mentioned in the stem. For example:

In paragraph (or line) _____, the word _____ means . . .

But even if the stem is not so explicit, you can recognize a vocabulary item from the fact that the word or phrase in question is printed in quotation marks or italics. Here is an example that relates to the passage above:

Native peninsulares are
a). Indian peoples of Mexico.
b). islanders of the Gulf.
c). descendants of Hernan Cortés.
d). people born in Baja California.

In this case, you may not know the word *peninsulares* because it is a Spanish word, but you can tell from the first sentence in paragraph 2 that it must refer to people:

. . . most native *peninsulares* prefer the more evocative Mar de Cortés . . .

Only people can prefer a name. This doesn't help you much with the item, however, because all the alternatives suggest people of different groups. You may at first be tempted by alternative (a) because the Indian peoples of North America are often referred to as "native Americans," but that would be to ignore the word *peninsulares* altogether. In addition, there is no other indication in the passage that the writer is thinking of Indians—in fact the Spanish name Mar de Cortés together with the word *peninsulares* suggests that the reference is to Spanish speakers. So you should reject (a) and think more about the other, primary, meaning of *native*: "born in (a particular place)." This would lead you to reject (c) because it has no reference to any place at all. Your choices are now reduced to (b) or (d). At this point you will have to think about the related English word, *peninsula*, because *peninsulares* are probably people of the peninsula. If *peninsula* means "island," then (b) is attractive. However, you don't know that this is what *peninsula* means, whereas you do know from the first sentence of the passage that, whatever it means, Baja California is one:

> One hundred miles of water, more or less, divide the *peninsula* called Baja, or Lower, California from the rest of Mexico . . .

This makes (d) the best alternative because joining it to the stem makes a closely corresponding statement:

> *Native peninsulares* are people born in Baja California.

So (b) is another distractor (and, as it happens, *peninsula* does not mean island).

Inference

An inference item requires you to complete a statement that is *not made* in the passage but is a logical conclusion from it. The correct alternative, however, is closely related to the words on the page—you are likely to choose the wrong one if you rely on information that is not given, even though you know that information to be true.

Inference items are clearly indicated by their stems, phrases such as these:

> The writer/passage *implies* that . . .
> The writer/passage *suggests* that . . .
> We can *infer* from the passage that . . .
> It *seems* from the passage that . . .
> From the information given we can *conclude* that . . .
> It is *probably* true that . . .

Following is an example of an inference item:

> The passage suggests that Hernan Cortés is best known for
> a). discovering Baja California.
> b). conquering Mexico.
> c). collecting pearls.
> d). naming the Vermilion Sea.

Alternative (a) states that Hernan Cortés discovered Baja California. But this idea is not indicated in any way in the passage, which only says that he went there: Baja California could easily have been discovered by someone else, who then told Cortés about it. So we cannot infer that Cortés discovered it, still less that he was well known for doing so. Alternative (c), on the other hand, does describe something that Hernan Cortés did, for we are told that he

> . . . came here hunting pearls in 1535 . . .

However, this information is presented toward the end of the sentence, which is where writers usually put information that you are *not* expected to know—and if you are not expected to know it, then you cannot infer that this activity is what Cortés is best known for. Similarly, alternative (d) echoes information given in the passage:

> Cortés may have called the Gulf the Vermilion Sea.

But the information is again given as if it is new to you, and the words *may have* show that it is not even certain that Cortés did this. That leaves us with alternative (b), which forms this statement:

> The passage suggests that Hernan Cortés is best known for conquering Mexico.

This statement is supported by the fact that Cortés is introduced in this way:

> . . . Hernan Cortés, the conqueror of Mexico . . .

The word *the* suggests that you already know that Mexico was conquered by somebody, and that Cortés was the one, so it is a logical inference that this is what he is best known for.

Tone or Mood

Items that focus on the tone of a passage usually offer as alternatives a set of words describing how a passage might make you feel, and the correct one indicates how you are supposed to feel on reading this particular passage—or, to put it another way, how you think the writer felt when writing it. The alternatives are usually quite different from each other, and the correct one picks out some fairly obvious characteristic of the text, so items of this kind are not particularly difficult; but a problem can occur if you don't know the words given

as alternatives. Here is a list of words that are commonly used in these
items. A good way of learning what they mean would be to use them,
in discussion with your instructor, to describe the selections that you
have already read in this book.

accusing	ironic
ambivalent	mocking
angry	morbid
bitter	objective
cheerful	optimistic
critical	outspoken
cruel	pessimistic
depressed	playful
depressing	positive
detatched	religious
distressed	romantic
enthusiastic	satirical
formal	sentimental
humorous	serious
indignant	straightforward
informative	sympathetic

Here is an example of an item on tone:

> This description of Baja California can best be described as
> a). romantic.
> b). bitter.
> c). satirical.
> d). playful.

The evidence for choosing an alternative is in specific words and images used in the passage. There is nothing at all to suggest that the
writer is bitter, satirical, or even playful, whereas the words *dreamlike*
and *evocative* and the references to the "haze above the Sea of Cortés"
and the "blood red" color of the sea suggest that the writer is sensitive
to the romantic beauty of the place. That makes (a) the correct alternative—even if the subject is not one you personally associate with ro-
mance.

Using the Exercises

The rest of this chapter consists of eight exercises that are modeled on real tests. Each exercise consists of a reading passage and five test items. Your instructor may ask you to do all or several of the exercises at one sitting—as if it were a real test—or one at a time. Either way, you should try to spend no more than four minutes on each exercise. This is quite a generous amount of time for the first ones, because the passages are short, but you will find that as you progress through the exercises you are pushed for time. This is appropriate, for that is exactly what happens in real tests. If you can do the later exercises comfortably in four minutes—and get all the answers right—you are doing well.

*

PRACTICE EXERCISE 5-1

Madeira is the largest of a group of Portuguese islands of about nine-hundred square kilometers, in the Atlantic about seven-hundred kilometers from the coast of Morocco. The only inhabited islands in the group are Madeira and Porto Santo. Madeira is a volcanic island with steep hills and cliffs, and a warm, mild climate which has made it a famous tourist center. The lower slopes of the hills are terraced for growing vines (for the special Madeira wine), sugar cane, bananas, pineapples, and other fruit which is exported to Europe. Dairy products from cattle are important, and fish is exported.

Circle the correct way of completing each statement.

1. The purpose of this passage is to

   a). give a general description of Madeira.
   b). compare Madeira and Porto Santo.
   c). explain Madeira's relationship with Portugal.
   d). discuss Portuguese islands in the Atlantic.

2. According to the passage, Madeira and Porto Santo are different from other islands in their group because

   a.). they belong to Portugal.
   b). they have people living on them.
   c.). they are bigger than the others.
   d). they are nearer to Morocco.

3. People visit Madeira because it has

   a). good weather.
   b). a big volcano.
   c). famous wine.
   d). beautiful terraces.

4. In Madeira, crops are cultivated

   a). wherever the land is flat.
   b). on the tops of the cliffs.
   c). down in the valleys.
   d). on the sides of the hills.

5. According to the passage, Madeira produces all the following except

   a). fruit.
   b). milk.
   c). wine.
   d). meat.

PRACTICE EXERCISE 5-2

Something is wrong with the state of children's television in this country. I have been saying that ever since 1974. Back then, broadcasters' service to children was merely considered unsatisfactory. Today it is little short of a national disgrace. There is virtually no programming offered to serve the educational or informational needs and interests of youngsters. Children spend more time watching television—an estimated fifteen hundred hours each year—than they do attending school or engaging in any single activity except sleeping. However, with the notable exception of some very good public-broadcasting programs, such as the now-legendary *Sesame Street*, the medium of broadcast television has largely failed to deliver any worthwhile educational content for youngsters.

Circle the correct way of completing each statement.

1. The main point that the writer is making is that
   a). children should not spend so much time watching television.
   b). the only program that children should watch is *Sesame Street*.
   c). television should be used more in schools.
   c). there should be more educational programs on television.

2. The writer asserts that since 1974 children's television
   a). has deteriorated.
   b). has remained the same.
   c). has improved slightly.
   d). has improved considerably.

3. According to the passage, children spend most of their time
   a). sleeping.
   b). attending school.
   c). watching television.
   d). engaging in games.

4. The word *now-legendary* indicates that *Sesame Street*
   a). is of educational value.
   b). has developed a reputation.
   c). will soon be a thing of the past.
   d). is based on fiction, not fact.

5. The tone of the passage as a whole is
   a). objective.
   b). enthusiastic.
   c). critical.
   d). emotional.

PRACTICE EXERCISE 5-3

The sidewinder is a rattlesnake found in mostly sandy, arid areas from southern California and Nevada to Sonora, Mexico. It received its name from its sidewinding locomotion—an efficient method for escaping over soft sand by looping the body forward in the shape of an S that contacts the ground at only two points, then "rolling" each loop ahead by shifting those points of contact back along the length of the body, by which means the snake may reach a top speed of about 4 kmh (2.5 mph). Sidewinders average less than 60 cm (2 ft) long, but some may exceed 75 cm (2.5 ft). They are generally a sandy color with grayish or brownish blotches, and the scale above each eye is developed into a hornlike projection. Sidewinders are primarily nocturnal and feed on lizards and small rodents.

Circle the correct way of completing each statement.

1. A suitable title for this passage would be:
   a). Snakes of the desert.
   b). How snakes get their names.
   c). Characteristics of the sidewinder.
   c). Strange ways of moving.

2. Sonora is in
   a). California.
   b). Nevada.
   c). Mexico.
   d). the United States.

3. The most interesting thing about the snake described is
   a). what it looks like.
   b). how big it is.
   c). what it eats.
   d). how it moves.

4. You would be most likely to find a sidewinder
   a). in a forest by day.
   b). in a forest by night.
   c). in a desert by day.
   d). in a desert by night.

5. Sidewinders eat
   a). mammals and reptiles.
   b). insects and worms.
   c). seeds and leaves.
   d). birds and eggs.

**PRACTICE
EXERCISE
5-4**

The beavers at the Minnesota Zoo seem engaged in a Sisyphean task. Each week they fell scores of inch-thick saplings for food. And each week zoo workers surreptitiously replace the downed saplings, anchoring new ones in the iron holders so the animals can keep on cutting. Letting the beavers do what comes naturally has paid off: Minnesota is one of the few zoos to get them to reproduce in captivity. The chimps at the St. Louis Zoo also work for a living: They poke stiff pieces of hay into an anthill to scoop out the baby food and honey that curators cache away inside. Instead of idly awaiting banana hand-outs, the chimps get to manipulate tools, just as they do in the wild. In 1988, when thirteen gorillas moved into Zoo Atlanta's new $4.5-million rain forest, they mated and formed families—a rarity among captives. "Zoos have changed from being mere menageries to being celebrations of life," says John Gwynne of the Bronx Zoo. "As the wild places get smaller, the role of zoos gets larger, which means intensifying the naturalness of the experience for both visitors and animals."

Circle the correct way of completing each statement.

1. A suitable title for this passage would be

    a). The Habits of Beavers.
    b). Beavers, Chimps, and Gorillas.
    c). Zoos of the United States.
    d). Imitating Nature in Zoos.

2. We can infer that the beavers at Minnesota did not reproduce before because

    a). they were not given the right kind of food.
    b). they had no wood for making their nests.
    c). they could not practice their natural behavior.
    d). they were disturbed by visitors to the zoo.

3. At St. Louis Zoo, the chimps are fed on

    a). banana handouts.
    b). ants and ant eggs.
    c). baby food and honey.
    d). stiff pieces of hay.

4. According to the passage, the distinctive feature about the gorillas at Zoo Atlanta is that

    a). they are expensive to keep.
    b). they have begun to breed.
    c). they are especially rare.
    d). they are relatively numerous.

5. The tone of the passage is

    a). ambivalent.
    b). critical.
    c). optimistic.
    d). pessimistic.

PRACTICE EXERCISE 5-5

The settlement areas in the Northeast and the South around Jamestown have one characteristic in common: they were mainly colonized by pioneers from the southwestern and eastern parts of England. But the making of American English is by no means just a tale of English emigration. In the Middle Atlantic state of Pennsylvania there was a new, rowdy element of English speakers, hard-bitten, land-hungry frontiersmen from Scotland and the Ulster settlements of Northern Ireland. And further south, in Charleston, named after Charles II, there were, in addition to a thriving population of Irish and Scots-Irish emigrants, boatloads of Black slaves from Africa and the Caribbean, many of them speaking pidgin English. In the end, American English was to be influenced by these and many other peoples, in a series of vital transfusions.

Circle the correct way of completing each statement.

1. The main idea of this passage is that

    a). the most important settlers in America were from England.
    b). Pennsylvania was dominated by people from Scotland and Ireland.
    c). American English developed from many varieties of English.
    d). an increasing proportion of Black slaves spoke pidgin English.

2. According to the passage, most of the pioneers in both northeast and south came from

    a). eastern and southwestern England.
    b). Scotland and Ireland.
    c). Africa and the Caribbean.
    d). many different places.

3. The description of the people from Scotland and Ulster suggests that they were particularly

    a). skilled.
    b). dogmatic.
    c). oppressed.
    d). aggressive.

4. The word *transfusions* refers here to

   a). political movements.
   b). transfers of slaves.
   c). medical operations.
   d). waves of immigration.

5. The author seems to think that the influence of so many peoples on American English has made it

   a). impure.
   b). lively.
   c). difficult.
   d). poetic.

PRACTICE EXERCISE 5-6

"I play more in Carnegie Hall than anybody else," says Franz Mohr. "But I have no audience." Seeing him alone on the stage hours before a concert, one might mistake him for a virtuoso improvising on a nine-foot grand. Instead, Mr. Mohr, the chief technician for Steinway & Sons, is tuning it. He goes where the pianos go: when Rudolf Serkin takes a Steinway on tour, Mr. Mohr goes along, checking a key here, tightening a string there. But the first strings he loved were on a violin. A native of Duren, West Germany, he gave up playing when he realized he would never be another Heifetz. He could not give up music, so he became an apprentice with the piano manufacturer Ibach & Sons in 1950, at the age of twenty-three. Twelve years later he moved to New York. He has been at Steinway's headquarters, a few steps from Carnegie Hall, ever since.

Circle the correct way of completing each statement.

1. This passage is mainly about

   a.). a man who works behind the scenes.
   b). why Mr. Mohr did not become a violinist.
   c). people who play in Carnegie Hall.
   d). how to take care of pianos.

2. Mr. Mohr is

   a). a virtuoso concert pianist.
   b). a teacher of piano and violin.
   c). an apprentice with Ibach & Sons.
   d). a technician who looks after pianos.

3. When Rudolf Serkin goes on tour, Mr. Mohr goes too in order to

  a). accompany him.
  b). play in the concerts.
  c). take care of his Steinway.
  d). help with publicity.

4. We can infer that Heifetz was

  a). a piano technician.
  b). a great violinist.
  c). a famous pianist.
  d). a brilliant composer.

5. Mr. Mohr gave up playing the violin because

  a). he realized he had no musical ability.
  b). he knew he was not a great player.
  c). he decided he preferred the piano.
  d). he could earn more money as a technician.

PRACTICE EXERCISE 5-7

Western civilization has, for more than a millennium, been based on a Judeo-Christian religious foundation that views human beings, and the planet we inhabit, as the central focus of God's province. This comfortably egocentric view was challenged more than four centuries ago when Nicolaus Copernicus dared to suggest that the earth was not the center of the universe, but only one of several planets revolving around a fairly small star. During the first three decades of the seventeenth century, first Kepler and then Galileo confirmed what Copernicus had suggested, and the gathering storm broke, with both church and state condemning the astronomers for their heresy. Galileo was called before the Holy Inquisition and forced to renounce his findings, but the true nature of the physical universe became more and more apparent through the continued pursuit of science, and eventually the established view was overthrown. Our planet is indeed a humble body in a vast array of solar systems and galaxies. Science had begun its erosion of the Judeo-Christian view of the world.

Circle the correct way of completing each statement.

1. The main topic discussed in this passage is

  a). early challenges to the traditional European worldview.
  b). Judeo-Christian beliefs about the universe.
  c). discoveries in astronomy in the seventeenth century.
  d). opposition to the ideas of Copernicus, Kepler, and Galileo.

2. Copernicus was working

   a). more than a thousand years ago.
   b). in the first third of the seventeenth century.
   c). before the end of the sixteenth century.
   d). at a time that is not indicated.

3. The "small star" mentioned in lines X–X is

   a). the earth.
   b). the sun.
   c). the moon.
   d). an unnamed planet.

4. According to the writer, Galileo's teaching was condemned because it

   a). was unpopular.
   b). falsified the facts.
   c). contradicted Copernicus's.
   d). challenged existing ideas.

5. The writer seems to regard Judeo-Christian beliefs as

   a). of no significance whatsoever.
   b). significant only for historical reasons.
   c). important to our understanding of the world.
   d). the only true basis of civilization.

PRACTICE EXERCISE 5-8

In ancient Greece, slaves were often conquered enemies. Since city-states were constantly conquering one another or rebelling against former conquerors, slavery was a threat to everyone. Following the Trojan War, the transition of Hecuba from queen to slave was marked by her cry "Count no mortal fortunate, no matter how favored, until he is dead." Nevertheless, Greek slaves were considered human beings, and they could even acquire some status along with freedom. Andromache, the daughter-in-law of Hecuba, was taken as slave and concubine by one of the Greek heroes. When his legal wife produced no children, Andromache's slave son became heir to his father's throne. Although slaves had no rights under law, once they were freed, either by the will of their master or by purchase, they and their descendants could become assimilated into the dominant group. In other words, slavery in Greece was not seen as the justified position of inferior people. It was regarded, rather, as an act of fate—"the luck of the draw"—that relegated a victim to the lowest class in society.

Circle the correct way of completing each statement.

1. The purpose of this passage is to show that slavery in ancient Greece was

    a). particularly cruel.
    b). like slavery in the United States.
    c). necessary to society.
    d). relatively humane.

2. According to this passage, slaves in ancient Greece were regarded as

    a). the equivalent of domestic animals.
    b). people who had had bad luck.
    c). enemies who must be subdued.
    d). human beings with certain rights.

3. Hecuba was

    a). a queen who became a slave.
    b). a slave who became a queen.
    c). a concubine who became a legal wife.
    d). an enemy who became heir to the throne.

4. Andromache's son is mentioned to show

    a). the status that freed slaves could achieve.
    b). the extent to which Greek slavery is misunderstood.
    c). the miserable life that slaves had.
    d). the typical experience of Greek heroes.

5. According to the passage, slaves who became free

    a). became influential leaders.
    b). were especially respected.
    c). could become full members of society.
    d). were the lowest class in the community.

Appendix

Graphs for Recording Speed and Scores

The graphs on the following pages are provided for you to record your progress increasing your reading speed and comprehension using the reading selections in Chapters 1 and 2. On the top graph, write the selection number at the top of the left-hand column, the date in the space below it, and an X across the vertical bar on the horizontal line that represents your speed. Then use the bottom graph in the same way to mark your first score on the Comprehension Check. Use a ruler to connect the X's each time you fill in the graphs. (See the sample completed graphs on page 286.)

284

Appendix   Graphs for Recording Speed and Scores

Passage														
Date														

wpm

380

360

340

320

300

280

260

240

220

200

180

160

140

120

100

First Score

10

9

8

7

6

5

4

3

2

1

Passage														
Date														

wpm

380														
360														
340														
320														
300														
280														
260														
240														
220														
200														
180														
160														
140														
120														
100														

First Score

10														
9														
8														
7														
6														
5														
4														
3														
2														
1														

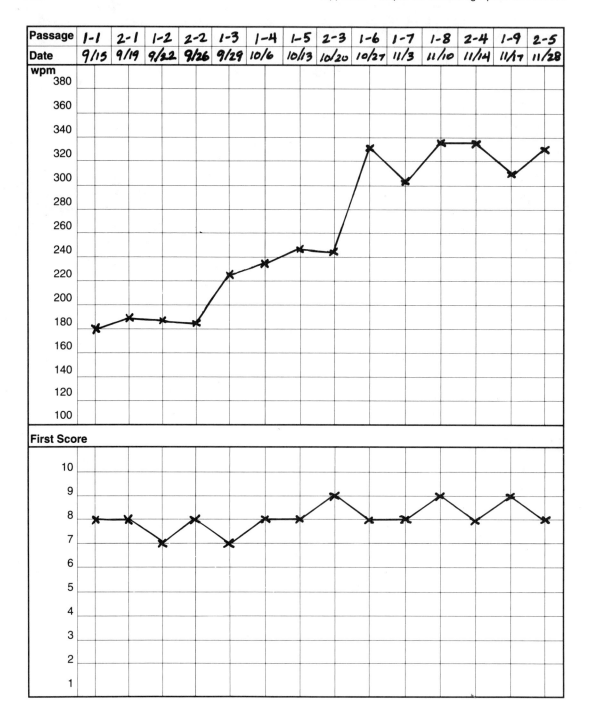

Passage	1-1	2-1	1-2	2-2	1-3	1-4	1-5	2-3	1-6	1-7	1-8	2-4	1-9	2-5
Date	9/15	9/19	9/22	9/26	9/29	10/6	10/13	10/20	10/27	11/3	11/10	11/14	11/17	11/28

Index